The New South Faces the World

The New South Faces the World

Foreign Affairs and the Southern Sense of Self, 1877–1950

Tennant S. McWilliams

Louisiana State University Press
Baton Rouge and London

For Paige and Lanier

10 9 8 7 6 5 4 3 2 1

Designer: Diane Batten Didier
Typeface: Linotron Sabon
Typesetter: Composing Room of Michigan, Inc.
Printer: Thomson-Shore, Inc.
Binder: John H. Dekker & Sons, Inc.

Library of Congress Cataloging-in-Publication Data

McWilliams, Tennant S., 1943–
    The new South faces the world.

    Bibliography: p.
    Includes index.
    1. United States—Foreign relations—1865–
2. Internationalists—Southern States—History.
3. Southern States—Intellectual life—1865–
4. Southern States—Relations—Foreign countries.
I. Title.
E661.7.M34 1988 327.73 87–32485
ISBN 0–8071–1402–2 (alk. paper)

The paper in this book meets the guidelines for permanence and durability of the
Committee on Production Guidelines for Book Longevity of the Council on Library
Resources. ∞

Contents

Acknowledgments

In researching and writing this book I have received important assistance from many people. Numerous scholars have helped me in ways they perhaps will not remember, by attending meetings of the Southern Historical Association and offering questions and comments in response to my papers on southerners and world affairs. I find it hard to believe that there is a more nurturing organization in American academe than the Southern Historical Association. I have also found expertise and friendship among the staffs of many libraries and archival facilities—those of Yale University, Harvard University, the University of North Carolina, the University of Virginia, Duke University, the University of Michigan, Emory University, the University of Georgia, Florida State University, the Library of Congress, the National Archives, the Alabama Department of Archives and History, the Mobile Public Library, the University of South Alabama, and the Linn-Henley Research Library of the Birmingham Public Library.

Also deeply satisfying remains the encouragement I have received for this and other scholarly projects from the University of Alabama at Birmingham; the faculty, the students, the staff of the Mervyn H. Sterne Library, and all levels of the administration have provided the right environment for scholarship. Especially am I grateful to the UAB history faculty, my excellent colleagues; to the UAB Graduate School for the award of essential research and travel funds; and to James H. Woodward, senior vice-president for University College, for his constant friendship and guidance.

The individuals who critiqued my manuscript or discussed the project with me in exceptionally helpful ways include Joseph A. Fry, Edward P. Crapol, William F. Holmes, Margaret E. Armbrester, C. Vann Woodward, William H. Harbaugh, Paul M. Gaston, Michael Thomason, George E. Mowry, Robert E. May, J. Wayne Flynt, Randall Woods, Samuel L. Webb, Paige Wainwright McWilliams, Thomas G.

.

Dyer, Willard Gatewood, James C. Cobb, David E. Harrell, Howell Raines, Blaine A. Brownell, Virginia V. Hamilton, E. Culpepper Clark, James Rachels, Clarence Mohr, and certainly John M. Cooper, Jr. Three individuals—Debra Givens, Patricia S. Jeffery, and Katherine Watson—provided expert staff support during the entire researching and writing project. Jeanne Holloway gave the manuscript the benefit of her noted magic on the word processor. Finally, Margaret Dalrymple, Catherine Barton, and the other good people of the Louisiana State University Press gave me their expertise and patience throughout the entire publication process, and Barbara Williams provided first-rate copy editing.

The New South Faces the World

Introduction
The Mission and the Burden

Amid the avalanche of international changes occurring after World War II, C. Vann Woodward began to critique American idealism, counterposing two viewpoints: the expansionism springing from the American mission to spread its "way of life" to the rest of the world and the caution about American expansionism that might be instilled by recent southern experiences—the burden of southern history. He began with two powerful essays: "The Irony of Southern History" (1953) and "The Search for the Southern Identity" (1958). Here he argued that cold war Americans were a problem for the world. Although they possessed the brute strength to make a lasting contribution to world peace, their ideological biases and misperceptions of history tended to prohibit such a contribution. They worshiped the American way of life as something nearly perfect, and most showed little of the "common base of experience and suffering" so essential to understanding other nations' pasts. As a result they could easily misjudge the nature of European dilemmas, react in a purely ideological way to the tensions of the cold war, and ultimately help lead the world into a third major war. The notion of America's mission to expand its influence in the world and the corollary idea of American exceptionalism could prevail in a devastating way.[1]

Nevertheless, Woodward hoped that American idealism could be modified into a realistic, though not amoral, outlook—a modern viewpoint—and that at least some key southern intellectuals and a few other southern cosmopolitans, functioning perhaps as a revived south-

1. On Woodward and mission, see, for example, C. Vann Woodward, *The Burden of Southern History* (Rev. ed.; Baton Rouge, 1970), 205–209, 231–32. "The Irony of Southern History" and "The Search for the Southern Identity" are reprinted in Woodward's *The Burden of Southern History,* 187–212 and 3–26, respectively. See also "The Burden of Southern History Thirty Years Later" (Audiotape of lecture, November 1, 1982, in possession of E. Culpepper Clark, Birmingham, Ala.); and Woodward's *Thinking Back: The Perils of Writing History* (Baton Rouge, 1986), 101, 104.

ern intellectual renaissance from the 1930s, might be instrumental in the change. As southerners had moved through the ages of Thomas Jefferson, Andrew Jackson, slavery, and Civil War and Reconstruction, they had encountered the failure, poverty, guilt, defeat, and ridicule so universal in the human experience. In this way, southern history seemed at odds with the romantic notions of innocence and invincibility that supported the idealized American way of life. Because of this "un-American" past, at least some straight-thinking southerners might not be so infused with the national dream and hence might develop a relatively discerning view about America's contacts in the world. More specifically, Woodward referred to a latent realism that possibly remained lodged in the folkmind of the South.[2]

By *folkmind* he seems to have meant, simply, an honest comprehension of history. Surely this fits with the emergence of Woodward's own existential modernism, his sense of obligation about turning to history for the values that allow comprehension of reality.[3] It also fits with Woodward's general dissatisfaction with clinical approaches to history, ideas with which he had ample contact while pursuing graduate study in the 1930s in the classroom of Howard W. Odum at the University of North Carolina. Indeed, connecting Odum's noted concept of *social continuum* to Woodward's folkmind, as some have done, obscures the central dynamic of the burden thesis. Although Woodward recalls clearly that he encountered folkmind while studying with Odum, the doctoral student "resisted a good bit" of Odum's method as well as his traditionalist race view. Instead, at Chapel Hill and afterward, Woodward showed growing interest in art forms that employed, rather than analyzed, symbol. He recalls that he was inspired by fiction. In fact, perhaps the best example of this inclination was his

2. Woodward, *The Burden of Southern History*, 22–25, 210–11. On the southern intellectual renaissance, see *ibid.*, 108–109; Richard H. King, *A Southern Renaissance: The Cultural Awakening of the American South, 1930–1955* (New York, 1980).

3. Woodward's continued use of the term *folkmind* appears when he retraces his steps through the problem of southern iconoclasm. See "The Aging of America," *American Historical Review*, LXXXII (1977), 590. See also his "The Southern Ethic in a Puritan World," *William and Mary Quarterly*, XXV (1968), 343–70, and David Potter's "The Enigma of the South," *Yale Review*, LI (1961–1962), 142–51. On Woodward's modernism, consult Daniel Joseph Singal, *The War Within: From Victorian to Modernist Thought in the South, 1919–1945* (Chapel Hill, 1982), xi, 301, 337, 374, 385 n. 17. On the southern folkmind, see Numan V. Bartley, "Writing About the Post–World War II South," *Georgia Historical Quarterly*, LXVIII (1984), 18.

developing attachment to Robert Penn Warren and his fascination with Jack Burden, the tortured protagonist in *All the King's Men* upon whom the phrase "burden of southern history" probably was mod- Later, Woodward reflected similar interests with his close analysis of the fiction of Herman Melville, Henry Adams, and Henry James, Yankee writers whose former-Confederate characters criticized values implicit in nineteenth-century American nationalism. Thus it was in a metaphorical sense, indeed a poetic sense, that Woodward seemed to describe the South's burden, which is to say the southern intel- ligentsia's burden: to tap into its sectional folkmind and develop a modern understanding of the region's past and thus the nation's past; to release this understanding into the polity of regional and national society; and to encourage a revised, nonidealized national identity before it was too late. As Jack Burden might say, "the enormous spider web" of connections between past, present, and future must be made to prevail.[4]

Conceived more in the context of contemporary international af- fairs than of southern history, this thesis had major implications for a changing foreign policy and deserves full review from this perspective. Under the realistic southern influence, Americans might begin to de- velop a sense of humility that would make them more compatible with the vast assortment of humanity around the globe. Because the influ- ence would include the southern experience in Civil War and Recon- struction, it might encourage Americans to have a greater understand- ing of how idealistic aims at the start of a war can easily be forgotten at the end of conflict. The sectional force might even make Americans ponder the problems of a foreign policy aimed at "disfranchising old ruling classes, . . . indoctrinating liberated people, . . . eradicating ra- cial dogma," and invoking reconstruction inadequately attuned to "the hazzards of reaction." Finally, using words reminiscent of Charles Beard, Woodward hoped that the southern influence might allow Americans to "realize the fallacy of a diplomacy based on moral big- otry and one that relies on economic coercion through the fancied indispensability of favored products."[5]

4. Robert Penn Warren, *All the King's Men* (New York, 1946), 189–90. On the influence of literature in Woodward's life, see Woodward, *Thinking Back*, 19, 21, 23, 109, 111, 114, 117–18, 146.
5. Woodward, *The Burden of Southern History*, 205–10.

This modern realism about the world failed to appear—and Woodward was among the first to say so. In "The Age of Reinterpretation" (1960), Woodward suggested that all Americans, including southerners, still had major readjustments to make. They were passing out of an "age of free security"—of physical isolation, weak neighbors, and abundant natural resources—and into a time of economic scarcity, rapid transportation, and, therefore, increasing contact with the world. The self-centered yet missionary outlook, Woodward implied, was one of the first things that had to go; it was neither realistic nor effective in an interdependent world. Although as late as 1968 Woodward continued to depict the South as a potential source of realism, and was in no mood to issue a retraction, he took southern attitudes toward the Vietnam conflict as reason to question whether the potential would ever be realized. As he explained in 1968, such cosmopolitan southerners as President Lyndon B. Johnson had helped expand America's intrusion in Southeast Asia, evoking the themes of invincibility and cultural superiority resting at the heart of America's missionary mentality. Later, he would place General William Westmoreland in the same context. More important, in Congress and in grass-roots sentiment he saw southerners reflecting ideas about the world that seemed traditionally American. On the left, southern doves (those who opposed the Vietnam intervention) reflected an attachment to American innocence. On the right, southern hawks (interventionists) mirrored the image of invincibility. Both views lacked grounding in historical fact and therefore realism.[6]

Less than a decade later, Woodward's tone of caution had turned to disappointment. In "The Aging of America" (1977), a bicentennial address before the American Historical Association, Woodward acknowledged that, except for William Faulkner, Robert Penn Warren and a few other noted intellectuals of the 1930s, 1940s, and 1950s, southerners had not emerged as the positive influence for which he had hoped. This was to say that the potential realism of the southern folkmind, even in a metaphorical sense, had remained dormant and that southerners as a whole embraced the nation's ethnocentric and

6. C. Vann Woodward, "The Age of Reinterpretation," *American Historical Review*, LXVI (1960), 1–19; C. Vann Woodward, "A Second Look at the Theme of Irony," Chap. 10 in Woodward, *The Burden of Southern History*; Woodward, *The Burden of Southern History*, 219, 221, 230; on Westmoreland as an afterthought, see 114.

expansionist view of the world. The region's uncritical responses to Watergate and the bicentennial celebration pointed to this. Even more suggestive was southern sentiment toward the later stages of American involvement in Vietnam. Southerners had continued to participate in the national gut response, reflecting the notion of invincibility on one side, the idea of innocence on the other, and the ensuing struggle that occurred between them. That was disappointing for Woodward. "The South has let down its fellow countrymen," he lamented, "and even failed its own legitimate heritage." It seemed that southerners along with others in the nation would have to experience something comparable to "the trials of Job" to gain a realistic outlook. Woodward now called the burden of southern history "the *sorrowful* burden" of southern history. Surely there was added irony and tragedy in this, the most recent of the South's failures.[7]

As Woodward perceived the essential failure of a modern southern view of the world, beginning in the late 1960s he also began to focus on factors possibly responsible for that failure. In the aftermath of World War II, many southerners demonstrated a strong sense of patriotism. Leaders of this sentiment were white, middle-class business types who found significant social and economic mobility in the postwar "bull-dozer revolution" and the "Great Barbecue" of profits it produced. Modern industrial America was good to these people, and they developed an almost blind faith in the nation because of it. Many southern whites who, for one reason or another, failed to call at the "Great Barbecue" also exhibited this patriotism. Woodward did not digress into the sources of their sentiment, but it seems safe to conjecture that it stemmed from victory over Japan and Germany as well as from the pending conflict with Soviet Russia. Woodward also suggested that any southerner who aspired to national office, as did Lyndon B. Johnson, felt compelled to shed his regional identity and take on the ideological trappings of the nation at large, to develop a "spurious nationalism" that Yankee leaders would find appealing. As the civil rights movement slowed in the late 1960s, Woodward spotted still another possible source of southern nationalism. Although forced to accommodate themselves to Negro mobility, many white southerners,

7. Woodward, "The Aging of America," 583–84, 591–94; C. Vann Woodward, interview with author, New Haven, Conn., June 21, 1982. On Warren and Faulkner, see Woodward, *Thinking Back*, 109–10. Italics are mine.

like other white Americans, began to exude a "treasury of virtue" attitude; that the civil rights movement had achieved partial success was taken as an indication that American life was after all something open and good, innocent and invincible, and certainly worth exporting. Finally, a strain of Woodward's own southernism, the fatalistic attitude, appeared in his explanation of why southerners failed to develop a critical view of the nation and the world. "When there is a choice between the 'right' lesson and the 'wrong'," he said, "mankind has a strong predilection for the latter."[8]

In the 1970s and 1980s Woodward returned to this topic and offered still other explanations for the lack of southern realism. He noted that the period since World War II had witnessed, as predicted, the end of "the age of free security" but, unfortunately, no commensurate alteration in American attitudes. Instead, "God, Luck or History"— that is, nuclear power, Pax Americana, and "fabulous increments of national wealth and power"—had "bailed out" southerners and other Americans every time they appeared on the verge of having to adjust their self-serving view of the world. Indeed, during this period the nation had experienced "enhanced illusions of national virtue," and these cold-war illusions provided a mighty reinforcement for other missionary strains in the South's sense of nationalism. Although southerners exhibited some of the national guilt over Vietnam that appeared during the mid-1970s, they nevertheless contributed to the resurgence of that "old time assurance" embodied by the Reagan administration.[9] Thus most southerners (or at least most white southerners) of the early 1980s appeared unburdened over much of their past and confident about their mission to extend the American way of life to the world. Determined to be part of the story of American progress, innocence, and invincibility, they lived essentially disconnected from the web of experiences constituting their past.

These thoughts about the American mission and the burden of southern history encourage focus on unanswered questions about the

8. Woodward, *The Burden of Southern History*, 223–31.
9. Woodward, "The Aging of America," 589–90. Woodward does not specify Southerners at this point; I include them because of the strong contextual implication. C. Vann Woodward, "The Fall of the American Adam," *New Republic*, CXXXV (December 2, 1981), 14–16; Woodward interview; Jan DeBlieu, "A Past Apart," Emory Magazine, LI (October, 1984), 12; Woodward, *Thinking Back*, 115–116.

recent South and world affairs. Woodward traced the southern failure to a "spurious nationalism" developing in the region during the cold-war period. However, could something else, not so much on the contemporary scene as in the past, help explain the recent South's belief in America's special mission to influence other people? Were the same factors of race, politics, economics, and patriotism that he isolated in the contemporary scenes of the 1960s, 1970s, and 1980s actually evolving throughout the postbellum period? Were there other historic elements, too, which could help explain the South's inability to reject American exceptionalism and "cold warriorship"? In short, what happened between the end of the Civil War era and the beginning of the cold war to further explain the failure of realism to make at least some inroads on the South's embrace of American expansionism?

Previous interpretations of southern foreign policy sentiment both elucidate and complicate these lines of inquiry. According to older analyses, the South was known in the eras of World War I and World War II as a region of strong internationalist sentiment that then turned its back on this relatively broad view of world affairs by adopting a strident, unilateral cold warriorism. More recently, some have argued that southern internationalists of the Woodrow Wilson and Franklin D. Roosevelt years actually never had been *true* internationalists. Instead, such prominent leaders as senators John Sharp Williams of Mississippi and Tom Connally of Texas were less than cosmopolitan thinkers who had simply latched onto Wilsonianism—the League of Nations, later the United Nations—to serve their historic sectional interests of racism, militarism, and export economics. In the late 1940s and early 1950s, concludes the revisionist analysis, Wilsonian programs no longer served southern interests, and southern "internationalists" went public, revealing their sectionally based unilateralism in the form of an aggressive cold warriorship.[10]

The revisionist approach has problems. Despite the general acceptance of militarism as a constant thread of southern thought, there has

---

10. For analyses of the "traditional," accepting view of southern internationalism as well as strong revisionist challenges to it, see Paul Seabury, *The Waning of Southern "Internationalism"* (Princeton, 1957); Charles O. Lerche, *The Uncertain South: Its Changing Patterns of Politics in Foreign Policy* (Chicago, 1964); and George C. Herring and Gary R. Hess, "Regionalism and Foreign Policy: The Dying Myth of Southern Internationalism," *Southern Studies*, XX (1981), 247–77.

never been full, scholarly documentation of this outlook. In fact, recent studies of southern history indicate a consistent inclination toward violence but a dislike of organized military activity. Still, the confused stereotype lives on. One scholar recently wrote, "The militant South, the military South prone to shoot first and answer questions later, did and still does exist." Note the mixing of "military," which connotes anything but a shoot-from-the-hip approach, and an inclination toward violence. Perhaps one of the chief reasons that scholars of the World War II and cold war eras have misperceived southern militarism is the acceptance of a highly impressionistic (though significant) work by John Temple Graves II.[11] For this and other reasons, caution should be associated with the implication that southern internationalists were somehow uniquely dishonest when compared to internationalists of the Northeast—people such as Nicholas Murray Butler of Columbia University and James T. Shotwell of the Carnegie Endowment for International Peace.[12] Nevertheless, the challenges to a genuine southern internationalism do indeed sharpen the focus on the question of the uniqueness of southern Wilsonianism. And considering that much of the recent American foreign outlook has found expression through the Wilsonian ideal—the spread of America's uplifting influence through international organization—any study of missionary, expansionist sentiment in the South ultimately must probe the role of Wilsonianism and, as it turns out, the influence of Wilson himself.[13]

11. For example, see Robert E. May's effective critique of the emphasis on southern militarism in "Dixie's Martial Spirit," *Historian*, XL (1978), 213–34. See also Dickson D. Bruce, Jr., *Violence and Culture in the Antebellum South* (Austin, 1979). Quote from Joel Williamson, *The Crucible of Race: Black and White Relations in the American South Since Emancipation* (Chapel Hill, 1984), 19. See John Temple Graves II, *The Fighting South* (New York, 1943). See also James C. Bonner, "The Historical Basis of Southern Military Tradition," *Georgia Review*, IX (September, 1955), 74–85, for comments on *The Fighting South*.

12. John Frank Greco, "A Foundation for Internationalism: The Carnegie Endowment for International Peace, 1931–1941" (Ph.D. dissertation, Syracuse University, 1971); Robert D. Accinelli, "Militant Internationalists: The League of Nations Association, the Peace Movement and U.S. Foreign Policy, 1934–1938," *Diplomatic History*, IV (1980), 19–38.

13. On Wilsonianism, see Arthur S. Link, "Woodrow Wilson: The American as Southerner," *Journal of Southern History*, XXXVI (February, 1970), 3–17. On modern American idealism and Wilsonianism, see Cyril E. Black, "Theories of Political Development and American Foreign Policy," in Gene M. Lyons (ed.), *The Role of Ideas in American Foreign Policy* (Hanover, N.H., 1971), 47–65.

Also pertinent to the rise of "spurious nationalism" in the southern outlook are investigations of America's late nineteenth-century experiment with formal imperialism in the Caribbean and the Pacific. There have been strong arguments for a racially motivated anti-imperialism emanating from the postbellum South. Fear of "mongrelization" enunciated by the vituperous Senator Benjamin R. Tillman of South Carolina is the classic example. Imperialist sentiment has received even more attention. With Alabama's senator John Tyler Morgan in the lead, southern imperialists employed nationalistic, racial (the internationalization of Jim Crow), and business arguments to advocate southern growth through expansionism. Fully attuned to the antebellum South's experience with expansionism, Morgan sought to connect the postbellum South to the imperialistic programs associated with Henry Cabot Lodge and other northeasterners. Through that connection southerners might reap the benefits of textile and other markets in the Caribbean and Pacific—markets that could free southern enterprise from what he considered the controlling influence of northeastern capitalists. Further, in advancing the growth of the American realm, southerners could help heal the wounds of the Civil War and reestablish themselves in the mainstream of American patriotism. Morgan was less an original thinker than a publicist; his force was never as great as Wilson's. There was no "Morganism." Yet the Alabamian and his followers led in urging expansionism among southerners and received international attention for advocating the isthmian canal and American intervention in Cuba.[14]

What is lacking in studies of southern anti-imperialism and imperialism, however, is treatment of the competition between the two. Moreover, both attitudes raise questions about other matters. What does this regional experience with imperialism and anti-imperialism tell about the development of Wilsonianism in the more recent South? And what connections do the rival positions suggest between Wilsonianism and cold warriorship?

14. See Christopher Lasch, "The Anti-Imperialists, the Philippines, and the Inequality of Man," *Journal of Southern History*, XXIV (1958), 319–31. On expansionism see Tennant S. McWilliams, "The Lure of Empire: Southern Interest in the Caribbean, 1877–1900," *Mississippi Quarterly*, XXIX (1975–1976), 43–63; Joseph A. Fry, "John Tyler Morgan's Southern Expansionism," *Diplomatic History*, IX (1985), 329–46.

These questions frame this book. Of the various groups composing the postbellum South—laborers of farm and industry, professionals of the middle and upper classes, agriculturalists and industrialists, black and white, the impoverished, the secure, and the wealthy—this examination focuses on one particular group and its attitude toward foreign policy and the world. That group is the generally white and middle class leaders associated with the movement for a New South—people whose outlook and values have come ultimately to dominate the region.

Change and continuity in the New South movement are central to this story. Perhaps the first advocates of progressive Southern change can be located in the 1830s and 1840s, when, unaware of anything to be called "the New South," southern unionists strove to blunt ideas about secession and in varying degrees urged economic diversification.[15] Connections between these proto–New South advocates and subsequent proponents of the movement need considerable investigation, as does the New South idea during the years of actual civil war. However, it is clear that at some point in the late 1870s or early 1880s another wave of "forward thinking" southerners surfaced under the leadership of such journalists as Henry W. Grady and employed the words *New South* in describing their plan to bring progressive change to their defeated region. As several scholars have emphasized, this wave of Gilded Age southerners advocated programs, in a highly publicized creed for change, that were essentially in contradiction with each other: industrialization, racial harmony, and sectional reconciliation alongside deep allegiances to the old order of white supremacy, elitism, and to a lesser degree sectionalistic politics and agrarianism. Indeed, such contradictions inherently limited the amount of substantive change that the New South movement of the Gilded Age could accomplish.[16]

Many of these same internal inconsistencies also characterized the third wave of the New South movement appearing in the Progressive

15. John McCardell, *The Idea of a Southern Nation* (New York, 1979), 36–39, 293–94, 301–304, 311–13, 321. See John K. Kneebone, *Southern Liberal Journalists and the Issue of Race, 1920–1944* (Chapel Hill, 1985), 214, 231.

16. Paul M. Gaston, *The New South Creed: A Study in Southern Mythmaking* (New York, 1970); Wayne Mixon, *Southern Writers and the New South Movement, 1865–1913* (Chapel Hill, 1980); Michael Perman, *The Road to Redemption: Southern Politics, 1869–1879* (Chapel Hill, 1984), 68ff.

Era. Granted, Walter Hines Page, Hoke Smith, and other Progressives placed greater emphasis on efficiency than did their counterparts in the second wave, and they also added public education, improved health, and other social projects to the creed. However, as those who helped implement legalized segregation, they perpetuated the old and imbedded institutions of racism and elitism and thus reinforced many of the self-defeating aspects of the creed. They proclaimed genuine social progress when on many fronts there was none. Moreover, New South interests that persisted through the hectic social changes of the 1920s were probably of the same Progressive orientation, reinforced by the noted economic and urban boosterism of the era.[17]

With the Great Depression and the New Deal, the New South movement broadened and deepened. The precise dynamics of this evolutionary step remain to be fully explored. Nevertheless, it is clear that the fourth wave included college professors and other intellectuals such as Howard W. Odum who worked alongside well-educated businessmen such as Donald W. Comer and journalists such as Virginius Dabney. When this more intellectual breed of leadership met the unavoidable realities of economic prostration, the New South movement, now led by people who often called themselves liberals, began to exhibit in many respects a hard, realistic outlook on the Southern way of life. Distancing themselves from earlier New South advocates, these leaders charged that previous programs for social change in their region had accomplished little; political, economic, and social elitism of the old order lived on. Significant change away from farming and toward industry had not occurred; taxes remained low and unable to provide the funds necessary for quality education and health care for both blacks and whites; intellectuals of the region had daily confrontations with intolerant, defensive civic leaders. Indeed, lynchings alone precluded anyone's claiming the actual accomplishment of a New

---

17. C. Vann Woodward, *Origins of the New South, 1877–1913* (Baton Rouge, 1951); George Brown Tindall, *The Persistent Tradition in New South Politics* (Baton Rouge, 1975); John M. Cooper, Jr., *Walter Hines Page: The Southerner as American, 1855–1918* (Chapel Hill, 1979); Dewey W. Grantham, *Southern Progressivism: The Reconciliation of Progress and Tradition* (Knoxville, 1983). George B. Tindall, "Business Progressivism: Southern Politics in the Twenties," *South Atlantic Quarterly*, LXII (1963), 92–106 shows the movement persisting with greater strength than I have described. See also his *The Emergence of the New South, 1913–1945* (Baton Rouge, 1967), 219ff.

South. To solve these problems and many others, they offered a spectrum of social planning projects supported by devoted liberal organizations such as the Southern Conference for Human Welfare. Yet here most of them stopped—if not in time, at least in the development of an idea.[18]

In the late 1940s and early 1950s most New South liberals collided with a force they inadvertently had helped to form but which they could not accept, much less promote: the black civil rights movement. Indeed, as this program for a genuine change in race relations rapidly gained momentum, most southern liberals recoiled at the whole notion of regional change. In turn the New South movement lost momentum and cohesiveness. Some southern leaders, such as John Temple Graves, who had been fearing a campaign for civil rights throughout the war years, reacted so strongly that they eventually attacked many of the programs for social change that they earlier had endorsed. Others simply stood still, bewildered yet honestly analytical and articulate about their confusion.[19]

That ended the story of the evolving New South movement, if one focuses on the racial absolute in defining the New South creed. Beginning in the 1960s most southerners advocating the progressive development of their region asked for substantive progress in race relations and worked hard for desegregation. On the other hand, if one does not look upon the race issue as the central ingredient of the New South movement but, rather, emphasizes the more general notion of seeking to bring progressive change, whether with the old caste system or not, then it is possible to trace yet another wave of New South activity moving over the region in the 1960s, 1970s, and 1980s. This movement, which can be identified with what have been called "New Liberals," has racial integregation and perhaps urban development as its key goals.

One of the less recognized and understood aspects of the persisting New South movement is its relationship with American expansion.

18. Morton Sosna, *In Search of the Silent South: Southern Liberals and the Race Issue* (New York, 1977); Kneebone, *Southern Liberal Journalists*. On liberals whose views continue to evolve, see Joel Williamson, *A Rage for Order: Black–White Relations in the American South Since Emancipation* (Chapel Hill, 1986), 257–71.

19. Kneebone, *Southern Liberal Journalists*; Margaret E. Armbrester, "John Temple Graves: A Southern Liberal Views the New Deal," *Alabama Review*, XXXII (1979), 203–13.

Exploration of this relationship can help answer some of the questions about sources of southern foreign affairs sentiment that are posed above—questions arising from the burden of southern history and thoughts on the cold-war South. This exploration can demonstrate the genuinely significant role that expansionism has played in the developing movement for a New South. In fact, it can suggest that connecting the South to the course of world events has been a major element in the New South creed.

As a path to this exploration, here are offered five case studies of New South leaders responding to expansionism and the world beyond Dixie. The Pacific adventure of Congressman James H. Blount of Georgia, who conducted a controversial fact-finding assignment on the issue of Hawaiian annexation, discloses the prevailing outlook of the Gilded Age, when America rose to world power. A classic New South newspaper, the Mobile *Register*, and the contradictory thoughts of its editor, Erwin Craighead, reveal other attitudes of New South leaders of the late Gilded Age as the Spanish-American War approached. This story continues into the early Progressive Era with the China market craze and one of its leading publicists, Daniel Augustus Tompkins, the Charlotte, North Carolina, textile baron. New South advocates in the era of World War I are examined with an account of Anglo-Saxonism in the Wilsonian diplomacy of John W. Davis, a West Virginian. An analysis of the Southern Council on International Relations, an organization of ministers, businessmen, and academics based at the University of North Carolina, reveals what happened to New South foreign policy sentiment during World War II and the early cold-war years.

This case-study approach is offered as more than a collective biography, more than select accounts of certain southerners reacting to the world at certain times. It includes examples associated with congressional voting patterns and other general indicators of southern foreign affairs sentiment over the course of a century. The case studies also focus on the types of individuals most representative of the succeeding waves of the New South movement. Here are not only the journalists, politicians, and businessmen who dominated the movement in the early years, but still other journalists as well as attorneys, diplomats, ministers, and intellectuals—the types who led the movement in its later years. Certainly in most cases better-known figures in history could have been selected. John Tyler Morgan, Cordell Hull, and Tom Connally come readily to mind. But by offering examples from the ranks of the less well known and less written about, and connecting them to the better recognized, the general body of knowledge about the South is expanded. In fact, with the exceptions of James H. Blount and John W. Davis, here are the first published, scholarly treatments focused on these people; and previous studies of both Blount and Davis do not treat the southernism in their respective foreign affairs outlooks, as this study does.[20] In short, because most of the subjects herein represent a level of power and influence below that of a Morgan or a Hull, they provide a relatively rare opportunity to examine the interplay of ideas and actions among people of the midlevel of southern society. Too often historical subjects of the midlevel exist in scholarship as statistics gleaned from government reports; in this study they are offered as they were, active people who helped reflect the depth and the breadth of New South foreign affairs sentiment.

Clearly this study of New South advocates moves into that treacherous interpretive territory known as "uniqueness." The study, however, begins with two cautious thoughts. First, missionary nationalism and expansionism are far from unique to the American experience; they are powerful strains in most Western societies and many others as well.[21] Second, in the broad American experience with expansion, Southern uniqueness is at most a matter of degree. When it is argued that a certain generation of New South leaders rejected or embraced a particular American position on world affairs because of their southern experience, it may be presumed that influences common to all Americans worked in the minds of the southerners as they exhibited the results of a unique sectional experience.[22] These premises are especially important underpinnings to Chapter 6, "The Expanding South."

20. See Osmos Lanier, Jr., "'Paramount' Blount: Special Commissioner to Investigate the Hawaiian Coup, 1893," *West Georgia College Studies in the Social Sciences*, XI (1972), 45–55; William H. Harbaugh, *Lawyer's Lawyer: The Life of John W. Davis* (New York, 1973).

21. A. P. Thornton, *Doctrines of Imperialism* (New York, 1965).

22. For examples, consult Sheldon Hackney, "The South as a Counterculture," *American Scholar*, XLII (1973), 283–93; Fifteen Southerners, *Why the South Will Survive* (Athens, Ga., 1981); and James C. Cobb, "No North, No South: Southern Writers and the Northern Model," 1985, typescript in possession of Tennant S. McWilliams, Birmingham, Ala.

Attuned to Woodward's own thoughts regarding the "notoriously elusive" notion of distinctiveness in culture, this concluding essay nevertheless suggests certain historic sources and dimensions of the cold-war South's sense of self, its identity—factors emphasizing the relative uniqueness of the South's experience with world affairs and with history.[23]

23. Woodward, *The Burden of Southern History,* ix.

James H. Blount
Paramount Defender of Hawaii

Ironically, the first wave of New South advocates generally rejected the idea of American expansion. Granted, Alabama's senator John Tyler Morgan headed a small clique of southerners who often worked with northeastern expansionists; but most "forward-thinking" southerners of the immediate postbellum period—those who lived by the creed of sectional reconciliation, industrialism, and traditional social values— saw no need to thrust America into the hectic mainstream of the nineteenth-century competition for empire. Rather, they sought to modernize the South without resorting to expansion and conflict. This sectional outlook has been attributed to Democratic opposition to Republican programs and to a southern racist fear of contact with nonwhites of the Caribbean, the Pacific, and beyond.[1] Although such attitudes within the southern middle class had considerable impact on the foreign affairs of the era, much more than race and party politics was involved in the dominant New South viewpoint of the Gilded Age. The short diplomatic career of James H. Blount helps elucidate this point.

1. On southern insularity, see Edwina C. Smith, "Southerners on Empire: Southern Senators and Imperialism, 1898–99," *Mississippi Quarterly*, XXXI (1977–1978), 89–107; Osmos Lanier, Jr., "Anti-Annexationists of the 1890s" (Ph.D. dissertation, University of Georgia, 1965); Lala Carr Steelman, "The Public Career of Augustus Octavius Bacon" (Ph.D. dissertation, University of North Carolina, 1950); Christopher Lasch, "The Anti-Imperialists, the Philippines, and the Inequality of Man," *Journal of Southern History*, XXIV (1958), 319–31; and Edward W. Chester, *Sectionalism, Politics, and American Diplomacy* (Metuchen, N.J., 1975), 128ff. On southern expansionism, see Patrick J. Hearden, *Independence and Empire: The New South's Cotton Mill Campaign, 1865–1901* (De Kalb, 1982). On race and national anti-imperialism, see Robert L. Beisner, *From the Old Diplomacy to the New, 1865–1900* (New York, 1975), 148–49. Also consult the fine thesis on "republicanism" and southern foreign-affairs sentiment, Gregory Lawrence Garland, "Southern Congressional Opposition to Hawaiian Reciprocity and Annexation, 1876–1898" (M.A. thesis, University of North Carolina at Chapel Hill, 1983).

In 1893 President Grover Cleveland appointed Blount as special commissioner to investigate America's role in the "Hawaiian revolution" of that year. One of the first scholars to examine Blount's mission, Julius W. Pratt, suggested that the special commissioner—a former Georgia congressman and former Confederate—acted in a most peculiar way. Instead of reflecting the "southern" racial and economic support for expansionism characteristic of the loud-talking Senator Morgan, Blount recommended that the president condemn Americans involved in the Hawaiian revolution and reinstate Queen Liliuokalani as the rightful royal authority over the islands.[2] An assessment of the Georgian's developing career, however, and a close analysis of his Hawaiian investigation suggests that Blount and many other southerners could hardly have thought any differently.

The "peculiar" envoy was born in Jones County, Georgia, in 1837. Early in the history of North Carolina and Virginia his relatives lived as planters and lawyers, and Blount had every intention of continuing the family tradition. After graduating from the University of Georgia in 1857, he devoted two years to the reading of law with a prominent attorney in Clinton, Georgia, and then moved to Macon, where he quickly established a thriving general practice. When the Civil War erupted, Blount volunteered for service with the Floyd Rifles and saw action on several fronts. By 1864 he had resigned that role to accept election as lieutenant colonel of the First Battalion of the Georgia Reserve Cavalry.[3] Although annals of the war reveal no exceptional drama for Colonel Blount the soldier, postbellum politics show Colonel Blount the lawyer and planter as an earnest warrior for the cause of the New South.

From his Macon law office, Blount won election as a Jones County delegate to the state constitutional convention of 1865. Held under the auspices of Presidential Reconstruction and led by an array of Con-

2. Julius W. Pratt, *The Expansionists of 1898: The Acquisition of Hawaii and the Spanish Islands* (Baltimore, 1936), 128, 136; Osmos Lanier, Jr., "'Paramount' Blount: Special Commissioner to Investigate the Hawaiian Coup, 1893," *West Georgia College Studies in the Social Sciences*, XI (1972), 45–55. Considerable racism also tainted northeastern responses; see statements by U.S. Representative Elijah H. Morse (Rep.-Mass.), in *Congressional Record*, 53rd Cong., 2nd Sess., 1879.

3. See also Macon *Evening News*, March 9, 1903; and Lillian Henderson (comp.), *Roster of the Confederate Soldiers of Georgia, 1861–65* (6 vols.; Hapeville, Ga., 1957–1964), VI, 797.

federate veterans including Blount, John B. Gordon, and Joseph E. Brown, the group drafted a document designed to extend the "stability" of antebellum race relations and politics into a new era of diversified economic life. From that experience Colonel Blount emerged with a statewide reputation as an attorney "devoted to his southland [and] . . . valiant in its defense."[4] Such efforts were frustrated with the advent of Congressional Reconstruction in 1867. As a man who undoubtedly perceived the Yankee occupation of Macon as "not possessed of a single magnanimous quality or liberal sentiment," Blount joined Alexander H. Stephens and other prominent Georgians in opposing the subsequent "Republican rule" in his homeland. It was not surprising that, when Georgia reentered the Union in 1872, Colonel Blount, at age thirty-five, won election to the United States House of Representatives and maintained his position there for the next eighteen years.[5]

During the 1870s Congressman Blount lived much as other southerners in Washington did, socially segregated from a capital-city mainstream dominated by northeastern Republicans and prominent Union veterans. Still, even by the time of James A. Garfield's presidency, Blount showed outward mastery of the difficult, bifurcated existence so essential for the southerner seeking national acceptance and political effectiveness in the back rooms of Washington power. He developed the art of working with his former enemies on key national issues while maintaining a strong identity as a southerner with the folks back in Jones County. To that local constituency he always remained Colonel Blount—the stocky, five-foot-eight-inch, ruddy-complexioned, "spotless" gentleman (white hair, white suit) who represented their every petition for relief, their every river improvement project, their every request for an interview with a Washington dignitary.[6] He also owned

4. Atlanta *Constitution*, March 9, 1903; *Confederate Records of the State of Georgia* (4 vols.; Atlanta, 1911), VI, 135, 451; I. W. Avery, *The History of Georgia, 1850–81* (New York, 1881), 348, 373, 420.
5. Quote from John C. Butler, one of Blount's close friends. See John C. Butler, *Historical Record of Macon and Central Georgia* (Macon, Ga., 1879), 287. Blount's continual reelection can be traced in Avery, *History of Georgia*, 502, 511, 520, 581; and in *Biographical Directory of the American Congresses, 1774–1971* (Washington, D.C., 1971), 605.
6. Dolly Blount Lamar, *When All Is Said and Done* (Athens, Ga., 1952), 59, 45, 51; Macon *News*, March 9, 1903; Ida Young *et al.*, *History of Macon, Georgia* (Macon,

extensive acreage outside Macon, not the least of which was a 3000-acre cotton plantation that in time would bear the name Hale Nue, Hawaiian for "big house." With his wife and four children, he returned to the plantation or to a smaller place in Macon for every vacation, where he entertained and maintained first-name relationships with his people.[7]

On the other hand, among prominent nonsoutherners living in Washington, whether Democrat or Republican, this Georgian—though he may have been called "Colonel" Blount—nevertheless enjoyed a reputation as "one of the ablest members of the House." For James G. Blaine, Grover Cleveland, Benjamin Harrison, Joseph G. Cannon, Richard Olney, and the New York *Times*, Blount was a man known not so much for southern "graces of oratory" (which he actually lacked) as for "sturdy integrity" and "a logical turn of mind."[8] His devotion to the national Democratic party was exceeded only by loyalty to principles and to "a sense of fair play," which he often identified with the southern way of life. A "deep thinker," he was known to be preoccupied—perhaps more than his Yankee colleagues realized—with the honor and the dignity of the American government. As he lectured an 1883 session of Congress: "It is . . . the right and duty of the Government to see to it that Government . . . shall do no act that shall affect the honor of the American name. . . . The Government of the United States has a position to maintain among the nations of the earth; her dignity and her honor [are] to be upheld."[9]

Ga., 1950), 354, 360, 387, 393. On Blount's advocacy of legislation designed to aid his constituency, see *Congressional Record*, 43rd Cong., 1st Sess. (seven bills); 44th Cong., 1st Sess., 593 (river improvement); and 47th Cong., 2nd Sess., 994 (Brunswick, Georgia Customs House). See also Savannah *Morning News*, March 4, 1875, September 4, 1890; James H. Blount to James A. Garfield, n.d., in James O. A. Clark Papers, Special Collections, Woodruff Library, Emory University, to James A. Garfield, September 29, 1879, in James A. Garfield Papers, Library of Congress, and to Grover Cleveland, November 15, 1887, in Grover Cleveland Papers, LC.

7. Lamar, *When All Is Said and Done*, 83; New York *Tribune*, March 9, 1903; Macon *Evening News*, March 9, 1903, obituary.

8. New York *Times*, March 9, 1903; Joseph Cannon, *Uncle Joe Cannon: The Story of a Pioneer* (New York, 1927), 131; New York *Times*, February 5, 1893; Henry Thurston Peck, *Twenty Years of the Republic, 1885–1905* (New York, 1929), 329; New York *Daily Tribune*, February 5, 1893.

9. *Congressional Record*, 47th Cong., 2nd Sess., 1297; see also New York *Times*, February 5, 1893.

Thus this high-minded politician who always did his homework for committee hearings rose rapidly within congressional ranks. In the Forty-fourth Congress he served on the Appropriations Committee and fought inefficiency in government expenditures. In the Forty-seventh Congress he left Appropriations for the Foreign Affairs Committee. Still later he chaired the Post Offices Committee. Finally, in the Fifty-second Congress, he headed the Foreign Affairs Committee. Throughout this service he acted as a nationalistic reformer determined to make government responsible to "the people"—and quite different from the way he recalled it to have been during "the dark days" of Yankee occupation and Reconstruction in the South. He favored bimetalism, civil-service reform, the interstate commerce commission, and the Sherman Anti-Trust Act. He fought against the McKinley Tariff and all the other measures of protectionism. He spoke constantly about the need for a "good America," a nation suitable for others to emulate *if* they so chose.[10]

On the specifics of foreign affairs Blount displayed much of the same moralism. He attacked Senator Morgan's Nicaraguan-canal strategy as too aggressive; the internal markets of the nation were more than ample for the envisioned productivity of the New South. He criticized American aggressiveness and the "improprieties" of American Minister Patrick Egan in the Chilean crisis of 1891 through 1892. He also opposed federal subsidies for ships and the expansion of America's diplomatic offices abroad. In short, he considered the new plans for greater American influence in the world, through both territorial growth and commercial aggressiveness, contrary to American tenets of self-determination and constitutionalism and also as unnecessary for the progress of his nation and region.[11]

Certainly a southern-style nineteenth-century race view figured

10. New York *Times*, March 9, 1903; Albert C. Westphal, *The House Committee on Foreign Affairs* (New York, 1942), 117–18; Hiram Harvie Britt, "The Georgia Delegation in Congress, 1880–1890" (M.A. thesis, Emory University, 1930), 37, 48–49, 54, 57, 63, 66; New York *Daily Tribune*, December 19, 1878.

11. *Congressional Record*, 44th Cong., 1st Sess., 1046, 49th Cong., 2nd Sess., 2163, 50th Cong., 2nd Sess., 87–88, 257–58, 264, and 51st Cong., 2nd Sess., 1001–1002. See also New York *Tribune*, December 24, 1893; Blount to Benjamin Harrison, May 6, 1892, and Harrison to Blount, May 7, 1892—both in Benjamin Harrison Papers, LC; Young *et al.*, *History of Macon*, 356; Garland, "Southern Congressional Opposition," 21.

prominently into this outlook. Just as he had fought the civil rights acts of the 1870s with delicately phrased arguments based on black inferiority, he explained his opposition to American commercial expansion into Venezuela with the pithy pronouncement, "We have nothing in common with those people."[12] Yet the connection between his Georgia experiences and his attitudes toward the world beyond could indeed reflect more than views on race. Blount perceived the Civil War and Reconstruction as resulting not only in violence for the nation but in a burden, a humiliation, a denial of basic constitutional rights for white southerners. As a Victorian-era advocate of the New South, he worked quietly and steadily to incorporate these lessons about the evils of Yankee aggressiveness into the critical foreign-policy developments of his time.[13] Colonel Blount's New South of industrialism and nationalism would not follow the northeastern pattern of economic modernization, which usually included foreign expansionism. His economically diversified South would follow what he considered the more traditional American approach to progress: change hinged on minimal connections with the world beyond. To foster that type of growth, he determined to work not just at home but abroad.

Blount declined renomination to Congress in 1892. To the press and to congressional colleagues he announced his retirement from public life. The plantation waited. To his family and a few close friends in Macon and Washington, however, he expressed the fervent hope of obtaining some type of diplomatic appointment and then perhaps making a run for the Senate. Many in Georgia, including those controlling the Atlanta *Constitution,* hoped to see Blount as Cleveland's secretary of the interior. However, Blount refused to compete for that long-term appointment. After all, he was at the peak of his career—age fifty six—and the first generation of postbellum senators from Georgia, John B. Gordon and Alfred H. Colquitt, were not far from retirement. Blount probably hoped to succeed Colquitt in 1894.[14]

12. *Congressional Record,* 49th Cong., 2nd Sess., 2163. On civil rights views see, for example, *ibid.,* 43rd Cong., 1st Sess., 411, and 2nd Sess., 977–78. For similar views of other southerners, see Garland, "Southern Congressional Opposition," 26–27.

13. *Congressional Record,* 43rd Cong., 1st Sess., 410–11, and 47th Cong., 2nd Sess., 2401.

14. Blount to Walter Quintin Gresham, March 6, 1893, in Walter Quintin Gresham Papers, LC; Washington, D.C.; Macon *Telegraph,* March 16, 1893; Atlanta *Constitution,* December 16, 1893. A. O. Bacon ultimately won the Senate seat. Dewey

Moreover, Blount was part of a group of southern Democrats to whom Cleveland, confronted with populism, felt the need to give at least token (and temporary) encouragement in the form of appointments. Perhaps most important, Cleveland's inner circle of advisors knew Blount's extraordinary ability as a finder of facts, a talent well suited for American diplomacy regarding the Hawaiian Islands.[15]

An object of American commercial expansion since the 1850s, those islands had reemerged as an issue in American foreign affairs most recently in response to the revolution of 1893. Rumors told of critical American influence behind the deposing of the Hawaiian queen. No sooner had the new provisional Hawaiian government taken charge than, on February 3, 1893, its president and commissioners—Sanford B. Dole and other Americans—arrived in Washington to negotiate Hawaii's annexation to the American union. The Republican administration of President Benjamin Harrison welcomed the proposed expansion of America's realm. Secretary of State John W. Foster drafted the necessary treaty and by February 14 had guided the document through approval in the Senate Foreign Relations Committee. When the treaty next moved to the Senate as a whole, however, it encountered a well-organized Democratic opposition. Key Democrats in the Senate and the House of Representatives sent word to Cleveland, only two weeks from inauguration, that the president-elect should make clear at least to them what his thoughts were on the issue of Hawaiian annexation. One powerful Democrat, Kentucky congressman James B. Mc-Creary, assumed that as Blount's successor to the chair of the House Foreign Affairs Committee he should do even more. Through newly appointed Treasury secretary John G. Carlisle, a Tennessean and old friend from Congress, McCreary urged that consideration of the treaty be postponed until after the inauguration. At that time Cleveland could appoint a fact-finding mission to determine the exact nature of American influence in the Hawaiian revolution.[16]

Grantham, *Hoke Smith and the Politics of the New South* (Baton Rouge, 1958), 54; Atlanta *Constitution*, December 16, 23, 1893.

15. New York *Daily Tribune*, February 5, 1893; New York *Times*, March 16, 1893; C. Vann Woodward, *Origins of the New South, 1877–1913* (Baton Rouge, 1951), 271; Hugh B. Hammett, *Hilary Abner Herbert: A Southerner Returns to the Union* (Philadelphia, 1976), pp. 142–43; and Matilda Gresham, *The Life of Walter Quintin Gresham* (2 vols.; Chicago, 1919), II, 74.

16. New York *Tribune*, March 21, 1893; Pratt, *The Expansionists of 1898*, Chaps.

Although Cleveland's thoughts about the sentiment on the Hill remain unclear, the president—who would soon write journalist Carl Schurz that he was not opposed to annexation "in all circumstances"—accepted McCreary's advice.[17] In late February the president-elect convened his cabinet appointees to plan the transition in administrations. Carlisle presented the McCreary plan, and all voiced approval. Carlisle then relayed the decision to key Democratic leaders in Congress, who blocked further action on the treaty during the remaining days of the Harrison administration. Finally, on March 4, one day after the inauguration, the new president formally withdrew the treaty from the Senate and turned to his cabinet for a specific plan to gather the facts of the Hawaiian revolution.[18]

It is not surprising that the new cabinet recommended the now "retired" Colonel Blount for this delicate assignment. Three of Blount's southern friends were in the cabinet—Carlisle (Treasury), Hoke Smith (Interior), and Hilary Herbert (Navy)—and they personally opposed America's territorial expansion and knew he shared their sentiment. Indeed, Congressman McCreary had advised them that Blount, in his final month with the Foreign Affairs Committee, had been approached by Secretary of State Foster as well as by Lorrin B. Thurston, representative of the provisional government, about using his influence on that committee to help bring about positive Senate action on the treaty. Blount had refused to cooperate, telling McCreary

2–4; Ernest R. May, *Imperial Democracy: The Emergence of America as a Great Power* (New York, 1961), 13–23; and Charles S. Campbell, *The Transformation of American Foreign Relations, 1865–1900* (New York, 1976), Chap. 10; Garland, "Southern Congressional Opposition," 12. The *Tribune* interview implies that Blount may have called upon Cleveland to present an initial version of the McCreary plan.

17. That Cleveland was a moralistic anti-imperialist is urged in E. Berkeley Tompkins, *Anti-Imperialism in the United States: The Great Debate, 1890–1920* (Philadelphia, 1970), 39–40; and in Campbell, *The Transformation of American Foreign Relations*, 187. His pragmatism as well as his general interest in expansionism are presented in John A. S. Grenville and George Berkeley Young, *Politics, Strategy, and American Diplomacy: Studies in Foreign Policy, 1873–1917* (New Haven, 1966), 106–10; and in Walter LaFeber, *The New Empire: An Interpretation of American Expansion, 1860–1898* (Ithaca, N.Y., 1963), 203–205. See also George F. Pearce, "Assessing Public Opinion: Editorial Comment and the Annexation of Hawaii—A Case Study," *Pacific Historical Review*, XLIII (1974), 332; and Thomas J. Osborne, *"Empire Can Wait": American Opposition to Hawaiian Annexation, 1893–1898* (Kent, Ohio, 1981), 10–13.

18. Grenville and Young, *Politics, Strategy, and American Diplomacy*, 108; Gresham, *The Life of Walter Quintin Gresham*, II, 744–45.

he did "not like the looks" of that effort. This episode, plus Blount's reputation with antiannexationists Richard Olney (attorney general) and Walter Gresham (secretary of state) as a superior researcher and an anti-imperialist, guaranteed the Georgian's unanimous recommendation to the president. It is likely that Gresham also considered Blount's mission an excellent opportunity to discredit the Harrison wing of the GOP, Gresham's primary political enemies since he had left the Republican party in the 1880s.[19]

Therefore on Friday, March 10, Cleveland instructed Hoke Smith to telegram his friend Blount, in Macon, with the message, "I ask you to come here immediately prepared for confidential trip of great importance to the Pacific Ocean." Blount accepted the telegram.[20] Undoubtedly suspecting the nature of the mission, he arrived in the capital on Sunday morning and went immediately to the State Department for a briefing with secretaries Smith, Gresham, and Herbert. In the afternoon the four joined Cleveland at the White House for further talks. The president showed no "position" regarding Hawaiian annexation—only a desire for "information." Gresham, however, indicated at several points during the day that he had severe reservations about the legality of the American flag flying over Honolulu. On Monday morning Gresham gave Blount the specifics of his instructions. As special commissioner with "paramount" authority over all American affairs in Hawaii, he would investigate American influence in the recent revolution. These instructions did not direct him to lower the flag, but Gresham advised Blount orally that he was empowered to do this if he

19. On the Foster-Thurston approach, see *Senate Reports*, 53rd Cong., 2nd Sess., No. 227, pp. 386, 404–05; New York *Times*, January 30, 1893; Macon *Telegraph*, March 16, 18, 1893; William Adam Russ, *The Hawaiian Revolution (1893–94)* (Selingsgrove, Pa., 1959), 167; and Michael J. Divine, "John W. Foster and the Struggle for the Annexation of Hawaii," *Pacific Historical Review*, XLVI (1977), 43. Views of the cabinet members are summarized in Grenville and Young, *Politics, Strategy and American Diplomacy*, 102ff.; Pratt, *The Expansionists of 1898*, pp. 124–29; Ralph S. Kuykendall, *The Hawaiian Kingdom* (3 vols.; Honolulu, 1966–68), III, 535; and Charles W. Calhoun, "Morality and Spite: Walter Q. Gresham and U.S. Relations with Hawaii," *Pacific Historical Review*, LII (1983), 292–311. For strikingly accurate contemporary accounts of these views, see, for example, Macon *Telegraph*, March 16, April 3, 1893; New York *Times*, March 16, 1893; and Atlanta *Constitution*, November 22, December 15, 1893.

20. Hoke Smith to Blount, March 10, 1893, in *Senate Reports*, 53rd Cong., 2nd Sess., No. 227, p. 385.

saw it as justified and necessary. Blount's report would be submitted to the president through the secretary of state. In the afternoon, Gresham officially presented Blount to the president, sitting with the full cabinet. This meeting of one minute included virtually no reference to Blount's assignment. Gresham announced his appointment as special commissioner to Hawaii, and Cleveland bid him farewell: "Now, Blount, you will let us hear from you."[21]

Such casualness, whether intentional or not, was at best superficial. On March 11, a full day before Blount had even arrived in Washington, Cleveland had cabled President Sanford B. Dole about Blount's pending visit to Hawaii, and Gresham had provided similar information to Minister John L. Stevens. Neither communication to the islands, however, mentioned Blount's paramount authority over American affairs in Hawaii or the future of the flag; the Blount mission would be simply a fact-finding enterprise. Administration statements to the press and others were equally incomplete.[22]

Domestic politics figured prominently in the deception. If the Georgian's truly paramount authority had been known before Blount left Washington, Senate Republicans and their colleague, the imperialist Mr. Morgan, could have called for confirmation hearings on Blount, as they could with other high-ranking diplomatic appointments. In these hearings they might have grilled Blount and Gresham on the exact nature of Cleveland's Hawaiian policy and increased their chances for keeping the partisan upper hand in the popular cause of Hawaiian annexation. As his appointment stood in the public eye, however, Blount served as no more than an executive agent of the president, a role not necessarily subject to Senate approval since no

21. U.S. Department of State, *Foreign Relations, 1894*, App. II, "Affairs in Hawaii," 467–69; *Senate Reports*, 53rd Cong., 2nd Sess., No. 227, pp. 386–87, 395, 407; Robert McElroy, *Grover Cleveland: The Man and the Statesman* (2 vols.; New York, 1923), II, 55; Calhoun, "Morality and Spite," 296; New York *Tribune*, March 16, 1893; New York *Times*, March 15, 16, 1893; Macon *Telegraph*, March 16, 1893; *Senate Reports*, 53rd Cong., 2nd Sess., No. 227, p. 407; New York *Times*, March 15, 1893; Macon *Telegraph*, March 15, 1893.

22. See Grover Cleveland to Sanford Dole, March 11, 1893, in *Foreign Relations, 1894*, App. II, 467–69; Walter Q. Gresham to John H. Stevens, March 11, 1893, in U.S. Department of State, Instructions: Hawaii, National Archives; and Hilary Herbert to Rear Admiral John S. Skerrett, March 11, 1893, in *Senate Reports*, 53rd Cong., 2nd Sess., No. 227, p. 400. Also see New York *Times*, March 16, 1893, and Atlanta *Constitution*, November 25, 1893.

oath of office was involved. Other possible explanations for the deception include the State Department's need for time to anticipate British or Japanese designs and its need to avoid further solidification of the Dole government.[23]

Considering all this, little doubt remains about Blount's awareness of his role. His duties were an important secret, and after twenty years in Congress he must have understood that partisan politics as well as national interest were responsible for the secrecy. Yet he always maintained that, when he accepted the mission, he was convinced that President Cleveland earnestly wanted the truth on America's role in Hawaii so that he could do what was right.[24] That commitment to truth inspired the moralistic colonel—so much that he would deliver more truth than the administration probably had ever wanted.

Anxious to get to work, Blount departed Washington for San Francisco on Tuesday, the day following the cabinet meeting. Accompanied by his wife and a confidential stenographer of the State Department, Ellis Mill, he boarded the train in an "air of inscrutable mystery." In California, after acting "dumb as an oyster," he boarded the USS *Richard Rush* and headed for Hawaii.[25]

Arriving at Honolulu on March 29, Blount established his household in a cottage and set immediately to work. On the morning of April 1 he called upon Dole in order to advise that on that very afternoon the American flag, flying over Honolulu since January, would be replaced with the Hawaiian flag and that American marines from the USS *Boston,* stationed in government buildings since the revolution, would return to their ship in the harbor. Before Admiral John S. Skerrett could implement this order, Minister Stevens called on Blount with the "grave" message that Japanese forces, standing off the coast,

23. Macon *Telegraph*, March 16, April 15, 1893; Peck, *Twenty Years of the Republic*, 331; George F. Hoar, *Autobiography of Seventy Years* (2 vols.; New York, 1903), II, 49; *Senate Reports*, 52nd Cong., 2nd Sess., No. 227, p. 388; William Michael Hogan, "The Anti-Japanese Origins of the Hawaiian Annexation Treaty of 1897," *Diplomatic History*, VI (1982), 23–44; and Osborne, *"Empire Can Wait"*, 43. Blount's ultimate authority as an executive agent would become a precedent for presidential appointments of special commissioners in foreign affairs. See Henry Merritt Wriston, *Executive Agents in American Foreign Relations* (Baltimore, 1923), 292–303, 816–19.

24. *Senate Reports*, 53rd Cong., 2nd Sess., No. 227, p. 387; Macon *Telegraph*, March 16, 23, 1893; McElroy, *Cleveland*, II, 55.

25. Macon *Telegraph*, March 16, 17, 1893; New York *Times*, March 21, 1893; New York *Daily Tribune*, March 9, 1903; *Senate Reports*, 52nd Cong., 2nd Sess., No. 227, p. 409.

planned to enter the harbor and reinstate the queen under their influence should the "American protectorate" be eliminated. Japan had no such plans, as Blount quickly determined. Admiral Skerrett therefore removed the flag and troops.[26]

Convinced that his initial actions had produced no extreme excitement on the islands, Blount felt quite confident about the investigation.[27] He soon wrote Secretary of State Gresham that his paramount powers should be made public; concurring, Gresham made the appropriate announcement. Then he went further. Gresham removed Stevens as American minister to Hawaii and named Blount to fill the position. Twenty years in Congress told Blount that the title Envoy Extraordinary and Minister Plenipotentiary, predicated on an official oath of office, might well compromise the supposedly objective nature of his investigation. Blount accepted the new appointment, took the oath, and then sent Gresham his resignation by the same vessel that had brought the letter of appointment.[28]

More important, Blount began to gather facts on what had happened in Hawaii. He used three principal sources: petitions from any party wishing to make an opinion known to him; statements or letters offered in the same way; and private interviews with individuals of his selection. Above all, he sought information from all shades of political opinion. He decided to avoid holding public hearings or making premature public statements for fear of agitating a delicately quiet mood on the islands.[29]

26. Sanford B. Dole, *Memoirs of the Hawaiian Revolution* (Honolulu, 1936), 93–94; *Senate Reports*, 53rd Cong., 2nd Sess., No. 227, p. 411; Blount to Walter Q. Gresham, April 6, 1893, in Cleveland Papers; Luther Severance (Consul General, Honolulu) to W. F. Wharton, [No. 198?], April 5, 1893, in Consul Despatches: Honolulu, NA; Macon *Telegraph*, April 15, 1893; *Senate Reports*, 53rd Cong., 2nd Sess., No. 227, pp. 391, 399.

27. On the vociferous responses of the American press to Blount's action, see New York *Tribune*, April 18, 1893; and Tompkins, *Anti-Imperialism*, 41–42. See also Macon *Telegraph*, April 15, 1893.

28. Walter Q. Gresham to Blount, April 25, May 22, 1893, in Instructions: Hawaii; Luther Severance to Josiah Quincy, May 22, 1893, in Consul Despatches: Honolulu; *Senate Reports*, 53rd Cong., 2nd Sess., No. 227, p. 411; New York *Times*, May 10, 11, 1893; New York *Tribune*, May 11, 23, 1893. On Blount's powers, the Nordoff incident, and the noted playing of "Marching Through Georgia," consult Kuykendall, *The Hawaiian Kingdom*, III, 625ff.; *Senate Reports*, 53rd Cong., 2nd Sess., No. 227, p. 413; clippings in Severance to Quincy, June 21, July 10, 1893 in Consul Despatches: Honolulu.

29. New York *Times*, April 14, 1893; Dole, *Memoirs of the Hawaiian Revolution*,

As the investigation proceeded through April, May, and June, Blount accumulated the abundant quantity of materials he anticipated. Files of petitions and other documents poured in from the annexationist side, showing President Dole, Hawaiian minister to the United States Lorrin B. Thurston, and American minister Stevens to be innocent of any wrongdoing; the "instability" of the queen's government led to the revolution, and the "stability" of Dole's new government represented progress for the islands. On the other hand, equally voluminous antiannexationist documents portrayed the queen as the devoted royal leader whose lands and people had been taken over by Americans long established in the economy of the islands and in great need of incorporation into the American system. According to this view, Dole had worked closely with Stevens to use the name and the troops of the United States to blunt the queen's possible counterattack against the revolting American interests.[30]

Although both Dole and the queen refused to be formally interviewed, in sessions behind closed doors in the cottage, stenographer Mill made transcripts of Blount questioning a wide range of islanders. Blount recalled "quite a mania" among the people to render transcripts that would be incorporated in an official United States government report.[31] These records provided Blount with an important understanding of the relationship between Hawaiian society and the islands' leaders. As transcripts, however, they also reflect the colonel's own deep concerns—indeed, his prejudice—about invasion, occupation, subjugation, and greed, things he felt he knew something about from his experiences as a southerner three decades earlier.

Astutely, Blount used the interviews to reconstruct social and economic conditions that might have encouraged an American coup in Hawaii. He discovered quickly that Americans and those of Hawaiian-American families had not only gained control of productive property

103; Blount to Walter Q. Gresham, No. 2, April 8, 1893, in *Foreign Relations, 1894,* App. II, 475–76.

30. This material is in Blount's final report, printed in *Foreign Relations, 1894,* App. II, 467ff.; see also Luther Severance to Josiah Quincy, May 4, 1893, in Consul Despatches: Honolulu.

31. *Senate Reports,* 53rd Cong., 2nd Sess., No. 227, pp. 393–96, 411, 415, 386, 389, 413; *cf.* Dole, *Memoirs of the Hawaiian Revolution,* 120–121, 142–43, which emphasizes an undocumentable one-sidedness to Blount's method of research.

but, by 1893, had become dependent upon the further economic development of the islands; that is, they owned the vast reaches of land suitable for sugarcane. Blount talked with one who opposed annexation, surveyor Albert B. Loebenstein.

> BLOUNT: Did the natives sell [their land]?
> LOEBENSTEIN: They sold it and they raised money on it by mortgages, and in some instances by foreclosures. . . . I should say that not over ten percent of the land originally conveyed to the Hawaiians [by the queen] or purchased by them from the Government has remained in their hands today. . . . The Hawaiian would get hard up. He wanted to raise money on his property, and of course the plantation was always ready to advance that money. . . . The man who had made him advances would want his interest or principal, and in the natural course of events it always came over to the corporation, and this is how they managed to obtain the whole or larger part of the land.[32]

As Blount proceeded, however, he discovered that monopolization of land was only the base for an expansionistic commercialism influenced by those who sought greater ties with America. For example, in an interview with William Blaisdell, an annexationist and planter, he asked if a John Wilcox was interested in sugar. Blaisdell replied: "Yes, sir. . . . In the sugar business he is estimated at being worth something like $1,000,000, and his plantation business I should think is something like half a million. . . . He has other interests besides. He is principal shareholder in the Interocean Steam and Navigation Company. [And] he has a great deal of stock outside of his own plantation. . . . His father was one of the early missionaries."[33]

Blount also discovered that the stake of the great sugar interests rested on solutions to two cost-accounting problems. The first, as planter, minister, and annexationist Sereno E. Bishop explained, involved an expensive contract labor system. That process had been necessary to attract Portuguese and Chinese workers, laborers perceived to be racially superior and more efficient than Hawaiian laborers. Ultimately, however, planters sought a means of avoiding contract labor.

32. *Foreign Relations, 1894*, App. II, 872.
33. *Ibid.*, 704.

> BLOUNT: You think contract labor could be done away with if there
> were annexation?
> BISHOP: It is so understood. . . . [There would be] a rapid immigra-
> tion here of energetic whites from America . . . which would follow
> annexation.
> BLOUNT: What would bring them here?
> BISHOP: The sense that they are going to the United States, that they
> are coming to their own country—the protection of the American flag.
> BLOUNT: They have that already. I mean what would bring them here?
> BISHOP: Attractions to land. Opening to enterprise. They are deterred
> from doing so now because of the political uncertainty of the country.[34]

The second problem revolved around the price of Hawaiian products
in the United States. The McKinley Tariff of 1890 discriminated
against foreign products while protecting, especially, Louisiana sugar.
Cattle and sheep rancher Fred H. Hayselden, another annexationist,
delineated the issue.

> BLOUNT: What do you think were the causes of the revolution?
> HAYSELDEN: Simply 2 cents a pound on sugar. . . . They did not see
> their way clear in the face of the McKinley bill.

Samuel S. Parker, the queen's foreign affairs minister and a strong
antiannexationist, gave a similar interview: "They said that unless
something is done . . . we are bankrupt."[35]
    Implicit to the economic rationale for annexation was the factor of
race. As Blount discovered in interviews on labor supply, many planters and merchants in Hawaii believed that the islands' economy and
their own personal fortunes could not expand without a racially superior white labor force. Considering Blount's experience with race relations in the postbellum South, it is not surprising that he probed race as
a corollary of economics in Hawaii and then expanded the discussions
to include race as a general factor in the island society. He showed
particular concern about possibilities for native Hawaiian suffrage if
the islands were incorporated into America. He talked with William
Hyde Rice, a cattle rancher.

> BLOUNT: Do you mean that the native element is not qualified for self-
> government?

34. *Ibid.*, 700–701.
35. *Ibid.*, 821, 904.

RICE: I mean that . . . no native is capable of carrying on business for himself, much less of carrying on government.[36]

Marvin M. Scott, an educator, gave broader context to Rice's type of outlook. "It is the people who want to make a living and bring up families," he told Blount, "who favor annexation. They recognize the Hawaiian is going. He will be nil. They recognize the fact that this country, left as it is, would become Asiaticized. With the dying out of this dynasty it must become Asiaticized or Americanized."[37]

In the same way Blount listened to Sereno E. Bishop describe Anglo control of Hawaiian legal institutions.

BISHOP: It has always been customary to have three white judges.
BLOUNT: Because they were learned in the law?
BISHOP: Yes; the natives were incapable of being learned in the law.[38]

Blount reflected nothing more than a matter-of-fact tone as he heard what annexationists had in mind for political rights after the proposed joining with America. He interviewed Hawaiian chief justice Arthur F. Judd, a man born in Hawaii but educated at Yale and Harvard universities.

BLOUNT: Could [the islands, after annexation] maintain a government such as obtains in . . . New York, for instance?
JUDD: . . . [A] republic of our own would not be at all successful. . . . Our natives are so likely to be influenced by demagogues.[39]

Other interviews indicated a plan to avoid the problem of native Hawaiian political rights in the American union by making the islands a territory without full voting rights. Sugar planter Henry P. Baldwin, an annexationist, dramatized the point: "My choice would be for a territorial government . . . and a limited franchise."[40]

Dole, Thurston, and other leaders of the provisional government had spread the word among annexationists that Blount's southernism would make him susceptible to racial reasons for annexation. From

36. *Ibid.*, 938.
37. See Pratt, *The Expansionists of 1898*, pp. 133, 137; Lasch, "The Anti-Imperialists, the Philippines, and the Inequality of Man"; *Foreign Relations, 1894*, App. II, 952.
38. *Foreign Relations, 1894*, App. II, 698–701.
39. *Ibid.*, 840.
40. *Ibid.*, 684. See also interviews with A. F. Judd and William Blaisdell, *ibid.*, 706 and 839–41, respectively.

talking with Hoke Smith and others, the provisional government had decided that the annexationists might advance their cause with the notion that incorporation would help the southerners "get rid of a portion of their colored population." Actually, the opposite viewpoint often prevailed among southerners; they discouraged annexation for fear of losing cheap labor while joining to the Union more nonwhites. Not once is there a record of Blount agreeing with the argument of nonwhite inferiority, but the colonel let those who used that argument talk.[41]

With a fair idea of what annexationists wanted—control over Hawaiian domestic affairs and the benefits of the expanding American economic realm—Blount also applied his inquiry to the issue of native Hawaiian sentiment. He found desires ranging from total independence to home rule, yet always including the protection of Hawaiian rights. Of one native, J. W. Kalua, Blount inquired, "Are the natives you represent in favor of annexation unless [without having?] they have the right to vote?" Kalua answered, "They are not." Antiannexationist Parker went even further, suggesting that native Hawaiian sentiment on behalf of annexation, with native suffrage as part of the arrangement, had been grossly overestimated through threat and manipulation. Urging the queen's position that most natives opposed annexation under any circumstances, Parker told Blount something the colonel must have found familiar in the context of upper-class control of lower-class political expression back home in Georgia. "You take the [sugar] plantations. . . . All laborers would do exactly as the overseers wanted. . . . The Wilder Steamship Company, rank annexationists, employ natives. They could intimidate these natives. If you gave them a secret ballot [however], they would vote as they felt." The annexationist Bishop elaborated, "Their preference would be to be ruled by their own people. . . . Things might go to the dogs, [but] they would adhere to that."[42]

In short, during the late spring and early summer of 1893, Blount's investigation—especially the interviews—revealed a set of circumstances ripe for an American coup in Hawaii. Yet for the experienced

41. Charles L. Carter to Sanford P. Dole, March 21, 1983, in Stephen Spaulding Memorial Collection, University of Michigan Library, Ann Arbor.
42. Foreign Relations, 1894, App. II, 846–47, 910–11, 690–91.

analyst of public affairs, motivation was not enough. Blount probed for facts showing these motivations acted upon.

During April, in his first full week of interviews, hints of such evidence were already surfacing. The same Mr. Bishop who had told of native sentiment on behalf of native rule talked with Blount as if he knew the special commissioner to be racially biased in favor of annexation: "Experience had taught the [white] people that no confidence was to be placed in any royal promise; that there was only one thing to be done—to make clean work and sweep the monarchy away."[43] Such a determination by a minority to force its will on a majority was nothing new to Blount. In America he had experienced these dynamics from two decidedly different perspectives: as a member of the southern white elite determined, both before and after Reconstruction, to impose its control over other southern whites as well as blacks, and as a white southerner of the Reconstruction days—defeated, occupied, removed from national and regional authority by invading Yankee soldiers, politicians, and capitalists. It is not surprising that he appeared fascinated and more than a little ambivalent as he assembled the right and the wrong of the Yankee takeover in Hawaii.

American minister Stevens played a key role in what Blount increasingly perceived as an American coup in Hawaii. On Stevens' activities, Blount heard the testimony of the annexationist Antone Rosa. "The evening before [the arrival of the troops] I had heard from two members of the cabinet that Mr. Stevens had told them [that] troops were to be landed to protect people and *to keep the Queen in office.*" The special commissioner, however, refused to take this version of Stevens' pro-queen stance at face value. Circumstances surrounding the actual arrival of the American troops from the USS *Boston* helped clarify what the minister did. Crister Bolte, another annexationist, told Blount that the revolutionary group had urged Stevens to call in the troops to protect property owned by Americans in the event that violence erupted.[44] This picture of Stevens and the troops became even clearer as Blount interviewed Robert W. Wilcox, a longtime advocate of Hawaiian "reform."

43. *Ibid.*, 695–96.
44. *Ibid.*, 723–26, 944–45.

BLOUNT: Now, when the Provisional Government was recognized by
Mr. Stevens, what was the effect on the Queen and her followers?
WILCOX: They all gave up . . . on account of the recognition by Mr.
Stevens and the presence of the United States troops.[45]

In early July, with interviews completed, Blount sat down to draft
his conclusions on the whole Hawaiian affair. What he wrote, a document mailed to Gresham on Monday, July 25, remains a devastating
case against Stevens and other Americans in the manipulation of the
internal affairs of another nation. After a lengthy discussion of the
growth of foreign influences in Hawaii, he showed how the events of
1893 represented a culminating effort by Americans to take Hawaii
away from the Hawaiians. The report advances four critical conclusions: 1) native Hawaiians, in a ratio as high as five to one, opposed
annexation to America; 2) American capitalists in Hawaii, needing
improved economic connections with America, sought annexation
despite this native sentiment; 3) to achieve their goal, capitalists had
dethroned the queen and laid plans to govern the territory without
Hawaiian suffrage; and 4) American diplomatic and military influence
played a vital role in the annexationists' coup. On this fourth point,
Blount wrote with particular clarity: "The American minister and the
revolutionary leaders had determined on annexation to the United
States, and agreed on the part each was to act to the very end."[46]

Although he had satisfied the fact-finding mission Cleveland had
given him, Blount felt compelled to go still further. This white southerner generally praised the Hawaiian people, something annexationists simply had not counted on. Well over 50 percent of the native
Hawaiians were literate, the colonel wrote, a claim "no country in
Europe, except perhaps England and Germany," could make. Moreover, the Hawaiians were "over-generous, hospitable, almost free from
revenge, very courteous—especially to females . . . , [and] their talent
for oratory . . . was unusually marked." With "good features, and the
complexion of the brown races," he reported, "they have exhibited
such a small amount of thievery and . . . beggary" as to be "more

45. *Ibid.*, 1008, 1015. Wilcox favored annexation as a Hawaiian republic, but not
monarchy. See Kuykendall, *The Hawaiian Kingdom*, III, 623.
46. "Report of the Commissioner to the Hawaiian Islands," *Foreign Relations, 1894*,
App. II, 567–605, quoted passage p. 594. Blount to Walter Q. Gresham, July 17, 1893,
in *Foreign Relations, 1894*, App. II, 566.

marked than amongst the best races of the world." Wistfully, he noted, "what they are capable of under fair conditions is an unsolved problem." Still, he urged that they be left to their own "overwhelmingly Asiatic" ways.[47] These comments reflect distinct traces of the upper-class white paternalism of Gilded Age America, especially that of the South, and these values certainly affected Blount's attitude about American incorporation of Hawaii. Even so, his estimate of the Hawaiians also showed some of the "higher" principles associated with the anti-imperialist movement of the 1890s—a respect for self-determination, a sensitivity to traditional American notions about self-government, and an opposition to subjugation of a weak people by a stronger one. There was much in his past as a Civil War and Reconstruction southerner to make him look at the world in this way.

Blount's document did not find overwhelming applause in Washington, D.C., nor in many other places in America. For the "paramount" special commissioner had done more than nail a conspiracy on the Republican foreign policy of 1893. He had documented the case against *any* American administration, including the Democratic one that had appointed him, from ever annexing Hawaii. This was not necessarily what Cleveland had had in mind. Indeed, the president instructed Gresham to hold the report as a confidential document in the State Department and not even transmit it to the White House until after congressional elections in the fall. Stalling and thinking about what step to take next would be Cleveland's temporary solution to the problem. To the press, which knew that some type of report existed, Gresham advised that Cleveland would clarify the Hawaiian situation after the president had addressed himself to the economic depression and had recovered from an operation.[48]

In the interim Blount began to sense that he had overestimated Cleveland's commitment to the truth about Hawaii—that is, the truth according to James H. Blount. When Gresham indicated no immediate plans for action on his report, Blount advised the secretary of state that

47. *Foreign Relations, 1894*, App. II, 600.
48. New York *Times*, August 17, 1893; Atlanta *Constitution*, March 9, 1903; Ellis Paxon Oberholtzer, *A History of the United States Since the Civil War* (4 vols.; New York, 1917–1931; rpr., 5 vols.; New York, 1969), V, 336; Kuykendall, *The Hawaiian Kingdom*, III, 630; May, *Imperial Democracy*, 22–23.

"private affairs make it necessary for me to return home." Such business, it would turn out, had little to do with Macon, Georgia.[49]

Convinced that the islands were for the time being quiet, Blount packed up the raw materials of his report and boarded the steamer *Gaelic* on August 8. A week later the party disembarked at San Francisco and the next day began the eight-day train journey across America—not to Macon but to Washington. His return had the same air of mystery that his departure had had some five months earlier. The New York *Tribune,* a strong expansionist paper, reported that the colonel was "uncommunicative regarding the exercise of his 'paramount' powers in Hawaii."[50] There was one exception to his silence, however. In San Francisco, a *Tribune* writer reported having heard Blount state "emphatically" that "under our constitution we could not annex a country which had practically deprived the natives of all their lands."

The *Tribune* seized on the "unpatriotic" approach to the Hawaiian issue, ridiculing Blount with the suggestion that he "go and shrink in Georgia" and chronicling his arrival in Washington with sectionalist sarcasm remindful of the 1870s. "In order to make sure that nothing should escape him unawares, [Blount] resisted the temptation of hunting up his old friends at the Metropolitan hotel, where he was in the habit of living while in Congress, and put up at the Shoreham, which has less the appearance of a watermelon patch than did the famous Southern hostery of Washington, and is an infinitely better setting to the dignity of a Commissioner with 'paramount' powers." Digging still deeper, the paper noted Cleveland's plans not to return to Washington until September 1 and suggested that Blount might take advantage of the interim time to visit Georgia, where he could "hold sweet converse with Pod Dismukes, Bask Myrick, Dink Botts, and Pump Haskins." The special commissioner uttered no public response to these and other attacks in the press. He installed his wife in the Shoreham Hotel and went immediately to confer with Gresham.[51]

49. Blount to Walter Q. Gresham, July 31, 1893, *Foreign Relations, 1894,* App. II, 630.

50. Luther Severance to Josiah Quincy, August 8, 24, 28, 1893 in Consul Despatches: Honolulu; Atlanta *Constitution,* August 16, 1893; New York *Tribune,* August 16, 1893; Gresham, *The Life of Walter Quintin Gresham,* II, 741; New York *Tribune,* August 14, 1893, which described Blount as having achieved one of "the most sustained and brilliant burst[s] of silence known to history."

51. New York *Tribune,* August 14, 16, 23, 1893.

What words Blount exchanged with the secretary of state went unrecorded. Gresham undoubtedly perceived Blount's report as a problem for the president. Since the initiation of the mission in the previous March, the factors of economic depression, currency reform, and British expansionism in Venezuela had encouraged Cleveland to think about Hawaii in even more pragmatic terms. If the cause of Hawaiian annexation remained popular, he had to consider this as he plotted his administration through increasingly difficult times. Yet Blount's report, written on presidential authority, urged no more moves toward annexation of the islands, and the existence of that report—if not its actual content—was public knowledge. Did Gresham ask Blount to moderate his findings—to condemn the Harrison administration but not necessarily the future of annexation? If so, Blount refused to yield. What is known, at least, is that Blount always regretted the way the administration finally decided to handle the predicament; although opposed to annexation, Cleveland delayed and let Congress carry the burden of a decision.[52]

In mid-October, with Blount back in Macon and the new American minister, Albert S. Willis, reporting the stability of Hawaii under the provisional government, Cleveland nominally accepted Blount's conclusions. He requested Dole's government to resign in favor of the queen. He then sent Blount's report up to the Senate Foreign Relations Committee as a confidential indication of his rationale for royal restoration. Dole's government refused to abdicate, since the order came from a foreign authority, and Senator Morgan along with the young senator Henry Cabot Lodge called for hearings. On November 21 Gresham released the entire Blount document to the New York *Times* and other leading papers.[53]

This burst of long-awaited information about the Blount mission polarized public reaction. Since the time of Blount's appointment,

52. Grenville and Young, *Politics, Strategy and American Diplomacy*, 114; Atlanta *Constitution*, March 9, 1903.
53. Grenville and Young, *Politics, Strategy and American Diplomacy*, 112ff. Attorney General Richard Olney strongly dissented from the impracticality of Cleveland's plan. The entire Blount document was printed in the papers, an action international lawyer John Bassett Moore considered highly detrimental to the antiexpansionist cause. Atlanta *Constitution*, November 20, 22, 1893; New York *Tribune*, November 21, 1893; Charles Callahan Tansill, *The Foreign Policy of Thomas F. Bayard* (New York, 1940), 405–406.

northeastern anti-imperialists, of both Democratic and Republican loyalties, had urged Cleveland to restore the queen regardless of what the special commissioner found. Now, with a report advocating what they wanted, Thomas M. Cooley, Carl Schurz, E. L. Godkin, and Thomas B. Reed applauded Grover Cleveland's administration for its courageous pursuit of truth and responsible action. Feeling a strengthened minority support for restoration of the queen and an end to annexationist plans, they heralded Blount's position as one that all moral, patriotic Americans should embrace. The New York *Times,* New York *Herald,* and Chicago *Herald* led the contingency of the national press that echoed these sentiments.[54] In the South, most major papers also praised Blount's assessment and opposed Hawaiian annexation. While they could reflect a blatantly racist opposition to incorporating Hawaii—an attitude often associated with the tirades of South Carolina's senator Benjamin Tillman—the southern papers also showed nonracist, if equally partisan, support for Blount's conclusions. As the Charleston *News and Courier* wrote, "It will go hard with [the Republicans] to give up Hawaii; it went hard with them to get out the South." The better-known Atlanta *Constitution* employed a more personal tact in bolstering Blount's work. "It is not consistent with our honor and dignity to put the world upon notice that Stevens is guilty of a high crime against the governments of the United States and Hawaii; and then take no steps to bring him to the bar of justice. . . . There should be no loophole of escape for this man, if he be guilty."[55]

Curiously, the *Constitution* has been described as an annexationist paper, based apparently on one editorial appearing in February, 1893. This sentiment was transitory. Throughout the winter of 1893, as the Hawaii issue heated up, the Atlanta paper urged, "Let Hawaii alone! . . . We have no right to make our authority felt in those is-

54. Walter Q. Gresham to Carl Schurz, November 21, 1893, in Gresham Papers; Tompkins, *Anti-Imperialism,* 50–59; Hans L. Trefousse, *Carl Schurz* (Knoxville, 1982), 276; Samuel W. McCall, *The Life of Thomas Brackett Reed* (Boston, 1914), 235.; Oberholtzer, *A History of the United States,* V, 336–37.

55. "Newspapers and the Issue of Imperialism," *Literary Digest,* XVII (July 9, 1898), 32, 36–37; Lasch, "The Anti-Imperialists, the Philippines, and the Inequality of Man"; Savannah *Morning News,* as cited in McElroy, *Cleveland,* II, 58; Pearce, "Assessing Public Opinion;" 337; Charleston *News and Courier,* clipping in Gresham Papers; Atlanta *Constitution,* December 6, 1893.

lands." The Macon *Telegraph* had long argued a similar point. "We have no place in our system for colonies. . . . A Republican newspaper [the New York *Tribune*] that believes that Southern Negroes should rule the United States denies [the Hawaiians] a voice in saying whether or not the independence of their country shall be taken away . . . a despicable hypocrisy."[56]

While the prominent Kentucky editor Henry Watterson could make public utterances favorable to Hawaiian annexation—a view that is often considered his only view—it is more likely that he vacillated on the issue. Indeed, Watterson ultimately wrote Gresham that "nothing could be more incisive . . . than your Report on the matter of Hawaii. The position is impregnable I think from both the standpoints of justice and policy." Moreover, in February, 1893, Watterson met with Gresham to discuss problems the administration faced. Considering Watterson's power in Democratic circles, it is unlikely that the southerner Blount would have been given the Hawaiian assignment if Watterson had strongly favored annexation.[57]

Still other views, nevertheless, jabbed at Cleveland's administration and represented personal attacks on its now notorious southern colonel. Led by two New York papers, the *Sun* and the *Tribune*, these attacks reflected the new influence of Alfred Thayer Mahan, whose article "Hawaii and Our Future Seapower" had appeared earlier in the year. Blount suffered condemnation not only for denying America her "first fruit" but for having "churlish manners." The *Tribune* suggested that Blount's report aimed to establish a monarchy of "idolatry and depravity." The New York *World* criticized the plan to reinstate the queen—which Blount never advocated openly—as one that "might apply in Utopia." Theodore Roosevelt, still in New York, had a singularly visceral reaction: "*That* Blount who lowered the flag."[58]

In Congress a similar polarity prevailed. In his annual message of December 4, 1893, Cleveland had told the joint session that Blount's report compelled him "to restore *as* far as *practicable* the status exist-

---

56. See May, *Imperial Democracy*, 169. Macon *Telegraph*, April 11, June 1, 1893.
57. Henry Watterson to Walter Q. Gresham, November 12, 1893, in Gresham Papers; Gresham, *The Life of Walter Quintin Gresham*, II, 740.
58. Oberholtzer, *A History of the United States*, V, 337; Peck, *Twenty Years of the Republic*, 333; Candice Stone, *Dana and the Sun* (New York, 1938), 349–50; *Selections from the Correspondence of Theodore Roosevelt and Henry Cabot Lodge, 1884–1918* (2 vols.; New York, 1925), II, 252; Tompkins, *Anti-Imperialism*, 42–43.

ing at the time of our forcible intervention." He then delivered a more detailed account of Blount's role in a special message to Congress on December 18. This message implied that restoration might not be practicable. Even before the second address, however, Senator George F. Hoar of Massachusetts proposed a resolution questioning the constitutional legality of the colonel's instructions as well as his general conduct in Hawaii. Hoar, later a leading anti-imperialist, urged annexation. (Hoar's opposition to Blount may have been personal; they had fought each other as early as 1875 on the civil rights act.) The resolution was referred to Senator Morgan's Foreign Affairs Committee, which addressed the issue during January, 1894.[59] As Blount prepared to leave Macon in early January, 1894, to appear before Morgan's committee, he wrote Gresham that he anticipated the hearings to be "an outrage . . . he [coaches] the witnesses of one side and even these are deeply implicated in the so called revolution."[60]

Morgan did indeed lead witnesses for annexation and personally advocated annexation, but he also permitted Blount ample time to speak on behalf of the report.

> MORGAN: Was your judgement . . . influenced by your desire either to promote or to prevent or retard the annexation of Hawaii to the United States?
>
> BLOUNT: I would hate to think so. I had the idea that I was to conduct myself in decency and pursue the inquiry with fidelity. I had confidence in the integrity and the high purposes of the President [who sent me]. . . . I was rigidly loyal to the idea that I was not there except to report information.[61]

On one occasion the Alabama senator even led Blount.

59. Grenville and Young, *Politics, Strategy, and American Diplomacy*, 112–13; Campbell, *The Transformation of American Foreign Relations*, 188–89; Pratt, *The Expansionists of 1898*, p. 175; Richard E. Welch, Jr., *George Frisbie Hoar and the Half-Breed Republicans* (Cambridge, Mass., 1971), 208. See *Congressional Record*, 43rd Cong., 2nd Sess., 977–79.

60. Blount to Walter Q. Gresham, January 3, 1894, in Gresham Papers.

61. *Senate Reports*, 53rd Cong., 2nd Sess., No. 227, pp. 388–89, 391. On Morgan's position favoring annexation, see Pratt, *The Expansionists of 1898*, pp. 183–85. Cf. August C. Radke, "John Tyler Morgan, An Expansionist Senator" (Ph.D. dissertation, University of Washington, 1954), 200–28, which argues (questionably) that Morgan may not have actually wanted annexation. See also Tompkins, *Anti-Imperialism*, 59–60.

BLOUNT: I understand that I am subject of a great deal of criticism, which is legitimate. . . .
MORGAN: You mean to say that the right to criticize you is a legitimate one?
BLOUNT: Yes.[62]

Other senators advocating annexation showed the colonel less respect. They continually ridiculed the "paramount" authority Cleveland had vested in him, arguing that by law such paramountcy necessitated confirmation hearings, which Cleveland and Blount had skirted. This in turn prompted the assertion that Blount's report, rendered by an illegal agent, should be given no credence.[63] More caustic was Senator Shelby Cullom of Illinois, one of the builders of the Republican party during the Civil War and Reconstruction. He accused Blount of being a "detective, . . . a spy upon a foreign government . . . [a practitioner of] Falstaffian diplomacy . . . [who] descecrated our flag in Honolulu . . . a humiliation to Americans." Cullom described Blount's lowering of the flag as no less treasonous than Confederate soldier William B. Mumford's removing the American flag flying over Yankee-occupied New Orleans. And he suggested that this former Confederate from Georgia deserved the same punishment: death by hanging.[64] Indeed, hearings in Morgan's committee and debate in the Senate as a whole included precious little defense of Blount. Only his old friend, former Confederate general John B. Gordon, picked up the gauntlet. "I deplore beyond the power of expression that this debate should make it necessary, for party reasons or any other reasons, to involve the high reputation of a man whose whole life stands like a polished pillar without a blot or blemish upon it." [65]

62. *Senate Reports,* 53rd Cong., 2nd Sess., No. 227, p. 416; Tompkins, *Anti-Imperialism,* 59–60.
63. The arguments over Blount's legal authority remain of significance in the context of executive agents in foreign policy. See Wriston, *Executive Agents in American Foreign Relations,* 292–303, 816–19.
64. Gresham, *The Life of Walter Quintin Gresham,* II, 808; *Congressional Record,* 53rd Cong., 2nd Sess., 1232–33; James G. Randall and David Donald, *The Civil War and Reconstruction* (Boston, 1961), 335. For a similar sectionalistic tone, see New York *Tribune,* December 26, 1893, and the attack by Senator John N. Dolph (Rep.-Oreg.), Atlanta *Constitution,* December 6, 1893. See also Gresham's "Notes" on senators critical of Blount, in the Gresham Papers; Hoar, *Autobiography,* II, 200; and William C. Widenor, *Henry Cabot Lodge and the Search for an American Foreign Policy* (Berkeley, 1980), 102–105.
65. *Congressional Record,* 53rd Cong., 2nd Sess., 204.

While the Senate continued this dissection of the Americanism and morality of Paramount Blount, the report moved expeditiously from debate to vote in the House of Representatives. In February, Congressman McCreary of Kentucky offered a resolution designed to defend his old colleague: "The people of [Hawaii] should have had absolute freedom and independence in pursuing their own line of policy." On that premise he called for repudiation of Minister Stevens and an end of American efforts to annex Hawaii. Congressman William F. Draper of Massachusetts opposed the resolution with "stepping-stone" and idealistic arguments based on the writings of Mahan. But Maryland congressman Isidor Raynor countered with a scathing attack on annexation as un-American, and so did Georgia congressman Henry George Turner, who spoke like an eastern anti-imperialist. "An entrance upon that system of imperialism is inconsistent with the spirit of our institutions." McCreary's resolution passed.[66] Here was one of the few formal expressions of public support Blount ever received, and it came from the man who helped send him to Hawaii in the first place.

Although Morgan could treat his fellow former Confederate with politeness, he would not allow meaningful affirmation of Blount's actions to emerge from the Senate. Morgan's report of late February, 1894, reflects his precarious political status as a minority element in the Senate in 1893: a Democrat from the South who advocated expansionism. Although he personally favored annexation, pragmatic politics as well as sectional loyalty dictated that he hedge. His report found nothing wrong with what Cleveland and Blount had done or with what Stevens had done. However, if the provisional government appeared more stable than the queen's following, he argued that annexation could occur. With Republican members of the committee dissenting from the report's softness toward Cleveland and Blount, and Democrats of the committee dissenting from the omission of any criticism of Stevens, the report made its way to the Senate as a whole but never received a vote. Finally in May, 1894, Senator David Turpie of Indiana proposed a resolution opposing restoration of the queen, opposing intrusion into the affairs of the Dole government, and opposing American action that could lead immediately to annexation. Here was

66. Pratt, *The Expansionists of 1898*, pp. 180–82; Russ, *The Hawaiian Revolution*, 310; Tompkins, *Anti-Imperialism*, 61–62.

something for just about everyone—except the people of Hawaii. The resolution passed the Senate by a vote of 55 to 0, though Roger Q. Mills of Texas (paired and therefore not voting) talked against it with the futile argument that America was obligated to "tear down the oligarchy which it had established by force" and stand behind the revived Hawaiian government.[67]

The Cleveland administration took no further action on the Blount report. The president has been faulted for delivering a confused foreign policy on Hawaii and for unsuccessfully using Blount's mission and report to rake the Republican party. This criticism remains questionable. Nevertheless, whatever Cleveland's motives, Hawaii had become a source of great frustration for him, and he began to focus increasingly on the depression, the Venezuelan boundary dispute, and the coming presidential election.[68]

As for James H. Blount, the paramount defender of Hawaii went home to Georgia. Only once more did he seek a personal role in the Hawaiian affair. In the summer of 1894 he returned to Washington and sought to visit Cleveland. Earlier, through Secretary Gresham, he had sent the president the message that he had "remained quiet under criticism . . . [but was] not reluctant to assume any responsibility which you may think best. I am at your service if desired." Cleveland had no such desire. In calling at the White House Blount "penetrated no further than the anteroom." After that he decided to stay in Georgia for good.[69]

With his time divided between being a retired politician living in Macon and an elder planter overseeing cotton fields stretching out from Hale Nue, the plantation, Blount stayed isolated during his last years. He looked upon himself as one who had attempted to apply a standard of fair play, of justice, and of self-determination to America's evolving role as a world power. He also viewed himself as a defender of

---

67. Pratt, *The Expansionists of 1898*, pp. 183–87. Thomas F. Bayard recalled Morgan's role as "sinister . . . one can never tell how he will act under any given state of affairs." Quoted in Tansill, *The Foreign Policy of Bayard*, 407. Gresham, like Blount, agreed. See Walter Q. Gresham to Bayard, January 21, 1894, in Gresham Papers.

68. Grenville and Young, *Politics, Strategy, and American Diplomacy*, 115–16; Campbell, *The Transformation of American Foreign Relations*, 192–93; cf. Osborne, "*Empire Can Wait*," 66–67.

69. Blount to Walter Q. Gresham, December 16, 1893, in Gresham Papers; New York *Times*, June 23, 1894.

the downtrodden and an ideological anti-imperialist, and he would always express great love for the Hawaiian people. As a former Confederate and a product of the Reconstruction South, he believed he had great sensitivity to the flaws of a self-righteous and aggressive America. If his prescription for regional growth included nationalism and economic diversity, it also reflected a strong sense of moralism and an insular approach to the world. He sought an expanded role in the polity of the nation to help his New South develop in a way different from the more aggressive style of Americanism. Nevertheless, even as the Hawaiian episode temporarily closed in 1894, he saw his career stymied. His regional and national ideals had probably been used to serve Cleveland's political expediency, and then his values as well as his regional personality had been ridiculed by those who opposed the president's policies.[70]

Still, as a man with twenty years in Congress, Blount understood the futility of personally seeking retribution for the misuse of his career and values. Only to his family and a few close friends did he ever reveal his inner, seething bitterness. When the Spanish-American War erupted in 1898, and annexationists made their final successful move on the incorporation of Hawaii, he repeatedly declined interviews with the press. "I am not in public life now, and my enemies may make the most of my public record. I am content to let it speak for me."[71]

Yet there were other southerners who openly advocated the position he had urged. Indeed, his son, the attorney James H. Blount, Jr., became a vice-president of the Anti-Imperialist League and worked to block Hawaiian annexation.[72] Perhaps more important, in the summer of 1898 when the joint resolution for annexation of Hawaii found the approval of Congress, a strong majority of southern leaders voted

70. Atlanta *Constitution*, March 9, 1903; Macon *Evening News*, March 9, 1903.
71. Atlanta *Constitution*, March 9, 1903; Macon *Evening News*, March 9, 1903; Lamar, *When All Is Said and Done*, 102; Americus *Weekly Recorder*, December 22, 1893.
72. Young, *et al.*, *History of Macon*, 366; and Tompkins, *Anti-Imperialism*, 40 (which confuses Blount, Jr. with his father). The younger Blount wrote extensively in opposition to American expansion. See, for example, James H. Blount, Jr., "Philippine Independence—When?" *North American Review*, CLXXXIV (January 18, 1907), 135–49; and "Philippine Independence—Why?" *North American Review*, CLXXXV (June 21, 1907), 365–77. He sought many positions in the U.S. diplomatic corps, where he was not a popular figure. As a judge in the Philippine Islands, he urged Philippine independence and was removed from his post.

nay. Although the House passed the resolution 209 to 91, southern representatives opposed the measure 65 to 25. This opposition included such future notables as Alabama's Henry D. Clayton, Oscar W. Underwood, and John H. Bankhead; Mississippi's John Sharp Williams; and Virginia's Claude A. Swanson. The minority of southern representatives who favored annexation included Alabama's William F. Aldrich, Kentucky's Albert S. Berry, and North Carolina's Richmond Pearson. In the Senate, where the annexation resolution passed 40 to 12, nine from Dixie voted yea and eleven nay. Those following Morgan's annexationist lead included his fellow Alabamian Edmund Pettus as well as South Carolina's John L. McLaurin, Mississippi's Hernando D. Money, and North Carolina's Jeter C. Pritchard. Opposing with great vigor were Augustus O. Bacon, his fellow Georgian Alexander S. Clay, and the Virginian John W. Daniel. Other leading southern opponents were the two senators from Louisiana, Donelson Caffery and Samuel D. McEnery, who of course represented the fear that duty-free Hawaiian sugar would have a devastating effect on their state's economy.[73]

Two years after Hawaiian annexation Colonel Blount suffered a stroke and died from a second one on Sunday, March 8, 1903. His old Yankee enemy, the New York *Tribune*, doggedly followed him into the grave with an obituary on "Paramount Blount." His marker in Macon's Rose Hill Cemetery, designed by a daughter who led the United Daughters of the Confederacy until the 1950s, offered another appraisal: "Lord, who shall dwell in Thy Tabernacle or who shall rest upon Thy Holy Hill . . . even he that leadeth an uncorrupt life and doeth the thing which is right and speaketh from the heart."[74]

73. *Congressional Record*, 55th Cong., 2nd Sess., 6019, 6712. See also Campbell, *The Transformation of American Foreign Relations*, 294; Pratt, *The Expansionists of 1898*, pp. 320–26; Also consult Smith, "Southerners on Empire", 89–107; Lanier, "Anti-Annexationists of the 1890s"; Steelman, "The Public Career of Augustus Octavius Bacon"; Lasch, "The Anti-Imperialists, the Philippines, and the Inequality of Man," 319–31; Chester, *Sectionalism, Politics, and American Diplomacy*, 128ff.; Hearden, *Independence and Empire*; Beisner, *From the Old Diplomacy to the New*, 148–49; Evans C. Johnson, *Oscar W. Underwood: A Political Biography* (Baton Rouge, 1980), 62; Francis Butler Simkins, *Pitchfork Ben Tillman, South Carolinian* (Baton Rouge, 1944), 353; George Colman Osborn, *John Sharp Williams: Planter-Statesman of the Deep South* (Baton Rouge, 1943), Chap. 6, "The Anti-Imperialist Raises His Voice"; and Garland, "Southern Congressional Opposition," 12–16.

74. Macon *News*, March 9, 1903; Atlanta *Constitution*, August 5, 1901, March 9,

This higher-principle view of Blount is not altogether accurate. Race figured prominently into his general outlook. Although he supported the cause of brown Hawaiians facing the imperialism of a predominantly white America and seemed genuinely enamored with the islanders, there was nothing inconsistent about this attitude and the white paternalism he exhibited on matters of race relations in his own region. Indeed, while his paternalism always was polite, there is no evidence to separate him from the premise of white superiority underlying the cruder expressions of racism associated with Senator Tillman. However, that Blount reflected racial paternalism as he looked abroad is no indication that his principled rejection of American expansionism, spawned in part by his experiences as a southerner, was anything but earnest.[75] In fact, the two lines of thought could reinforce one another in a mind dominated by nineteenth-century moralism and tormented recollections of Yankees in Georgia. Perhaps the most important thing about this type of southern outlook is that over the next century, as the paternalistic strain of antiexpansionism changed, the principled one did too.

1903; New York *Times*, August 5, 1901; New York *Tribune*, March 9, 1903; Interment Record, Rose Hill Cemetery, Macon, Ga.; Calder Payne to the author, July 30, 1983; Lamar, *When All Is Said and Done*. The inscription is based on Psalm 15.

75. It has been suggested that memories of an expansionist slave South helped motivate isolationism in Gilded Age America, especially in the Northeast. See Morton Keller, *Affairs of State: Public Life in Nineteenth Century America* (Cambridge, Mass., 1977), 98. This is ironic, for many southerners embraced isolationism and anti-imperialism in part because of *their* memories of Yankee aggressiveness. Garland, "Southern Congressional Opposition."

2

The Mobile Register
and Cuba Libre

As the turn of the century approached, the New South's consensual opposition to expansionism gave way to a tentative enthusiasm about America's growing, sometimes violent, role in world affairs. One of the most intriguing barometers of this evolving viewpoint was regional journalism. The late 1890s witnessed the continued influence of the New South editors. Although 1889 had brought death to two key figures—Henry W. Grady of the Atlanta *Constitution* and Francis W. Dawson of the Charleston *News and Courier*—their journals lived on through the turn of the century as powerful advocates of the New South creed. Moreover, other editors were on the rise. In Charlotte, North Carolina, Daniel Augustus Tompkins devoted almost as much effort to the *Daily Observer* as to his textile ventures. Equally important were the emerging full-time professional journalists such as Richard Hathaway Edmonds of the Baltimore *Manufacturer's Record,* Henry Watterson of the Louisville *Courier-Journal,* and a man not so well recognized by historians, Erwin B. Craighead of the Mobile *Register.*[1]

Although critics normally explain the significance of these journalistic impresarios by pointing to their personal dynamism, it is possible to consider their views on American expansion into Cuba (and other issues) as part of a broader and deeper current—the confluence of journalism and public opinion in the late nineteenth-century South. At that time the stability of American culture had been undermined by the

1. The experiences of the early New South journalists are synthesized in Thomas D. Clark, "Newspapers," in David C. Roller and Robert W. Twyman (eds.), *The Encyclopedia of Southern History* (Baton Rouge, 1979), 903–905; their lives are chronicled in C. Vann Woodward, *Origins of the New South, 1877–1913* (Baton Rouge, 1951); and in Paul M. Gaston, *The New South Creed: A Study in Southern Mythmaking* (New York, 1970). On the postbellum South and journalism, see E. Culpepper Clark, *Francis Warrington Dawson and the Politics of Restoration: South Carolina, 1874–1889* (University, Ala., 1980).

forces of science, industrialism, and urbanization. Perhaps southerners felt this disorientation even more intensely than did others because of the additional forces of change spawned by the Civil War and
Reconstruction. Yet government offered little help to southerners, or
to other Americans. Without modern bureaucratic tentacles, government remained weak and uninvolved, leaving people virtually on their
own to make order out of disorder. In this limbo of public uncertainty,
newspapers gained enormous power. With innovations such as
streamer headlines, large line illustrations, eye-catching advertise-
ments, the wire network of the Associated Press, and editors who
singlehandedly dominated their editorial pages, highly subjective journalism counseled southerners and other Americans on how to survive
and prosper in a rapidly modernizing culture. Such a large number of
Americans looked to the press that between 1880 and 1899 (while
population in cities of eight thousand or more grew only 52 percent)
daily newspaper circulation rose 323 percent. It is not surprising that
contemporary readers perceived the dynamic New South editors as
"metropolitan" and "unprejudiced."[2] In retrospect they stand as even
more. On a wide range of issues, including American expansion, these
editors appear as a pressure group—cosmopolitan and business-oriented—that advocated specific policies for "progress" and simultaneously supported a developing consensus attuned to upper-middle-class
values.[3]

The New South editors' counsel on the coming of the Spanish-
American War is especially helpful in understanding changing regional attitudes concerning expansionism. In view of their interest in
Yankee industry, it was predictable that these newspapermen would
often assume editorial positions reflecting business-oriented journals
of the Northeast. Beginning in the spring of 1895 with the outbreak of
the second Cuban revolution against Spain, Tompkins, Watterson, and
virtually all other New South editors did indeed echo their Yankee

2. Robert H. Wiebe, *The Search for Order, 1877–1920* (New York, 1967), Chaps.
1–6; Gerald F. Linderman, *The Mirror of War: American Society and the Spanish
American War* (Ann Arbor, 1974), 152–64; New Orleans *Times-Democrat*, as quoted
in Woodward, *Origins of the New South*, 145.
3. Woodward, *Origins of the New South*, 147–48; Linderman, *Mirror of War*, 152–
55. See also James Boylan, "Journalists and Foreign Policy," in Alexander DeConde
(ed.), *Encyclopedia of American Foreign Policy* (3 vols.; New York, 1978), II, 507–14.

counterparts. Patriotic, even belligerent, they urged Spain's removal from the Western Hemisphere. As the Cuban revolution continued, however, and chances for American intervention increased, these same southern journalists urged calmness and a patient, peaceful way of resolving the Cuban predicament. A Spanish-American war, they feared, would traumatize the stock market and retard recovery from the depression of 1893. Finally, when William McKinley's administration decided that declaring war was the only option, southern newspapermen endorsed the decision with a flurry of patriotism and began to focus on the economic benefits the conflict might produce—an end to uncertainty on the stock market and the opening up of former Spanish markets in the Caribbean and the Pacific.[4]

Yet there also were peculiar regional interests that made finding a position on this issue tormenting and contradictory for southern editors and their readers. Many of the antiexpansionist factors that had surfaced during the Hawaiian annexation controversy now reappeared, especially pacifism and Anglo-Saxonism. There were countervailing forces, too: the compulsion to appear patriotic and reconstructed in the first war since 1865, and the desire also to appear economically modern, that is, attuned to contemporary world affairs so as to deflect the criticism that southerners were backward. These and other uniquely sectional impulses made the thought of Caribbean intrusion strikingly complex for New South advocates during the 1890s. Although in 1893 most had rejected the idea of America's imperialistic takeover of Hawaii, just four years later—while they had

4. On conservative, anti-yellow press journals of the era see Marcus W. Wilkerson, *Public Opinion and the Spanish-American War* (Baton Rouge, 1932); Joseph E. Wisan, *The Cuban Crisis as Reflected in the New York Press* (New York, 1934); and Charles H. Brown, *The Correspondents' War* (New York, 1967). There is no effective synthesis of the southern press on the Cuban issue. One can piece together a pattern from the following studies: "Newspapers and the Issue of Imperialism," *Literary Digest*, XVII (July 9, 1898), 32–38; Richard E. Wood, "The South and Reunion, 1898," *Historian*, XXXI (1969), 415–30; Tennant S. McWilliams, "The Lure of Empire: Southern Interest in the Caribbean, 1877–1900," *Mississippi Quarterly*, XXIX (1975–1976), 43–63; and Martha Ashley Girling, "Southern Attitudes Towards the Cuban Craze" (M.A. thesis, Mississippi State University, 1960). The same pattern also appears in state studies such as George H. Gipson, "Attitudes in North Carolina Regarding the Independence of Cuba," *North Carolina Historical Review*, XLIII (1966), 43–65; and Katheryn McConnell, "Alabama and the Spanish-American War" (M.A. thesis, Auburn University, 1955).

not forgotten the implications of the Hawaiian coup—New South supporters grudgingly began to abandon the forbearance of James H. Blount. They began to accept the northeastern expansionist litany so long urged by their fellow southerner, Senator Morgan, and now applied to Cuba. That southern votes in Congress, as well as petitions sent to Washington by southern chambers of commerce, reflected much the same pattern of thought suggests that the New South editors were indeed acting and reacting in tune with their predominantly middle-class readership.[5]

The editorials of the Mobile *Register,* a paper with offices virtually looking out at Cuba, provided a daily, blow-by-blow account of the southern experience with journalism and world affairs and, in the process, established that paper as yet another of the classic New South mold. Like the Louisville *Courier-Journal* and other well-known papers, the Mobile *Register* prospered under the leadership of personalities living in the mainstream of the New South creed, men reflecting that convoluted blend of the Old South and modernizing America. The owner of the *Register,* John L. Rapier, was a Mobilian by birth. While a young Confederate soldier he saw action at Seven Pines, Second Manassas, Sharpsburg, and Fredericksburg, only to be captured some twenty miles from home when Yankees, in 1864, took Mobile Bay and Fort Gaines. At the end of Reconstruction, Rapier—age thirty-five—used a small inheritance and some savings to purchase the Mobile *Register* Company from the Old South diplomat, John Forsyth. Although Rapier had dabbled in journalism during the war and later served briefly as Forsyth's secretary, he was no writer. Rather, he was one of many old-family entrepreneurs determined to take advantage of

5. On southern insularity, see, for example, Edwina C. Smith, "Southerners on Empire: Southern Senators and Imperialism, 1898–99," *Mississippi Quarterly,* XXXI (1977–1978), 89–107; and Christopher Lasch, "The Anti-Imperialists, the Philippines, and the Inequality of Man," *Journal of Southern History,* XXIV (1958), 319–31. On southern expansionism, see Patrick J. Hearden, *Independence and Empire: The New South's Cotton Mill Campaign, 1865–1901* (De Kalb, 1982). On race and national anti-imperialism, see Robert L. Beisner, *From the Old Diplomacy to the New, 1865–1900* (New York, 1975), 148–49. Edward W. Chester traces congressional voting patterns in *Sectionalism, Politics and American Diplomacy* (Metuchen, N.J., 1975), 140ff. On petitions from businessmen, consult McWilliams (ed.), "Petition for Expansion: Mobile Businessmen and the Cuban Crisis, 1898," *Alabama Review,* XXVIII (1975), 58–63, which also touches on documents from Savannah, New Orleans, Charleston, S.C., and Jacksonville, Fla.

the boom developing in Mobile through the influx of Yankee capital.[6] Thus, for his newspaper to flourish and to help usher in the new era, he knew that he needed a professional journalist. He found one in Erwin B. Craighead.

A descendant of a noted Presbyterian minister from North Carolina, Craighead had experienced the Civil War as a youth in Tennessee. During Reconstruction he studied in Racine College in Wisconsin; read law at Nashville College, near his home; and then went abroad for further study in law and philosophy, first at the Middle Temple, Inns of Court, London, and later at the University of Leipzig. On returning to the United States in 1877, he moved immediately to New Orleans, where he used an inheritance to purchase half ownership in that city's *Daily States*. There he discovered not only his own significant talent as a writer but his great dislike for the business of running a newspaper. "Up and coming," fluent in German, yet slow-moving and "lanky" and "courtly" and preoccupied with the Civil War, young Craighead had just the combination of new and old ways to make Rapier's paper a success.[7]

In 1883, Rapier hired Craighead to come to Mobile as city editor. Quickly the young journalist developed a reputation as "Mobile's newspaperman" in part owing to an article he wrote in the *Register* on the death of President Ulysses S. Grant. Reprinted in prestigious journals nationwide, including the New York *Times,* the essay urged the New South cause of sectional reconciliation. By 1889, Rapier had named Craighead vice president of the *Register* Company and, three years later, editor-in-chief as well.[8] With equally cosmopolitan wives,

6. See "John Lawrence Rapier," in Marie Bankhead Owen (ed.), *The Story of Alabama* (5 vols.; New York, 1949), III, 163; *Mobile City Directory,* 1867 through 1905; Tennant S. McWilliams, *Hannis Taylor: The New Southerner as an American* (University, Ala., 1978), 13; and Records of Appointments of Postmasters—Alabama, 1889–1929, p. 384, in National Archives.

7. See "Erwin Craighead," in Owen (ed.), *The Story of Alabama,* III, 141–42; and "Erwin Craighead," *The South in the Building of the Nation* (12 vols.; Richmond, Va., 1909), XI, 234. See also John Wilds, *Afternoon Story: A Century of the New Orleans States-Item* (Baton Rouge, 1976), 49–50; and an unidentified clipping, in Erwin Craighead File, Mobile Public Library.

8. *Mobile City Directory,* 1883–1928; New York *Times,* February 5, 1932. See, for example, John C. O'Connell to the Editor, New York *Times,* December 9, 1927, a clipping included in John C. O'Connell to Craighead, December 9, 1927, in Erwin Craighead Papers, in possession of Mrs. Frank Plummer, Mobile; and Craighead to

Craighead and Rapier fitted neatly into Mobile's elite. Their regular social circle included the Mobile Chamber of Commerce, the Commercial Club, and the Cotton Exchange, not to mention the even more restricted Athelston Club and secret Mardi Gras societies. Rapier and Craighead saw "eye to eye on all."[9] But it was Craighead who wrote the editorials of the Mobile *Register* and who, on retirement in 1927, enjoyed a reputation among New York journalists as "perhaps the most scholarly . . . man at the head of any newspaper in the South" and, indeed, "one of the most forceful of the Southern editors."[10] Delivered in a precise, legalistic style, Craighead's editorials on *Cuba Libre* provide a rare opportunity to examine the ambivalence in the minds of many New South advocates as America, for the first time, went forth into the modern industrial world to fight a war.

At first the *Register* conveyed anything but confusion. On March 8, 1895, with the second Cuban revolution less than two weeks old, a Spanish gunboat fired blank shots across the bow of an American merchant vessel, the *Alliança*. Spain later apologized, saying that the *Alliança*, en route from Colón, Panama, to New York, had been suspected of carrying contraband to Cuban revolutionaries. Not waiting for the apology, Craighead swiftly joined the *Register* to the journalistic response nationwide—Spain was guilty of an atrocity. With an intricate discussion of "international waters" and many references to *Wharton's Digest of International Law,* the *Register* characterized the attack as "an outrage upon the American flag" and urged Madrid to reprimand the Spanish captain.[11] The same patriotism blared forth two weeks later in response to internal changes in the Spanish government. Conservative leader Antonio Cánovas del Castillo replaced the

Overton Fullton, November 1, 1930, in Stephens Gaillard Croom Papers, in possession of Stephens Gaillard Croom II, Mobile.

9. Mobile *Register*, February 4, 1932; Craighead to Emma Langdon Roache, April 15, 1931, in Craighead File; Adelaide Marston Trigg, interview with author, Mobile, July 16, 1982.

10. New Orleans *Daily States*, November 18, 1923; New York *Times*, December 9, 1927. Craighead maintained close contacts with well-known journalists and publishers. See for example William Gilmore Beumer (of Harper & Row) to Craighead, March 9, 1915, in Craighead Papers; and Craighead, "Lamon's Warning to Lincoln," New York *Times*, May 20, 1928.

11. French Ensor Chadwick, *Relations Between the United States and Spain: Diplomacy* (New York, 1949), 419–23; Mobile *Register*, March 16, 1895. For the national response, see Wilkerson, *Public Opinion and the Spanish-American War,* 18–20.

Liberal minister of state, Práxedes Mateo Sagasta, in a crisis touched off by press censorship. To Craighead, the change of government not only indicated that many "foreigners" failed to "understand the idea of an absolutely free press" but also that the Hispanics' unstable society lacked the ability to "rise above local prejudices." Sooner or later, he believed, Spain's decadence would be a problem in the Caribbean, and the Monroe Doctrine would need to be activated. Ultimately, Cuba would be brought into the American system through legal means— but not through "Hawaiian monkey business."[12]

The same tone persisted into the summer of 1895. Ever the trained attorney, Craighead stood forcefully behind the claims of Antonio Mora, a naturalized American citizen whose vast Cuban sugar estates had been confiscated by Spanish authorities.[13] Throughout this period, Craighead wrote repeatedly that Spain remained "backward" in its concepts of "law" and "rights" while America had "progressive" legal traditions. That Hannis Taylor, a Mobile attorney and close friend of both Rapier's and Craighead's, served as American minister to Spain at that time and moderated many of the developing Spanish-American disputes, only made the American flag wave more briskly on the pages of this New South journal.[14] So strong was this anti-Spanish sentiment that Craighead, an erudite man and one normally attuned to the subtleties of history, seemed unaware of the irony of his position—a journalist of the American South was criticizing nineteenth-century Spain for its inability to solve problems of localism and to function as a cohesive, progressive nation. Even more curious was his rapid reversal of this position.

In January, 1896, as Spanish-American tensions increased and some congressmen and journalists began to talk about the need for American intervention in Cuba, the *Register* recoiled from its earlier advocacy of the American rescue of Cuba. Cánovas, Spain's new minister of state, attempted to stymie the Cuban revolt by placing the island

12. Mobile *Register*, March 17, 19, 20, 29, April 6, 29, 1895. On this change of the Spanish government, see Ernest R. May, *Imperial Democracy: The Emergence of America as a Great Power* (New York, 1961), 94–99.

13. On the Mora claim, see Tennant S. McWilliams, "Procrastination Diplomacy: Hannis Taylor and the Cuban Business Disputes, 1893–97," *Diplomatic History*, III (1977–1978), 63–79.

14. Mobile *Register*, June 23, August 13, 25, 1895; McWilliams, *Hannis Taylor*, 9, 21, 21–33, 48–49.

under the control of General Valeriano ("the Butcher") Weyler. The new commander's concentration camps sparked a range of aggressive responses in the United States: calls for recognition of Cuban belligerency (which would legitimate American aid to the Cubans), calls for immediate American military intervention, even pleas for annexation of the island. Ignoring his recent references to the mission implied by the Monroe Doctrine, Craighead attacked his own senior senator, John Tyler Morgan, and other interventionists for being irresponsible. On the question of belligerency status for Cuba, Craighead warned, "It is well for us to know whither we are drifting."[15]

With the escalation of Spanish-American tensions, Rapier's antiwar sentiment sharpened, deepening and focusing on specific targets. In the spring of 1896, filibustering expeditions from the American coast began slipping weapons and supplies into Cuba. Much like business-oriented journals in the Northeast, and unlike the emerging yellow press, the *Register* blasted the filibusters as troublemakers.[16] In late April, when a Spanish gunboat apprehended one American-based blockade-runner, the *Competitor,* Craighead applauded the arrest of the seven adventurers, even though two were naturalized American citizens. In time Spain would release them. Not knowing their fate, however, Craighead argued that "those who render assistance by offering personal service and are caught in the act, have taken their lives in their [own] hands, for by the law of nations they are condemned." Indeed, he now portrayed General Weyler and his government as ethical and excessively tolerant. "If Weyler is the bloodthirsty man he is popularly supposed to be, why did he not hang the alleged filibusters from the yardarms of their vessel instead of bringing them to trial and causing all the present discussion? He could have said that they were found with arms in their hands, that they resisted arrest, [and that] they had been disposed by summary court-martial on deck. Being hanged they could not have refuted the statement!" Even if Spain had acted less prudently in the *Competitor* affair, Craighead would still have believed that Americans would have been unwise to let the epi-

15. May, *Imperial Democracy,* 98–107; Mobile *Register,* May 25, 1896.
16. May, *Imperial Democracy,* 84; Brown, *The Correspondents' War,* 38–40; Wisan, *The Cuban Crisis as Reflected in the New York Press,* 149–54, 220–21, 348, 456; Wilkerson, *Public Opinion and the Spanish-American War,* 20ff.

sode become an issue. Pointing to the relationship between Cuban difficulties and the Venezuelan boundary dispute, then in final stages of resolution, he suggested that it "would not be wise to take up new [diplomatic] trouble when the old one with Great Britain is in an unsettled condition." Rapier did not want war, especially when Britain could not be counted on as an ally.[17]

Developments in late 1896 and early 1897 explain why Craighead so swiftly embraced an antiwar view. In December, President Grover Cleveland attempted to quell growing war and annexation sentiment by proposing, in his annual message, that Spain grant autonomy to Cuba. Craighead praised the speech, saying that it would "command the respectful attention not of Spain only but of the civilized world."[18] More revealing is the *Register*'s defense of Cleveland when he was attacked by Senator Morgan. Leader of the small imperialist element within the New South elite that included Alabama congressman Joseph H. Wheeler, Morgan criticized Cleveland's policy as weak and urged all Americans to support, instead, a Cuban belligerency resolution recently introduced in the House of Representatives.[19] Craighead fought back.

> [Morgan] exhibits a fine contempt for our business interests and assumes a monopoly of right thinking. . . . The Mobile merchants declared that peace is essential to this recovery of the commercial interests of the country from the acute depression of the past several years, and that peace should not be endangered by the intrusion of our government into the domestic concerns of people foreign to us in race, language, and institutions. . . . There is a feeling of weariness [here] caused by the senator's heroics and Quixotic performances generally. He should strive to keep in touch with the commercial interests of Alabama.

A week later, on January 12, 1897, Craighead shot out again, "Senator Morgan is [ready] to throw commercial interests to the winds. . . .

17. Mobile *Register*, May 10, 14, 1896.
18. James D. Richardson (ed.), *A Compilation of the Messages and Papers of the Presidents* (20 vols.; New York, 1897), XIV, 6149–54; Mobile *Register*, December 8, 1896.
19. On Morgan's belligerency, see Joseph A. Fry, "John Tyler Morgan's Southern Expansionism," *Diplomatic History*, IX (1985), 340–41.

Fortunately, there are cooler and wiser heads in the senate, and there is a safe man at the helm of the state."[20]

Morgan may have worked for commercial growth by advancing the China market and a Nicaraguan canal. But, in the minds of Craighead and Mobile's business leaders, Morgan's position on the Cuban issue seemed to defeat certain basic interests of the New South. Morgan's "solution" to the Cuban problem would start a war with Spain. That war, in turn, not only would force America off the gold standard, discouraging investment and recovery from the depression of 1893, but result in an American victory leading to annexation of more non-whites and further racial tension in an already unsettled atmosphere. The same, standard antiwar arguments had appeared in the New York *Journal of Commerce* and other conservative organs of America's industrial and commercial expansion.[21] But Mobile's civic elite had an even greater stake in these arguments. Their goal was not just general Anglo-Saxonism and national recovery from the depression. They sought progress according to a complex racial and economic formula—they sought a New South. In view of these regional and national interests, Craighead determined that *Cuba Libre,* regardless of the Monroe Doctrine and America's mission to expand its influence, simply was not worth a war. He wrote, "War is a bad thing at any time, but a war begun in the wrong and in which victory, when obtained, will not confer glory upon our flag, is little less than a crime."[22]

Craighead spread the pacification message during the remainder of 1897. On August 8, Spain's minister of state, Cánovas, was assassinated. Although Craighead had once portrayed Cánovas as backward, he now eulogized the fallen leader. "It must be said to [Cánovas'] credit that Spain has prospered when conservatism prevailed, and but for the rebellion in Cuba and the Philippines, would be today in exemplary condition. Personally, he was a man of highest character, diligent, well-informed, and thoroughly patriotic. In his death Spain has suffered a

20. Mobile *Register,* January 6, 1897.
21. *Ibid.,* January 12, 1896. See also December 20, 1896, February 25, 26, March 2, April 20, May 18, 19, 1897. On antiwar sentiment, see McWilliams (ed.), "Petition for Expansion," 58–63; Julius W. Pratt, *The Expansionists of 1898: The Acquisition of Hawaii and the Spanish Islands* (Baltimore, 1936), 242; Wisan, *The Cuban Crisis as Reflected in the New York Press*; and May, *Imperial Democracy,* 77.
22. Mobile *Register,* February 26, 1897.

serious loss." He gave a similarly positive assessment of General Weyler, who was removed shortly thereafter from the Cuban command. "No matter what opinion Weyler's enemies may hold [of] him," he wrote, "it must be said [that] the Cuban governor-general vacated his place in a very graceful manner." America's yellow press showed no such kindness.[23] Nor did it share Craighead's optimism about Sagasta's return to the office of minister of state. In September, Craighead advised Mobilians of Sagasta's new approaches to the Cuban problem. Instead of seeking resolution through sheer force, Sagasta offered Cubans universal manhood suffrage and control over certain internal economic affairs. This was quite an offer considering Cuba's "polyglot" population, Craighead wrote. Even though Cubans rejected the reforms and kept fighting for full independence, Craighead emphasized the conciliation in Sagasta's offer and repeated the central point: "Spain is not out for war with [America]. The new premier uses language on this subject that should inspire action on the part of our administration worthy of [our] great and glorious republic."[24]

That depiction of a pacific American government found ironic contrast in Craighead's treatment of an impetuous grande dame of the Confederacy, Mrs. Jefferson Davis. Having once been a rebel herself, Mrs. Davis wrote to the queen of Spain, criticizing Spanish forces for imprisoning Evangelina Cisneros, a celebrated Cuban revolutionary. Craighead viewed her letter as premature: Cisneros "had not been tried, much less condemned." The editor would not even bow to Lost Cause notables as he urged a steady course of peace. Several months later, in February, 1897, the paper used the same approach in treating the case of Julio Sanguilly. Claiming to be an American citizen, Sanguilly had been residing in Havana when hostilities broke out in 1895. He was jailed by Spanish authorities; this act provoked a rage of American jingoism in Congress and in the yellow press. But when Weyler freed Sanguilly in February, 1897, Craighead offered the re-

---

23. May, *Imperial Democracy*, 125, 160; Mobile *Register*, August 10, 20, October 10, 1897; Brown, *The Correspondents' War*, 106–107.

24. Mobile *Register*, September 9, November 14, 1897. Sagasta's reforms are detailed in Tennant S. McWilliams, "United States Relations with Spain, 1893–97: A Study of the Ministry of Hannis Taylor" (M.A. thesis, University of Alabama, 1967), App.

leased man no sympathy; he explained that Sanguilly had misused American citizenship to aid the Cuban movement. When Senator Morgan praised Sanguilly, the *Register* retorted, "So Morgan goes sprouting on."[25]

Even as the critical year of 1898 arrived, the *Register* attempted to hold its antiwar position. On February 9, 1898, New York papers printed the famous letter of Dupuy deLome, in which the Spanish ambassador to the United States described the new president, William McKinley, as a weak leader unable to withstand war pressures. While many editors nationwide responded by urging that America declare war, Craighead stuck with highly conservative eastern papers and sought to defuse the issue. He argued that Madrid's quick recall of Dupuy deLome represented decisive action "taking the breath [out] of the jingos" and further indicated that Spain was "anxious to avoid trouble with us." "It is not possible," Craighead advised on February 15, "that any further unpleasant consequences will have to be noted" because of the deLome issue.[26]

Indeed, the same day he dispensed with deLome, the *Maine* exploded and Craighead still refused to flinch; he would not retreat from his pacifistic position. Subsequent investigation would trace the battleship's destruction to negligence on board the vessel. But when it blew up that afternoon in Havana Harbor, many politicans and editors blamed Spain for the resulting loss of more than 250 American lives and cried "*casus belli!*"[27] Craighead did not—at least not at first. On February 17 he lamented the "calamity that has befallen the . . . *Maine*," suggesting that no city in America experienced the tragedy's gloom more than Mobile did, for in the port town as public guests were many members of families with sons and husbands assigned to the battleship. On the same day, however, he also attacked the rumor that Cubans blew up the *Maine*: "We mention the theory in order to cover the whole ground, but we give it no great weight. People who are in a desperate position do not adopt such roundabout methods." If he

25. Mobile *Register*, February 27, March 2, September 1, December 15, 1897. On the Cisneros and Sanguilly cases, see May, *Imperial Democracy*, 134; and Chadwick, *Relations Between the United States and Spain*, 428–29, 481–90.

26. David F. Trask, *The War with Spain in 1898* (New York, 1981), 26–28; Brown, *The Correspondents' War*, 112–13; Mobile *Register*, February 12, 15, 1898.

27. Trask, *The War with Spain*, 24–25, 35; May, *Imperial Democracy*, 139–40.

was weak on that point, the day after he was stronger. "There are so far no evidences of treacherous conduct in connection with the loss of the *Maine*. We suppose that the news will have a calming effect upon those war-like spirits who have volunteered to help our country out of the peril in which they suppose it to be placed by the *Maine* incident. Their readiness to fight has never been questioned, but their readiness to volunteer suggests the idea that they are seeking cheap advertising for their valor." Also on February 18, he took on "Key West specialists"—yellow journalists—who had been reporting, contrary to fact, that Cubans were implicated because in the bottom of the vessel had been found a hole made by an eight-inch percussion shell, a type of shell that the *Maine* did not use. Craighead reminded readers that "there has been no diver sent down to examine the vessel" and that no one had any factual knowledge of "any hole in her bottom."[28]

On the other hand, that mid-February editorial represents Craighead's last clear effort on behalf of peace. Henceforth, as America moved closer and closer to war with Spain, Craighead showed deep ambivalence about his nation's and his region's role in the world. In fact, the *Register* seemed to embrace a superpatriotism while simultaneously cautioning about the flaws of jingoism. With the initiation of a joint Spanish-American investigation into the *Maine* disaster, Craighead, in late February, wrote: "If [Spanish] treachery be proved, the act of treachery will be *casus belli*." One day later, February 27, he declared: "The people of the South as represented by this truly typical Southern city are not anxious for war. . . . [Southerners] deprecate war, especially [war] that has no good cause behind it. . . . [In] case of war, commerce would be interfered with, if not stopped entirely for a time, and the present rapid development would receive a severe check. If we have to have war, we will bear our part in it with bravery, but we do not want war. *We know too well what war means*."[29] On February

28. Mobile *Register*, February 17, 18, 1898.
29. *Ibid.*, February 26, 27, 1898. A similar opposition to war and the military existed in rural areas often isolated from the daily influence of the New South publicists. Some of this sentiment, as William A. Williams has suggested, can be traced to populism; but it also appeared in less reform-oriented places owing apparently to unpleasant memories of war and Yankee military occupation. Joseph C. Kiger, "Social Thought as Voiced in Rural Tennessee Newspapers, 1878–1898," *Tennessee Historical Quarterly*, XI (1950), 153–54; Harvey H. Jackson, "The Spanish-American War as Reflected in the Clark County [Alabama] *Democrat*, 1895–99" (typescript in possession of Tennant S.

28, Craighead advanced a national antiwar argument. With an insightful analysis of American expansionism, he wrote: "We [Americans] are filled with an immeasurable and boundless feeling of our own importance, of our possessions, of our capacity to conquer and maintain, of our irresistibility. . . . A nation that is suffering from the bliss of over-estimation is simply preparing itself for a deep disappointment."[30]

Similar ambivalence appeared regarding the economic implications of the crisis. Throughout March and early April, as the McKinley administration and Congress expanded the American military, Craighead joined Richard H. Edmonds of the Baltimore *Manufacturer's Record* in noting with pleasure that there soon would be a Southern Division of the War Department. "This proper movement," Craighead wrote, "will in time give [our] part of the United States the attention that it deserves." By *attention* Craighead meant military expenditures and the development of bases in the South.[31] He appeared particularly excited about the potential for expanding Mobile's port using a $50-million war appropriation that came out of Congress in early March. Aware that Pensacola and New Orleans had the same idea, Craighead maintained a running account of why Mobile deserved the funds more than either of the other Gulf ports. When none of these ports won the wartime plums they anticipated, Craighead lamented the economic loss: "The South gets the hot end of the poker every time." Yet only two weeks before, he had used economics to argue against open conflict with Spain. "We are about to engage in another war without paying for the last one. . . . Heaven knows what our debt will be."[32]

Even in the last week before war, the ambivalence persisted. As late as April 20, Craighead was one of many New South advocates, including politicians in Washington, who reasserted pacifist lessons from the southern past. "The Southern people know what war is, and they keep

McWilliams), 15 ff.; William A. Williams, *The Roots of the Modern American Empire* (New York, 1969), 355 ff.; Ida Young *et al.*, *History of Macon, Georgia* (Macon, 1950), 363–64.

30. Mobile *Register*, February 28, 1898.

31. *Ibid.*, March 12, 1898. On McKinley, Congress, and the military buildup, consult Trask, *The War with Spain*, 33–34 ff. For examples of Edmonds' excitement, see the Baltimore *Manufacturer's Record*, XXXIII (April 8, 1898), 182.

32. Mobile *Register*, March 12, 25 (quotation), April 1, 3, 8 (quotation), 1898.

asking: What are we going to fight about? They do not as yet fully understand the necessity of spilling their blood for a lot of guerillas, bushwhackers, and barn burners." Three days earlier Craighead had argued, "If we whip Spain, and we surely will, it will give us no credit."[33] With his usual condescension toward sensationalist journalists, he proposed that if America had to fight Spain, "a batallion of war poets be turned loose" upon the enemy. America would have "an unfair advantage" in such a contest, but at least no actual lives would be at stake.[34]

Nevertheless, during this same climactic time the *Register* also reflected the increasing war sentiment that began to appear throughout the South as well as the East.[35] Early in April, Craighead wrote, "While we of the South deplore war . . . , and regret that the President finds he will not be able to settle the Cuban situation peacefully, we are for our country with a patriotism not excelled by that of any other part of the Union." On April 2, he wrote: "We are face to face with another irrepressible conflict." The economic perspective also shifted. A naval-reserve base should be established at Mobile, he wrote, for "a volunteer force may be needed to keep our port open to the world's commerce." By the second week of April, however, the war sentiment had exceeded these tones of resignation about the inevitability of conflict. "We hope the [enlistment] response will be by such numbers as to reflect credit upon our city," Craighead wrote on April 7. And on April 21 and 22, as diplomatic relations between Spain and America were disintegrating, Craighead offered a series of patriotic statements reflecting the nation's adventuresome, "Splendid Little War" outlook.

33. *Ibid.*, April 20, 17, 1898. For other examples of southern antiwar sentiment based on experience with civil war, see Edwina C. Smith, "Southerners on Empire: Southern Senators and Imperlialism, 1898–99," *Mississippi Quarterly*, XXXI (1977–1978), 98, 104–106; Lala Carr Steelman, "The Public Career of Augustus Octavius Bacon" (Ph.D. dissertation, University of North Carolina, 1950), Chaps. 9–10; and David E. Alsobrook ed., " 'Remember the *Maine!*': Congressman Henry D. Clayton Comments on the Impending Conflict with Spain, April, 1898," *Alabama Review*, XXX (1977), 229–31.
34. Mobile *Register*, April 21, 1898.
35. Charles S. Campbell, *The Transformation of American Foreign Relations, 1865–1900* (New York, 1976), 266–67; Pratt, *The Expansionists of 1898*, pp. 23–316; and Walter LaFeber, *The New Empire: An Interpretation of American Expansion, 1860–1898* (Ithaca, 1963), 385–406.

Give our navy a chance and it will prove itself worthy of the great confidence we place in it. . . . There shall be no more such scenes as those which have disgraced civilization on this continent through Spanish bad government.

The United States troops are coming in our back door . . . , and are not giving our people a chance to welcome them commensurate with the patriotic envoy which signalled their departure from the North. . . . But we are right heartily glad to have them here not alone as defence but as a sign that the old [sectional] feeling is dead. . . . Our interests are one and the same. . . . The New Era has indeed begun and we rejoice in it.

When you get your gun, Johnny, don't forget your mosquito net.[36]

Finally, by April 25 and 26, support for the war subsumed any lingering ambivalence in Craighead's writing. After the American blockade of Cuba and prowar votes among southerners in Washington, Craighead appeared unalterably committed to what was happening in both the internal and external affairs of the nation.[37] "The sight of a Confederate soldier wearing the stripes of a major general of the United States army will certainly do something to 'close the bloody chasm.' " This prediction was followed by an equally "modern" analysis of world conflict. A Spanish naval captain had challenged the *Maine*'s captain, Charles Dwight Sigsbee, to a duel because the latter continued to blame Spain openly for the explosion. To Craighead, this duel was symbolic of "ancient times when individual champions settled the quarrels of nations by personal encounter." However, he concluded, if "that method has its advantages, . . . we have outgrown it."[38]

In retrospect, what is important is not just Craighead's ultimate embrace of America as an expanding world power involved in war but the torment he experienced as he assumed this posture. Between his lines, the same questions always appeared. How aggressive should the nation be in its outward surge? What should be sacrificed at home for the sake of expansion abroad? What aspects of other societies should

36. Mobile *Register*, April 1, 2, 7, 21, 22, 1898.
37. Trask, *The War with Spain*, 108ff. A large majority of southern representatives and senators voted for the joint resolution, which amounted to a declaration of war. See *Congressional Record*, 55th Cong., 2nd Sess., 4040–41, 4105.
38. Mobile *Register*, April 25, 26, 1898.

give way to the march of American progress? What would Mobile stand to gain or lose through world power?

When chances of a Spanish-American war seemed slight, he and many other southern editors could give aggressive answers to these questions without apprehension. Spain, according to the *Register,* should get out of the Western Hemisphere and leave Cuba's progress to America and the Monroe Doctrine. National factors help account for such an attitude. In the mid-1890s, from San Francisco to Boston, middle-class business interests urged an open-door foreign policy, one that would enable American trade to encircle the globe. This expansionism would provide raw materials and markets for an American economy seeking to recover from the depression of 1893 and, simultaneously, would infuse many parts of the world with Anglo-Saxon leadership, capitalism, Protestant Christianity, and other progressive characteristics of commercial-industrial America.[39] As new encouragement for industrial capitalism came South after the Civil War, this type of economic nationalism began to capture the imagination of the region's civic elite—people such as Erwin Craighead and John Rapier.[40] Although some of these middle-class leaders had rejected "the Hawaiian monkey business," later in the decade, with the deepening of the depression and heightened interest in foreign markets, they appeared far more well disposed toward American expansionism, especially with regard to the Caribbean. Indeed, it is no coincidence that throughout the mid-1890s the *Register,* along with the Baltimore *Manufacturer's Record,* the Charlotte *Daily Observer,* and other New South papers, became a stronger and stronger voice of open-door expansionism—from expansion of railroads, the harbor, and the American navy to lower tariffs and the Nicaraguan canal.[41] Thus

39. The classic description of this national sentiment is LaFeber's *The New Empire.* See also Campbell, *The Transformation of American Foreign Relations,* 111, 121, 160.

40. Patrick J. Hearden, *Independence and Empire: The New South's Cotton Mill Campaign* (De Kalb 1982); McWilliams, "The Lure of Empire."

41. On transportation and harbor improvement, see, for example, Mobile *Register,* April 24, 1894, August 7, 1895; January 26, 1896, April 8, 1898; on naval expansion, September 22, 1895, November 1, 1896, April 1, 1898; on lower tariffs, December 6, 1893, October 26, 1894, March 5, 1895, January 24, 1896, May 5, 1897, January 30, 1898; on the Nicaraguan canal, May 17, 1894, January 22, 1897. Articles demonstrating interest in foreign markets—especially outlets for iron, coal, pine timber, grain, and cotton textiles—appeared in virtually every issue. For examples, see November 18, 1893, December 13, 1894, December 20, 1895, December 5, 1896, February 14, 1897,

Craighead's aggressiveness on the Cuban issue during 1895 can be viewed as part of a national, middle-class response to world affairs during the Gilded Age. On the other hand, uniquely sectional forces were also at work. In the Gilded Age, Mobile and other old southern commercial centers sought to recoup the golden era of antebellum days by rushing headlong into the new diversified economic life. No sooner had post–Civil War development permitted certain fragile achievements than the depression of 1893 returned such centers to their prostrated condition of the late Civil War years. Thus Craighead and other New South editors such as Watterson and Tompkins saw economic expansionism not just as a key to the nation's recovery from the depression but as essential to their region's final return to a prosperous and happy Americanism.[42]

Even so, when the Cuban issue heated to the point of threatening actual war, the *Register* suddenly opposed aggressiveness toward Cuba just as intensely as it had favored aggression before. Again, certain national forces appear to have been important. In late 1895 middle-class businessmen across America began to reverse their positions on Cuba, fearful that an aggressive American policy would result in war. They conjured up visions of interrupted trade, a silver-based currency, and a generally unstable stock market—all meaning slowed recovery from the depression.[43] The *Register* manifested this national outlook but also appeared quite southern as it embraced a virtually

February 1, 2, 1898. On the other New South papers, see Williams, *Roots of the Modern American Empire*; Thomas J. McCormick, *China Market: America's Quest for Informal Empire, 1893–1901* (Chicago, 1967); Hearden, *Independence and Empire*.

42. Hearden, *Independence and Empire*; McWilliams, "The Lure of Empire"; Tennant S. McWilliams (ed.), "New Southerner Abroad: General Joe Wheeler Views the Pacific and Beyond," *Pacific Historical Review*, XLVII (1978), 123–27; Tennant S. McWilliams, "New South 'Functionals' Look Outward: The Brunswick Seven and the Cuban Crisis, 1897," *Georgia Historical Quarterly*, XLIV (1979), 469–75. Craighead's sectional interest in expansionism also appeared in articles on commercial clubs, expositions, and competition with New Orleans. For examples, see Mobile *Register*, October 3, November 18, 1891, November 27, December 3, 1892, January 27, 1893, February 15–16, July 29, 1894, January 31, April 7, November 21, 1895, September 1, November 4, 1896, February 9, May 15, December 29, 1897, March 2, April 12, 1898.

43. Pratt, *The Expansionists of 1898*, pp. 233ff.; LaFeber, *The New Empire*, 384. Pratt and LaFeber differ as to exactly when midlevel businessmen began to support an antiwar position.

pacifist position. Craighead and other southern leaders—notably Georgia's senator Augustus O. Bacon—recalled what war could do to people, not just to Cubans or Spaniards but to Americans. Such earnest pacifism stemming from the Civil War was an ironic contrast to the South's historic image as a militarist section.[44] Equally ironic was the role of race in Craighead's type of isolationism. Anglo-Saxonism, which before armed conflict had threatened encouraged aggressiveness toward the encroaching Latins from the Iberian Peninsula, now prompted the Mobile editor to fear war. The timing of this racial threat is of critical significance. For a member of the southern elite, an individual welcoming the "stabilization" of race relations through legalization of segregation and disfranchisement, the new racial threat posed by Cubans must have been frustrating. Mobile, a Gulf Coast trading center easily accessible to the Caribbean, was especially vulnerable.[45]

Then there was Craighead's ambivalence early in 1898, when he was simultaneously held by an introspective isolationism and enthralled by the possibilities for a Spanish-American war. Although arguing that conflict would hurt economic recovery, he and other middle-class leaders of the South nevertheless saw war as inevitable and soon praised the business opportunities attendant to mobilization. Although arguing that southerners could not endorse open conflict, having experienced more than had other Americans the ravages of war, he nevertheless called on southerners to prove that the age of the Civil War and sectional discord had ended: they should don the blue uniform and fight for the nation. If, as Richard Hofstadter suggested, the Spanish-American War revealed Americans in a "psychic crisis" touched off by the Civil War and industrial revolution, the type of vacillation and contradiction Craighead manifested shows how New South advocates (with

44. *Cf.* C. Vann Woodward, *The Burden of Southern History* (Rev. ed.; Baton Rouge, 1970), 210–211. See also Willis Brewer to Robert McKee, April 23, 1898, in Robert McKee Papers, Alabama Department of Archives and History, Montgomery.

45. See Christopher Lasch, "The Anti-Imperialists, the Philippines, and the Inequality of Man," *Journal of Southern History*, XXIV (1958), 319–31; and Reuben Francis Weston, *Racism in US Imperialism* (Columbia, S.C., 1970), 91–95, 101–102. However, there is no careful delineation of the relationship between legalized segregation and the Cuban issue. One may infer such a relationship from David E. Alsobrook, "Alabama's Port City: Mobile During the Progressive Era, 1896–1917" (Ph.D. dissertation, Auburn University, 1982), Chap. 4. On imperialism and race, see Joel Williamson, *The Crucible of Race: Black and White Relations in the American South Since Emancipation* (Chapel Hill, 1984), 337.

the notable exception of Senator Morgan's imperialist clique) had an especially tortuous experience in this crisis.[46] Of course, for these southerners, resolution finally arrived much as it did for other Americans on the cutting edge of modernization and world power. Ultimately, the economic and patriotic advantages of expansionism were deemed more important than were the drawbacks.

In fact, with the war over and a Treaty of Paris that would make America an imperial democracy, Craighead joined Watterson, Tompkins, and Edmonds in exhibiting a critical adjustment to the issue of race in foreign affairs: segregation, as Senator Morgan had urged all along, could simply be exported to Cuba, Puerto Rico, and other parts of the new American realm.[47] This adjustment probably still represented a minority position among southern leaders. The treaty was ratified by a 57-to-25 vote in an executive session of the Senate—it received eleven yea votes from southerners and fifteen nays. Here were the usual influences: Morgan led a few other expansionists such as South Carolina's McLaurin, and Tillman and Bacon urged the antiexpansionist position along with avid followers such as Virginia's John W. Daniel and Florida's Stephen Mallory.[48] The adjustment,

46. Richard Hofstadter, "Cuba, the Philippines, and Manifest Destiny," in Hofstadter, *The Paranoid Style in American Politics and Other Essays* (New York, 1966), 145–87. Although there is no study of southerners and the introversion-aggressiveness dilemma, Hofstadter did place Henry Watterson and Walter Hines Page in the context of such a crisis: see pp. 180–81. See also Robert Dallek, "Imperialism: A Crisis in National Self-Confidence," in Dallek, *The American Style of Foreign Policy: Cultural Politics and Foreign Affairs* (New York, 1983), 3–31.

47. Craighead's support for the treaty is shown in Mobile *Register*, July 14, August 15, September 6, 27, December 28, 1899. Other New South papers supporting the treaty included the Baltimore *Manufacturer's Record*, the Louisville *Courier-Journal*, the Atlanta *Constitution*, the Atlanta *Journal*, the Charlotte *Daily Observer*, the Memphis *Commercial Appeal*, and the Richmond *Times*. See also Joseph Frazier Wall, *Henry Watterson: Reconstructed Rebel* (New York, 1956), 240.

48. Of the eleven yeas, several probably do not represent a genuine expansionist position. Louisiana's McEnery, known as an antiannexationist, voted for ratification when, it is alleged, Republicans promised him a federal judgeship. It is possible that three others, Mississippi's Sullivan, Georgia's Clay, and North Carolina's Butler, voted yea as part of the William Jennings Bryan strategy of seeking ratification to create a campaign issue for 1900. Some also have argued that McLaurin cast a spurious yea vote. This is doubtful, in view of McLaurin's strong advocacy of Hawaiian annexation and the China market. See *Journal of the Executive Proceedings of the Senate*, 55th Cong., 3rd Sess., 1284; Henry Cabot Lodge to Theodore Roosevelt, February 9, 1899, in *Selections from the Correspondence of Theodore Roosevelt and Henry Cabot Lodge* (2 vols.; New

nevertheless, would increase among southerners, especially those seeking a New South. In the near future many from the section would conclude, as Craighead had, that the new era of the South should include not just a closing of the "bloody chasm" but economic and social change as part of a national society moving progressively into the rest of world. In 1898 the Detroit *News Tribune* urged that "nothing short of an archaeological society will be able to locate the Mason-Dixon line."[49] In that year, and for some time to come, this statement was a gross exaggeration. Yet many New South advocates in 1898 were indeed involved in a critical change of thought about their section's relationship with the world—a change that would show little reversal over time.

York, 1925), I, 391–92; John K. Cowan to William McKinley, January 25, 1899, and Mark Hanna to William McKinley, February 7, 1899—both in William McKinley Papers, Library of Congress; Paola Coletta, "Bryan, McKinley and the Treaty of Paris," *Pacific Historical Review*, XXVI (1957), 131–46; George Colman Osborn, *John Sharp Williams: Planter-Statesman of the Deep South* (Baton Rouge, 1943), 83–105; Francis Butler Simkins, *Pitchfork Ben Tillman*, South Carolinian (Baton Rouge, 1944), 352–54; and Evans C. Johnson, *Oscar W. Underwood: A Political Biography* (Baton Rouge, 1980), 58–62.

49. Detroit *News Tribune*, quoted in Thomas A. Bailey, *The Man in the Street* (New York, 1948), 114n. For an earlier appearance of this viewpoint, see Paul H. Buck's classic, *The Road to Reunion* (New York, 1937), 318–20.

3

Daniel Augustus Tompkins
and China

In the wake of the Spanish-American War, New South business leaders joined the journalists in the evolving support for American expansion. The owners of steel and textile and lumber mills, the merchants parlaying the new products of modernization into middleman profits, reflected the additional expansionist influence of progressivism. Senator Morgan, who died in 1907, was not one of the New South leaders who made the evolutionary step to progressivism. Still, amid the feverish optimism and nationalism of this complex era of reform, it was Morgan's cause that both broadened and intensified as a tenet of the New South creed, and businessmen were an essential part of the story.[1]

Indeed, their role demonstrated some of the basic countervailing forces of the early twentieth century. Like their late-nineteenth-century counterparts, these businessmen could encourage quiet collaboration with Republicans of the Northeast. Such cooperative ventures probably increased as southerners embraced what had recently been a northeastern-based idea—expansionism. Moreover, in these days of the Democratic party before Woodrow Wilson, southern businessmen needed all the pragmatic political alliances they could find. Yet most of the "forward-looking" entrepreneurs of Dixie still carried indelible impressions of northeastern Republicans freeing the slaves and defeating the South, and increasingly they feared reputed efforts by the sons of the carpetbaggers to place a yoke of economic colonialism on their section. Thus New South business Progressives also sought economic expansion abroad as part of the sectional creed that would help cast off what they perceived as the new Yankee yoke.[2]

1. The New South movement and progressivism are analyzed in Dewey Grantham, *Southern Progressivism: The Reconciliation of Progress and Tradition* (Knoxville, 1983), 25, 419, and *passim*. The relationship between progressivism and expansionism is treated in Jerry Israel, *Progressivism and the Open Door: America and China, 1905–1921* (Pittsburgh, 1971).

2. Woodward's narrative of intersectional rivalry remains the classic argument that

In context such incongruity seems almost natural, for since its early postbellum conception, the New South creed had never known internal consistency. The creed had fostered economic progress but championed retention of vital values of the old order, and had produced a distinctively conservative blueprint for change. Now, with the rising tide of Progressive reform, that pattern of inconsistency and conservativism was only extended. To solve the social problems of industrialism while preserving the individualism of nineteenth-century lifestyles, widely divergent groups of Progressives from across the nation offered programs emphasizing collectivism and centralized government. Such were the ironies of a people searching for social order in an age of economic transformation. With these powerful national currents meeting those of the historic South, it is no wonder that the resulting conservative, contradictory outlooks in the South fostered political and economic actions equally complex and never really capable of offering a happy reconciliation between progress and tradition. So inwardly confused yet so outwardly optimistic, at least one group of southern Progressives, the New South businessmen, would therefore fight child labor laws while advancing the efficiency of railroad regulation, would implement segregation while seeking "broadened horizons."[3] More to the point, in this environment New South business Progressives would urge their region out into a world economy of competing nations and in the process both fight and support the infamous, expansionist Yankees.

Daniel Augustus Tompkins, the North Carolina textilist, provides a leading example of the conservative New South business Progressive who advanced expansionism.[4] Tompkins' many publications and

---

northeasterners sought to control the southern economy and, indeed, did so to a large degree. See C. Vann Woodward, *Origins of the New South* (Baton Rouge, 1951), esp. Chaps. 2 and 11; also George Brown Tindall, *The Ethnic Southerners* (Baton Rouge, 1976), 215–23; and Patrick J. Hearden, "New England's Reaction to the New South," *South Atlantic Quarterly,* LXXV (1976), 371–88. For the argument that indigenous southern conditions were critical determinants of this colonial relationship, see Gavin Wright, *Old South/New South: Revolutions in the Southern Economy Since the Civil War* (New York, 1986), Chap. 6.

3. Paul M. Gaston, *The New South Creed: A Study in Southern Mythmaking* (New York, 1970); Robert Wiebe, *The Search for Order, 1877–1920* (New York, 1967), Chap. 4. The relationship of the New South creed to the search for order and to modernization deserves considerable investigation. Emphasis on progress and tradition comes from various writings by Dewey Grantham.

4. For a general study of Tompkins' life, see Howard B. Clay, "Daniel Augustus

large collection of personal papers elucidate not only his own evolving viewpoint but also the ideas of many others who considered him a model New South leader. Business life was increasingly perceived as an interrelated worldwide phenomenon, and that perception was partially indebted to the span of southern history. In this context, Tompkins recalled his early years as nothing less than dramatic. Son of a "befallen" South Carolina planter, Tompkins was fourteen years old when the Civil War ended. The forces of his youth were in many ways those of the South seeking to overthrow Reconstruction. Yet, as Tompkins later recalled, much of what carpetbaggers had preached sounded similar to what Thomas Jefferson, Andrew Jackson, and James K. Polk had advocated—national expansion. Pragmatically bypassing antebellum differences over industry and labor, Tompkins would reflect on his early influences as the "strong" and "progressive" Yankee outlook reinforced by traditions of a "patriotic" and "expansionistic" prewar South, a region ranking "high in commerce, not only here at home, but in all markets."[5]

Precisely how these broad and merging forces helped mold Tompkins into a New South business Progressive is difficult to say. If, as he suggests, they caused him to look "outward," reinforcement of them must have occurred through more personal, concrete experiences. In 1869 he left South Carolina for Troy, New York. There he

---

Tompkins: American Bourbon" (Ph.D. dissertation, University of North Carolina, 1948). See also publications from this dissertation: Clay, "Daniel Augustus Tompkins and Industrial Revival in the South," and "Daniel Augustus Tompkins: The Role of the New South Industrialist in Politics," both in *East Carolina Publications in History: Essays in Southern Biography* (Greenville, N.C., 1965), II, 114–49, and III, 85–118, respectively. On Tompkins' significance in the context of more recent scholarship, consult Laurence Shore, "Daniel Augustus Tompkins and Blacks: The New South Faces the Race Question" (Honors essay, University of North Carolina at Chapel Hill, 1977); Gaston, *The New South Creed*, 48–52; Dwight Billings, Jr., *Planters and the Making of the New South: Class Politics and Development in North Carolina, 1865–1900* (Chapel Hill, 1979), 64ff.; and Patrick J. Hearden, *Independence and Empire: The New South's Cotton Mill Campaign, 1865–1901* (De Kalb, 1982), 64, 84, 104–105, 130–38, 141.

    5. This intellectual and social environment is discussed in Carl N. Degler, *Place over Time: The Continuity of Southern Distinctiveness* (Baton Rouge, 1977), 113; J. Mills Thornton, *Politics and Power in a Slave Society: Alabama, 1800–1860* (Baton Rouge, 1978); and in Woodward, *Origins of the New South*, Chap. 11. Quotes are from Daniel A. Tompkins, "Fourth of July Address at Gastonia," in George T. Winston, *A Builder of the New South: Being the Story of the Life and Work of Daniel Augustus Tompkins* (Garden City, N.Y., 1920), 287ff.

devoted four years to the study of engineering at Rensselaer Poly-technic Institute, and then stayed on in Troy and Brooklyn to test his new knowledge under the guidance of Alexander Holley, an innovative steel manufacturer and exporter. In 1874 Tompkins took employment with John Fritz, the Bethlehem, Pennsylvania, blast-furnace operator. Then in May, 1879, he journeyed under Fritz's direction to Germany to install a hoop mill at the Schwerte Ironworks in Westphalia. In the process Tompkins observed much of the industrial development in Great Britain, France, Belgium, and Germany. On returning to America in 1880, he served a short while as a superintendent in a Missouri glass factory and then contracted with the Westinghouse Corporation to represent this company along the Atlantic seaboard. By 1883 Tompkins was located in Charlotte, North Carolina, and was on his way to developing his own textile operations.[6]

In North Carolina, Tompkins' education in the ways of industrial-ism and foreign marketing never ceased. His growing wealth allowed him to return to England several times and also to visit regularly in such American commercial centers as Boston and New York. The wealth permitted him to buy books rare in North Carolina. During 1900 and 1901, for example, Tompkins ordered four works on nation-al and international trends in industrialism: Thomas J. Scherer's *Japan Today*, Jonathan Baines' *History of Cotton Manufacturing in Great Britain*, Frank H. Hitchcock's *Our Trade With Japan, China, and Hong Kong*, and J. C. Fernald's *The Imperial Republic*.[7] He subscribed to a costly clipping service, which provided articles appearing in New York and Washington, D.C., newspapers and relating to textile man-ufacturing and marketing on the world scene. He maintained active correspondence with manufacturers and their representatives world-wide—in Africa, Latin America, Europe, China. He stayed in constant communication with American state and commerce department offi-cials on projected world trade patterns. In one instance he even wrote

6. Clay, "Tompkins and Industrial Revival in the South," 115–18ff.

7. *Ibid.*; Tompkins to Van Nostrand & Co., March 7, April 26, 1901, to Superinten-dent of Documents, March 26, 1900, to Robert Clarke Co., August 16, 1901, Anna L. Twelvetrees (Secretary) to J. B. Lippincott, July 21, 1900, all in Daniel Augustus Tompkins Papers, Southern Historical Collection, University of North Carolina, here-inafter cited as Tompkins Papers, SHC.

Joseph Chamberlain, hoping to open discussions on the advantages of British industry and imperialism.[8]

With regard to his speeches and writings on public affairs, it has been suggested that "only a few insignificant pamphlets were actually written by Tompkins and that he relied heavily on hired researchers." This statement is probably a more accurate estimate of Tompkins' highly technical publications on textile manufacturing. His papers contain speeches and essays dealing with public affairs written and revised many times by his own hand. Moreover, on those occasions when he did employ researchers for public affairs writings, he often gave forceful directions. For example, to one of his principal assistants he wrote: "My desire is to . . . record an honorable history of a worthy people. If this cannot be truthfully done, then it is not only useless to publish a history but a postive injury to do so."[9]

By the mid-1890s Tompkins had taken on many characteristics of America's vibrant new cosmopolitan-elite. He found great mobility through industrialism and wielded an influence some have compared to that of Yankee industrialist Edward F. Atkinson. He would employ this power not just to make more money but to urge the regulation of railroads and monopolies, to oppose new labor laws, to keep abreast of world affairs, and to provide the foreign affairs leadership he understood to be essential for regional and national growth.[10]

In this relatively elite role, Tompkins came to comprehend the South as one among many societies in the world that was recovering from

8. Examples of Tompkins' international correspondence include Silas D. Webb to Tompkins, November 13, 1899, and Tompkins to Ulrico Hoepli (Milan), May 14, 1906; see also Tompkins to Joseph Chamberlain, January 2, 1903—all in Tompkins Papers, SHC.

9. Clay, "Daniel A. Tompkins: American Bourbon," 86ff.; Tompkins to C. Coon, April 20, 1899, in Tompkins Papers, SHC.

10. The term *cosmopolitan-elite* is adapted from Samuel P. Hays, "Political Parties and the Community-Society Continuum," in William R. Chambers and Walter D. Burnham (eds.), *The American Party System* (New York, 1967), 152–81. For use of this term in diplomatic history, see also Lloyd C. Gardner *et al.*, *Creation of the American Empire: U.S. Diplomatic History* (2 vols.; Chicago, 1976), I, 191–211; and James John Lorrence, "The American Asiatic Association, 1898–1925: Organized Business and the Myth of the China Market" (Ph.D. dissertation, University of Wisconsin, 1970), 1–5. Tompkins is compared to Atkinson in William A. Williams, *The Roots of the Modern American Empire* (New York, 1969), 525 n. 15. On Tompkins' role as a conservative business Progressive focusing on the domestic scene, see Grantham, *Southern Progressivism*, 146, 155.

war and simultaneously working for economic progress through industrialization. He focused on Germany as a good model for the New
South. With a clear echo of Herbert Spencer, whom he read inces-
santly, Tompkins told a 1903 Trinity College group: "We all know to
what depths of poverty Germany was left at the end of the Napolian
[*sic*] wars. We all know how little the rest of the world cared about
Germany and her fate and how utterly France despised her. The story
of Germany is wholly a story of education. It is a story of arduous
labor, of self-sacrifice, and of complete redemption. By acquiring
knowledge of natural laws, the people of Germany have developed."[11]

Although Tompkins developed heightened interest in the Protestant
ethic and in Darwinism as he observed recent world developments, he
realized that these values and the modern industrial life they might
deliver should not be restricted to a narrow regional base. The northeastern section of the United States and, to a lesser extent, other areas
of the nation were fostering industrial development. The surest path to
a New South was the coordination of southern progress with this
national experience. Benefits accruing to the South, he reasoned,
would certainly extend well beyond economic mobility. Taking a lesson from British imperialism as well as from Thomas Jefferson ("the
strong expansionist President"), and reflecting his devotion to a key
premise of progressivism, Tompkins became convinced that Christian,
Anglo-Saxon Americans could have a significant impact "through the
increase of freedom and the spread of liberty over the globe." White
southerners could participate in such missionary work by supporting
the cause of American industrialism and a foreign policy that extended
America's democratic, technological life to less fortunate peoples.[12]

As a New South advocate imbued with the ideals and self-interest of
America's progressive expansionism, Tompkins praised General Jo-
seph H. Wheeler and other southerners prominent in the Spanish-
American War. He reveled in Senator Morgan's vision and in ratifica-

11. Tompkins, "Address Before the Alumni Association of Trinity College," Charlotte,
N.C., April 7, 1903, copy in Tompkins Papers, SHC; Clay, "Daniel A. Tompkins:
American Bourbon," 164. See Billings, *Planters and the Making of the New South*, 97–
99, 212–13.

12. Tompkins to Bruce Craven, December 26, 1903, in Tompkins Papers, SHC;
Tompkins, "Fourth of July Address at Gastonia," 293–308; Tompkins, *American Commerce*, 12, 76ff. See also Stuart Anderson, *Race and Rapprochement: Anglo-Saxonism
and Anglo-American Relations, 1895–1904* (Rutherford, 1981).

tion of the 1898 Treaty of Paris that permitted America a foreign empire. He looked to the internationalization of Jim Crow to offset racial drawbacks of annexation.[13] And of primary concern here, he encouraged southerners to join the movement for an expansion of American influence among the "teeming millions" of China. It is not surprising that Tompkins viewed exportation of cotton products, especially southern textiles, as a proper medium for this progress.

In 1899, as America sent Europe the first Open Door note aimed at preserving free trade rights in China, Tompkins began to publicize the possibilities for his nation's progressive relationship with Asia. Speaking before the Southern Industrial League, the Interstate Commercial Conference, the New England Cotton Manufacturer's Association, and other business groups, Tompkins called for vocal support of the policies then being enunciated by President William McKinley and his secretary of state, John Hay. Tompkins depicted America as a civilizing world power with a large mission that included the expansion of "trade, commerce, Christianity, civilization, and good government." He also focused on a domestic economic factor. "The United States," he proclaimed, "has come to the period in her life when she must recognize . . . that she has developed her manufacturing interests to such an extent that her domestic market no longer absorbs her manufactured products." He advocated acquisition of more foreign markets through naval and merchant marine expansion, tariff reduction and reciprocity, consular reform, and a Central American canal.[14] He used cotton, the industry he knew best, to illustrate the problem: "The cotton crop is now about 10 million bales. About one quarter of this is manufactured in the United States. The remaining seven and a half million bales are sent abroad to be manufactured. If our export facilities [capabilities] should be equal to those of England and Germany, then the subject would be reduced to one of our ability to compete."[15]

13. Tompkins, *National Expansion* (Charlotte, 1899); Charlotte *Daily Observer*, July 4, 1900; Chattanooga *Tradesman*, CCCIX (June 1, 1898), 75, and XL (September 1, 1898), 1; New York *Journal of Commerce*, October 17, 1899, p. 6; New York *Commercial and Financial Chronicle*, LXVIII (May 20, 1899), 394; Winston, *A Builder of the New South*, 298. There is every indication that Tompkins consciously publicized what the Spanish-American War could do for the South. *National Expansion*, for example, was written and disseminated to businessmen with a plan. See Tompkins to James J. Hooker, October 31, 1899, in Tompkins Papers, SHC.

14. Tompkins, *American Commerce, Its Expansion*, 12, 24–25, 37, 39, 93–94.

15. Quoted in Gardner *et al.*, *Creation of the American Empire*, II, 264.

He focused more narrowly on southern textiles and China: "We hear about the competition between the South and New England in cotton manufacturing. . . . If we extend our markets . . . with the trade of China kept open, there will be more goods needed than we can make in America—New England and the South put together. If we fail to extend our foreign trade . . . none can prosper." This was Tompkins' way of saying that New South textile manufacturing would not falter before discriminatory activities of northeastern mill men. It also was his declaration that the South had a real stake in American penetration of China and should stand with the nation in this cause.[16]

Although Tompkins was a southern Democrat, certain Republican economic leaders of the Northeast warmed to him.[17] In November, 1899, John Foord, the guiding personality and perennial secretary of the American Asiatic Association (AAA) based in New York City, invited Tompkins to join his effort to pressure government for further development of the China market. Cautiously Tompkins befriended Foord, accepted the invitation, and rose rapidly in the hierarchy of the AAA. As a member of the Executive Committee from 1902 to 1910, Tompkins sought to bring southern textilists into the organization; this would provide added influence to the AAA's already intense efforts on behalf of international cotton trade.[18]

His task required concerted effort. Many southerners historically sympathized with California's objections to Chinese immigration,

16. Tompkins, *American Commerce*, 72, 93–94. Also consult Tompkins, "Early Southern Cotton Mills," *American Wool and Cotton Reporter*, XV (October 3, 1901), 1264; Tompkins to John Foord, October 31, 1899, in Tompkins Papers, SHC; and Lorrence, "The American Asiatic Association," 77–78. Tompkins' fear of Yankee discrimination appears in many respects justified. On the intersectional rivalry over labor laws, railroad rates, and foreign textile markets, see Hearden, "New England's Reaction to the New South," 371–88, and *Independence and Empire*.

17. Although Tompkins endorsed William Howard Taft for president in 1908, he always considered himself a southern Democrat, a loyal southerner. Clay, "Daniel A. Tompkins: American Bourbon," 300–301; A. B. Farquhar to William Howard Taft, January 13, 1909, in William Howard Taft Papers, Library of Congress.

18. John Foord to Tompkins, November 2, 1899, Tompkins to Foord, November 20, December 13, 1899, and October 10, 1902—all in Tompkins Papers, SHC. Tompkins is listed as an AAA member commencing February, 1900. See "The American Asiatic Association" [the constitution, statement of purpose, and a listing of initial members and officers], pamphlet in the general collection, LC; "Executive Committee" and "Membership" lists, in *Journal of the American Asiatic Association*, I (November 20, 1899) through XI ([May ?] 1911); and Lorrence, "The American Asiatic Association," 4, 6, 78–79.

which were based on considerations of race and labor. They feared that increased immigration and "mongrelization" would follow stronger economic ties between China and America. Still, there were small pockets of interest in China that Tompkins could approach. Since the end of the Civil War a few powerful southern planters and business-men had sought Chinese labor to ease worker shortages resulting from emancipation of the slaves and to encourage reciprocity through which southern textilists might tap the fabled China market.[19] More-over, as suggested by southern newspaper support for the Open Door note of 1899, some southerners who had opposed American expan-sion in the Caribbean and the Pacific apparently felt comfortable with the growth of American influence in China: the Orient's hold on the American imagination had affected at least some otherwise inward-looking southern Protestants.[20] In addition, the very distance between China and the United States made it unlikely that America would ever fight an extended war in the Orient or attempt to annex its people, thus alleviating lingering southern fears that expansion would lead to sub-jugation, racial tension, and conflict.[21]

19. Rowland T. Bertoff, "Southern Attitudes Toward Immigration, 1865–1914," *Journal of Southern History*, XVII (1951), 329, 359; Gregory Lawrence Garland, "Southern Congressional Opposition to Hawaiian Reciprocity and Annexation, 1876–1898 (M.A. thesis, University of North Carolina at Chapel Hill, 1983), 20. Although American cotton exports to China always represented a small portion of the nation's total export, the potential of the China market "staggered the imagination." Jack Blicksilver, *Cotton Manufacturing in the Southeast: An Historical Analysis* (Atlanta, 1959), 22–23. National export statistics were also encouraging: in 1893 the U.S. shipped 353,910 pieces of drill cotton to Shanghai; and in 1899, 1,521,240. Sun Jae Koh, "A History of the Cotton Trade Between the United States and the Far East," *Textile History Review*, IV (1963), 134–39. See also Charles S. Campbell, *Special Business Interests and the Open Door Policy* (New Haven, 1951); Thomas J. McCormick, *China Market: America's Quest for Informal Empire, 1893–1901* (Chicago, 1967), 91 n. 15, 107 n. 18, 201–207; and Richard H. Davis, "The Role of South Carolina's Cotton Manufacturers in the United States Far Eastern Policy, 1897–1902" (M.A. thesis, University of South Carolina, 1966). On southern planters and Chinese labor, consult Lucy M. Cohen, *Chinese in the Post–Civil War South: A People Without a History* (Baton Rouge, 1984).

20. Southern press opinion is addressed in Edward W. Chester, *Sectionalism, Politics, and American Diplomacy* (Metuchen, N.J., 1975), 138, and in Marilyn Blatt Young, *The Rhetoric of Empire: America and China, 1895–1901* (Cambridge, Mass., 1968). Church and missionary sentiment is summarized in Kenneth Scott Latourette, *A History of Christian Missions in China* (New York, 1929), and in Irwin T. Hyatt, Jr., *Our Ordered Lives Confess: Three Nineteenth Century American Missionaries in East Shan-tung* (Cambridge, Mass., 1976).

21. Julius W. Pratt, *The Expansionists of 1898: The Acquisition of Hawaii and the*

With this sentiment for encouragement, Tompkins set to work as the compulsive organizer. Calling upon several well-known southern Democrats—South Carolina senator John L. McLaurin, a committed China market advocate, and editors Clarence Poe and Richard H. Edmonds—Tompkins and his secretary, Anna L. Twelvetrees, developed a profile of virtually every southern trade organization. To these they mailed out literature propounding the potential of the China market. Logging hundreds of hours on the railroads, Tompkins often followed this paper barrage with formal addresses and private lobbying at business conventions. Most of his appearances were limited to the South Atlantic states in order to conserve travel time and reach clusters of textile mills; and it was within these states, especially South Carolina, that his AAA message found the warmest reception. Those who responded immediately included such powerful textilists as Ellison A. Smyth (Pelzer, South Carolina), Thomas I. Hickman (Augusta, Georgia), Thomas B. Dallas (Nashville), and Daniel Ripley (Galveston). Many others subsequently joined. Textile concerns consistently appearing on AAA membership lists during the years 1901 through 1909, Tompkins' most active period, included Anderson Cotton Mills (Anderson, South Carolina), Mills Manufacturing Company (Greenville, South Carolina), Abbeville Cotton Mills (Abbeville, South Carolina), and of course the D. A. Tompkins Company (Charlotte).[22]

Another of Tompkins' AAA endeavors went well beyond membership activity. He was an effective public-opinion maker for the group. When the Boxer Rebellion erupted in the spring of 1900, Tompkins was one among many who viewed it as an obstruction to the spread of general Western progress as well as a major intrusion on American economic activity in China. The AAA did its best to publicize the event, hoping to mobilize business sentiment in support of American intervention. Tompkins' chosen role was to delineate certain issues before southern audiences. Turning to other organizational contacts,

Spanish Islands (Baltimore, 1936), 270; Burton Beers, "Southern Americans and China: A Research Note," (Paper read before the annual meeting of the Southern Historical Association, 1976, copy in the author's possession).

22. Lorrence, "The American Asiatic Association," 79; Anna L. Twelvetrees to John L. McLaurin, March 19, 1905, Tompkins to E. S. Askew, July 23, 1900, Tompkins to John B. Cleveland, November 22, 1899, Twelvetrees to C. B. Aycock, April 16, 1901, Tompkins to Richard H. Edmonds, January 3, 17, 1900, Tompkins to Clarence Poe, September 13, 1901—all in Tompkins Papers, SHC.

he arranged for two Republicans, Thomas C. Search of the National Association of Manufacturers and John Barrett of the AAA, to address the Southern Cotton Spinners Association in Charlotte during May, 1900. Search reinforced the convention's gloomy appraisal of trade losses, while Barrett—one of the most articulate of the China publicists—hammered away at the relationship between Christian missions and American economic expansionism, the "mutually dependent" forces of civilization in China.[23]

At this meeting and others, Tompkins spoke along similar lines, but with a distinctively southern flavor. As one who believed that "people guided by Christian faith have a towering superiority," Tompkins suggested that Americans in China, as well as the pro-Western Chinese dynasty, were "besieged by the heathen mob" just as southern whites had been assaulted "by the anarchy" of Negroes during the "so-called Reconstruction." The relationship between race and efficiency clearly worried this New South Progressive, a preoccupation in which Yankees played both positive and negative roles. Moreover, he demonstrated the New South faith that, while black slavery had been discredited, Anglo-Saxon Christians still had a mission to guide the progressive movement of Western civilization, and that out of this movement could result a modern South.[24]

Tompkins also used the Charlotte *Daily Observer*, which he had owned since 1893, to heighten southern interest in the China problem. On July 7, 1900, T. I. Hickman wrote Tompkins, "It seems to me that the only thing that the United States can do in the [Boxer] crisis now pending . . . is to protect our interests thoroughly and to maintain as far as possible an open door policy." The following day Tompkins printed this letter in the *Daily Observer* and kept similar views of other

23. Campbell, *Special Business Interests*, 68–71; Tompkins to John Barrett, and to D. S. Franklin, April 20, 1901—in Tompkins Papers, SHC; New York *Journal of Commerce*, May 11, 1900; *Journal of the American Asiatic Association*, I (1900), 93. As a result of the Boxer revolt, exports of American sheeting and jeans dropped from an 1899 high of 5,700,000 pieces to 3,200,000 pieces in 1900. Search had similar figures available to make his point. Davis, "The Role of South Carolina's Cotton Manufacturers," 48; Salvadore Prisco III, *John Barrett, Progressive Era Diplomat, 1877–1920* (University, Ala., 1973).

24. Tompkins to Miss Anna [Twelvetrees], April 26, 1898, and unidentified newspaper clipping dated May, 1900—both in Tompkins Papers, SHC; Tompkins, "Fourth of July Address at Gastonia," 285–95.

southerners before his readers for the duration of the controversy. With the recently acquired services of the Associated Press, he also covered the breaking news: trade reverses, China specialist William W. Rockhill's counseling of John Hay, Senator McLaurin's interventionist sentiment, the eventual Western intervention in China, and finally the issuance of America's second Open Door note urging respect for China's territorial integrity.[25] When American troops entered China in 1900, Tompkins could make no specific claim to having incited the strong interventionist sentiment across the South. Yet he was still excited about having worked for the cause. As he wrote Richard H. Edmonds, "We should always stand responsible for the safety of those who volunteer as Christian missionaries and such inferior factors in our civilization as trade will take care of themselves." Thus Tompkins also linked Christianity to industrial capitalism as he called upon his region to find progress by looking outward.[26]

During Theodore Roosevelt's administration, the type of China sentiment that Tompkins had been helping to generate became focused on further threats to American interests there. Fearful of Russia's use of the Trans-Siberia Railroad and that nation's refusal to practice an Open Door policy in Manchuria—which received the bulk of American textiles sent to China—the *Journal of the American Asiatic Association* began a running account of Russian policy and economic activity in the Orient. Tompkins' *Daily Observer* followed these themes, emphasizing Japan as a force that might check Russian expansion. "The United States, England, and Japan . . . this combination," wrote Tompkins, "could be invincible—it could dominate the world." The editorial was accompanied by supporting views from Henry Watterson's *Courier-Journal*.[27]

25. Tompkins to Melville E. Stone, December 26, 1899, in Charlotte *Daily Observer*, July 8, 1900. For many more examples of attitudes like Hickman's, see Charlotte *Daily Observer*, May–August, 1900, and Williams, *Roots of the Modern American Empire*, 443.

26. Tompkins to Richard H. Edmonds, July 19, 1900, in Daniel Augustus Tompkins Papers, LC. See also Tompkins, "Early Southern Cotton Mills," 1243, 1264. On the South's interventionist sentiment, consult Young, *The Rhetoric of Empire*, 169, 277 n. 32; and Davis, "The Role of South Carolina's Cotton Manufacturers," 49–50.

27. Gardner *et al.*, *Creation of the American Empire*, II, 266–77; *Journal of the American Asiatic Association*, I (1900) through III (1903). Charlotte *Daily Observer*, August 16, 1900, and other issues from August, 1900, to February, 1902. Watterson, usually the Anglo-Saxon nationalist, felt that a Russo-Chinese alliance could be "very powerful," but not strong enough to win against an Anglo-American effort.

When Tompkins helped John Foord draft a petition urging the administration to protest Russia's monopolistic activities in Manchuria, he had little difficulty accumulating signatures of the majority of the members of the Southern Cotton Spinners Association. Then Tompkins, accompanied by Ellison A. Smyth, Senator McLaurin, and other AAA members, presented the document to President Roosevelt on December 18, 1901. Russian activities continued and American pressures mounted. Finally, on February 1, 1902, Roosevelt issued what some have termed a third Open Door note condemning further Russian control in Manchuria.[28] How importantly such organizational and media pressures figured in Roosevelt's statement is difficult to say; Roosevelt's primary consideration in Far Eastern affairs was balance of power.[29] But it seems certain that Tompkins and other southerners felt that they had a stake—markets for a modern economy—as they lobbied the president with their business cause.

While the McKinley and Roosevelt years found Tompkins advancing southern expansionism through highly publicized diplomatic episodes, they also saw him involved in a number of peripheral events, little known but still reflective of an intense expansionist outlook. In the spring of 1901, Tompkins arranged a meeting between Wu Ting Fang, Chinese minister to the United States, and major textilists of the southern states. Tompkins felt sure that the two-day gala held at Charlotte represented a major step toward increasing southern textile contacts with the China market.[30] He found less success, however, in efforts to send John Barrett, a textile export advocate, to represent the United States in China.

28. See *Journal of the American Asiatic Association*, II (1902), 20. In January, 1901, Tompkins and thirty-nine other southern textilists also had sent a petition to President McKinley, emphasizing problems they anticipated in Manchuria. *Senate Documents*, 56th Cong., 2nd Sess., No. 79, pp. 1–5; Davis, "The Role of South Carolina's Cotton Manufacturers," 52–54.

29. Raymond Esthus, *Theodore Roosevelt and International Rivalries* (Waltham, Mass., 1970), 25–27; Howard K. Beale, *Theodore Roosevelt and the Rise of America to World Power* (Baltimore, 1956), 170ff.; Michael H. Hunt, *Frontier Defense and the Open Door: Manchuria in Chinese-American Relations* (New Haven, 1973), 60–63.

30. Tompkins to Wu Ting Fang, April 4, 1901, and to John L. McLaurin, April 4, 9, 1901—all in Tompkins Papers, SHC; Charlotte *Daily Observer*, April 18–22, 1901. Wu also appeared before the New York Southern Society, the American Asiatic Association, and the National Association of Manufacturers. George E. Paulsen, "The Abrogation of the Gresham-Yang Treaty," *Pacific Historical Review*, XL (1971), 468.

Former minister to Siam, and a vocal member of the AAA, Barrett had a long-standing interest in a modernized South. As a student at Dartmouth College in 1889, he had become fascinated with Henry W. Grady's noted "New South" speech, particularly Grady's call for international commerce. Before working temporarily as a Pacific Coast journalist, Barrett also studied at Vanderbilt, where he was close to his mother's family and absorbed more of the New South optimism. His primary interest would become international affairs. Yet Barrett maintained an abiding interest in southern change through foreign policy, and Tompkins was naturally drawn to him when they first met while delivering China market speeches before an 1899 meeting of the Texas State Commercial Convention in Dallas.[31] As noted, Tompkins subsequently had Barrett praise the China market before a 1900 meeting of the Southern Cotton Spinners Association. Then in the spring of 1901, when it was rumored that aging Edwin H. Conger would retire from the post of minister to China, Tompkins joined other AAA members in working for Barrett's selection as the replacement. With little effort, Tompkins acquired endorsements of Barrett from several key southern newspapers: the Atlanta *Constitution,* the New Orleans *Times-Democrat,* the Baltimore *Manufacturer's Record,* and of course the Charlotte *Daily Observer.* He also obtained support for Barrett from southern manufacturing clubs and chambers of commerce.[32]

In a personal letter to President McKinley, Tompkins summarized Barrett's image in the New South: "This section is very much interested in trade with the Chinese and also in the subject of a mission to China. If a change should be made in the personality of the U.S. minister . . . we southerners feel that Barrett is familiar with the conditions of this

31. Barrett's New South interests are explored in Prisco, *John Barrett,* 2–5. On Tompkins' early contacts with him, see John Barrett to Tompkins, December 21, 1899, and Tompkins to Barrett, December 26, 1899—both in Tompkins Papers, SHC; and *Journal of the American Asiatic Association,* III (1903), 260. In May, 1900, Tompkins had helped rally southern support for Barrett's futile effort at obtaining the post of Commercial Commissioner for Asia. J. H. McAden to William McKinley, May 5, 1900, in John Barrett: Applications and Recommendations for Office, National Archives; and Prisco, *John Barrett,* 46–47.

32. Tompkins to John Barrett, April 20, 1901, and to D. S. Franklin, April 20, 1901, Barrett to Tompkins, May 14, 1901, and a memorandum on southern newspapers supporting the application—all in John Barrett Papers, LC; Southern Manufacturers Club to William McKinley, June 11, 1901, in John Barrett: Applications and Recommendations for Office, NA.

section; that he is equally familiar with the sentiment of the people of the United States; . . . and that he has had considerable contact with the East." To Tompkins' chagrin and that of many other southern members of the American Asiatic Association, these efforts proved futile. Conger did not resign as anticipated; and when he did resign four years later, he was replaced by the experienced China hand, William W. Rockhill.[33]

From 1904 to 1906 still another issue, Chinese exclusion, drew Tompkins' attention to the China market. The American policy of restricting Chinese immigration, embodied in the Gresham-Yang Treaty of 1894, was due for reconsideration by Congress beginning in December, 1904. As congressional debates developed and it became clear that President Roosevelt would support the West Coast's plea for extended exclusion, Chinese merchants made plans to boycott American trade. The State Department and most congressmen exhibited little concern about Chinese retaliation.[34] Tompkins nevertheless had deep interest in these issues and worked to get them before the public eye.

Although a majority of southern senators had supported the Gresham-Yang Treaty, exhibiting a bond with Californians on race that affected more than a few congressional debates, Tompkins and other southerners for some time had urged that racial concerns should not take priority over needs for cheap agricultural labor and trade. In 1900, Tompkins argued this case for improved relations with China before the United States Industrial Commission. Moreover, in 1902, as the Gresham-Yang agreement came under attack, Tompkins, other southern textilists, and the AAA futilely committed themselves to nonrenewal of the treaty for the sake of better trade.[35] Tompkins remained

33. Tompkins to William McKinley, May 31, 1901, in John Barrett: Applications and Recommendations for Office, NA; Prisco, *John Barrett*, 49.

34. George E. Paulsen, "The Gresham-Yang Treaty," *Pacific Historical Review*, XXXVIII (1968), 281–97; Paulsen to the author, August 3, 1979.

35. Paulsen, "The Gresham-Yang Treaty"; Paulsen to the author, August 3, 1979. The common position of southerners and Californians on the Chinese Exclusion Act of 1882 is examined in Bertoff, "Southern Attitudes Toward Immigration," 359, and with particular reference to the political machinations of Alabama senator John Tyler Morgan, in Ollen Lawrence Burnette, Jr., "The Senate Foreign Relations Committee and the Diplomacy of Garfield, Arthur, and Cleveland" (Ph.D. dissertation, University of Virginia, 1952), 106–107, 250–51, 361–66, 477, and 483. See also Chester, *Sectionalism, Politics and American Diplomacy*, 110. On Tompkins' 1902 activities, consult Davis,

undaunted as the treaty returned to congressional focus some two years later. On June 10, 1905, he published a letter in *Fibre and Fabric*, the textilists' major journal. There was nothing oblique about his approach; cotton manufacturers had to out-lobby exclusion advocates and secure passage of a compromise immigration bill. He suggested one that excluded "coolies" who competed chiefly with America's West Coast laborers, but one that admitted professional-class Chinese—doctors, merchants, and others with government contacts.[36]

Tompkins also worked through the AAA. John Foord cabled that he needed "four or six good cotton mill men." These, along with Tompkins, would join other AAA delegates in a meeting scheduled for June 17 to urge Roosevelt to adopt a compromise spirit. Tompkins cabled Foord his choices: James W. Cannon (Concord, North Carolina), B. Frank Mebane (Spray, North Carolina), Henry B. Jennings (Greenville, South Carolina), William Allen Erwin (Durham, North Carolina), and the president of the American Cotton Manufacturers Association, Robert M. Miller, Jr. (Charlotte). When word spread that this dramatic appeal would be made to the president, T. I. Hickman, Ellison A. Smyth, and other southern mill men seemed adamant about going to Washington, too. Thus the twenty-seven member AAA delegation that called on Roosevelt included nineteen of Tompkins' textile cohorts. The show of force did little good. The group received the same pragmatic response Roosevelt had given earlier— anti-Chinese sentiment on the West Coast would have to be considered.[37]

"The Role of South Carolina's Cotton Manufacturers," 56–59. Tompkins' belief that reciprocity should not be sacrificed for exclusionism and protectionism is demonstrated in his *The Tariff and Reciprocity*; and in U.S. Industrial Commission, *Finals Report* (19 vols.; Washington, D.C., 1897–1902), XIX, 974–75; Tompkins to John R. Commons, June 15, 17, 1901, in Tompkins Papers, SHC.

36. *Fibre and Fabric*, June 10, 1905; Tompkins. Letter, *Fibre and Fabric*, June 16, 1905, typed copy in Tompkins Papers, SHC.

37. Tompkins to John Foord, June 3, 1905, to W. C. Maxwell, June 6, 1905, to B. Frank Mebane, June 16, 1905, and to J. A. Smith, June 6, 1905—all in Tompkins Papers, SHC; *Journal of the American Asiatic Association*, V (1905), 167–68, 174–75; Charlotte *Daily Observer*, June 17, 27, 1905; Marjorie W. Young (ed.), *Textile Leaders of the South* (Anderson, S.C., 1963), 39, 61, 747, 620. The other textile leaders who accompanied Tompkins included W. M. Montgomery, F. W. Poe, J. M. Geer, J. M. Maxwell, S. M. Orr, J. A. Brock, J. J. Spaulding, J. Irving Westervelt, William P. Greene, I. B. Turner, C. W. Johnson, and R. T. Durham. *Journal of the American Asiatic Association*, V (1905), 167–68.

The American Asiatic Association now moved to other strategies. While Foord launched an intense search for potentially friendly senators and congressmen, Tompkins used his long-standing membership in the National Association of Manufacturers to bring that organization's powerful lobby into the cause for some type of compromise immigration measure. In mid-June, Tompkins also wrote Wu Ting Fang, now a private citizen in Peking, asking about the breadth of the boycott sentiment in China and the date the boycott might actually commence. Although the boycott began in July, Wu's reply, dated August 9, was far from anticlimactic. Surely aware of Wu's stance on exclusion, Tompkins nevertheless accepted the letter as accurate and as portending trouble for cotton traders. "The movement to boycott American goods," Wu wrote, "is now spreading all over the country, being backed by all classes of people. . . . If this should continue, it would seriously affect the export trade to China." The only way for Americans to ease the situation, Wu concluded, was for them to approve an immigration plan excluding lower-class Chinese and admitting professionals.[38]

Tompkins was depressed by general trade losses caused by the boycott and also by Wu's letter—which had suggested a strategy that had so far failed—when, in December, 1905, Foord reported a breakthrough. United States Representative David J. Foster, of Vermont, had agreed to advance a compromise bill in the House of Representatives, one very similar to Wu's proposal. The bill charged American officials in China with responsibility for determining which Chinese were "coolies," to be excluded, and which were acceptable professionals. While many exclusionists liked the provision giving Americans on-the-scene power, there was still the obstacle of exactly how the differentiation between types of Chinese could be made. Regardless, Tompkins viewed the plan as the most likely means of halting the boycott. On Foord's confident instruction, Tompkins coordinated southern petitions and press support for passage of the Foster bill. With T. I. Hickman's influence, the Georgia legislature passed a resolu-

<hr>

38. Tompkins to James Inglish, June 7, 1905, to John M. Carson, June 20, 1905, and to Wu Ting Fang, June 16, 1905, Wu to Tompkins, August 9, 1905, Tompkins to J.P. Caldwell, September 23, 1905, Anna L. Twelvetrees to Wu, June 26, 1905, Tompkins to minister from China, June 7, 1905, clipping from Norfolk (Va.) *Landmark,* October 11, 1905—all in Tompkins Papers, SHC.

tion endorsing the plan, and Tompkins arranged for this to be read before Congress.[39]

When the bill reached the House Foreign Affairs Committee on March 14, 1906, Tompkins and three other southern textilists joined Foord in giving supportive testimony. Tompkins was grilled on how "coolies" could be distinguished in the immigration application process. He replied that there were certain "natural" racial divisions in all societies. The questioner bore down: "But have you had any practical experience with the Chinese at all?" Tompkins answered, "No, sir, not a bit . . . yet we [southerners] have had plenty of experience with alien races of people." In short, Tompkins was drawing on his domestic racial experience. As a New South leader he had advocated for the home scene a pragmatic approach to race recently developed as part of southern progressivism: not slavery, for it was inefficient, illegal, and unpatriotic; not black and white equality, for it collided with Anglo-Saxon control; but what he (and the United States Supreme Court) saw as a compromise between these two extremes, segregation. Before the Congress he now called for a similar compromise with regard to yellow racism in order to protect trade he considered vital to the economic progress of the South. Even so, a more rigid variety of racism, California's anti–Chinese labor sentiment, prevailed. After what has been described as "quiet execution behind closed doors," the pragmatic measure was dropped in May, 1906, and exclusion was extended. Later, Roosevelt did his best to recoup business support by threatening American intervention in China if the boycott continued, and thus it ceased.[40]

Tompkins worked for expansionism only a few more years. His textile business and many others in the South apparently escaped

39. John Foord to Tompkins, December 11, 1905, *ibid*; Delber L. McKee, *Chinese Exclusion Versus the Open Door, 1900–1906* (Detroit, 1977), 171ff.; James John Lorrence, "Business and Reform: The American Asiatic Association and the Exclusion Laws, 1905–1907," *Pacific Historical Review,* XXXIX (1970), 43ff.; Charlotte *Daily Observer,* June 27, 28, 1905; Tompkins to Smith, June 6, 1905, and John Foord to Tompkins, March 3, 8, 1906—all in Tompkins Papers, SHC.

40. House Committee on Foreign Affairs, *Hearings on Chinese Exclusion,* 59th Cong., 1st Sess., 20–54; *Journal of the American Asiatic Association,* VI (1906), 67–76; Lorrence, "Businessmen and Reform," 54; Paulsen, "Abrogation of the Gresham-Yang Treaty," 469, 470–477; McKee, *Chinese Exclusion,* 181ff. See also Shore, "Daniel Augustus Tompkins and Race," 73–94.

undamaged by the boycott. After 1909, however, American cotton interests began to show declining profits from the China market, and although his records on this particular point are incomplete, there is no reason to view the North Carolinian's experience as an exception to the national trend. The general downturn of the American economy in 1908 resulted in major setbacks for southern textilists. Moreover, what oriental cotton markets the southerners could have developed during this time rapidly came under the Japanese control, and America's tobacco began to fare relatively better in China than its textiles.[41] While Tompkins saw real possibilities for tobacco as an alternative southern export, he made one last dramatic effort on behalf of southern textiles.

He was convinced that an individual well experienced in the textile business, rather than a diplomat, should be the chief American representative in the Orient at this critical time. Thus in 1909 Tompkins personally applied for the China post. The application had some foundation. He had met President William Howard Taft on several occasions; he had dealt with a few powerful Republican businessmen, including Silas Webb of the China and Japan Trading Company; and he had developed a national reputation as a China market advocate, bringing New South support to a cause—expansionism—currently identified with the Republican party. Yet the fact remained that Tompkins was a southerner and a Democrat in a political era of sectionalistic politics. At a time when virtually all diplomatic assignments were awarded on the basis of politics, he lacked sufficient contacts within the northeastern Republican hierarchy to capture an appointment from a Republican president. In addition, while Webb and other northeasterners needed a tentative alliance with New South leaders such as Tompkins, they feared that a prominent southerner in China would only create further problems for northeastern textilists competing with those in Dixie. The appointment went to another businessman, Charles R. Crane, a noted Republican from Illinois.[42] Here was a

41. McKee, *Chinese Exclusion*, 185–215; Shik-sham Ts'ai, "Reaction to Exclusion: The Boycott of 1905 and Chinese National Awakening," *The Historian*, XXXIX (1976), 95–110; Paul Varg, "The Myth of the China Market, 1890–1914," *American Historical Review*, LXXVIII (1968), 742–58; Beers, "Southern Americans and China," 4–8, 10–13.

42. The opposing forces are revealed in Walter Hines Page to Tompkins, November 3,

disappointing end for the aging Tompkins. With a declining China trade, not to mention his own deteriorating health, Tompkins after 1909 gradually removed himself from public life and devoted his remaining six years to private business.[43]

Tompkins' experience provides a number of insights into the developing New South outlook. In forming his rationale for an expansionistic South, he clearly rejected the inward views so dominant among many southerners in the immediate postbellum era. Affected by events of 1898—the warring patriotism, the racial "compromise," the search for markets, still other aspects of Morgan's type of message—and also influenced by modernizing societies abroad, he appeared to be fertile ground indeed for the ideas of efficiency, optimism, expanded government, and national mission characteristic of business progressivism. On the other hand, as a New South advocate ever needful of the past, he had to find historical *southern* legitimacy for the Yankee-based expansionism he urged upon his section. He did this by invoking the expansionist traditions of the Jeffersonian and Jacksonian Souths. Thus through the merging influences of section and nation, his New South expansionism in most ways fitted neatly into the mainstream of American expansionism in the era of Theodore Roosevelt.

In one way southern expansionism did not fit. Yankees were a persisting problem. Since 1860 the mass of white southerners had considered Republicans to be their enemies. In the early 1900s, these southerners blamed northeastern Republicans for prolonging sectionalism by seeking to control numerous southern industries and to stifle those which represented competition for the Northeast. Regardless, New South business Progressives, themselves part of the section's anti-Republican sentiment, attempted cautious rapprochement with expansionist interests in the Northeast. If this effort was led by individ-

---

1909, in Walter Hines Page Papers, Houghton Library, Harvard University; Tompkins to Nelson Aldrich, June 9, 1909, Henry E. C. Bryant to Tompkins, June 14, 1909, Lee S. Overman to Tompkins, June 25, 1909, Howard Ayres to Frances M. Huntingdon-Wilson, July 6, 1909, all in Daniel Augustus Tompkins: Applications and Recommendations for Office, NA; *Journal of the American Asiatic Association*, LX (1910), 357. See also Charles Vevier, *The United States and China, 1906–1913: A Study of Finance and Diplomacy* (New York, 1968), 91ff.; and Israel, *Progressivism and the Open Door*, Chap 3.

43. Clay, "Daniel A. Tompkins: American Bourbon," 316–17.

uals who were genuinely cosmopolitan by early twentieth-century standards, it nevertheless failed because of the powerful forces of sectionalism. So close to being a complete formula, New South expansionism in the early Progressive Era still lacked a political mechanism; Democrats remained splintered, and Republicans usually excluded southerners from the inner power circles. However, unknown to Tompkins and his New South colleagues, the critical mechanism was indeed on the horizon. While it would not be located in the Republican party, it would still be found where the New South had been looking since at least 1898.

4

The Anglo-Saxon Bond
of John W. Davis

On July 14, 1918, Congressman Robert L. Doughton of North Carolina stood up before a group of friendly Yankees convened in Trenton, New Jersey, and indulged in some grandiloquence about Americans and World War I. Doughton asserted that "grandsons of the men who wore the blue and . . . grandsons of the men who wore the grey were . . . now marching with locked shields and martial step to the mingled strains of Dixie and the Star Spangled Banner."[1] The congressman failed to note that those same shields, those same steps, had been finding a closer and closer harmony since the Spanish-American War. Yet he had the central point. By 1918 the spirit of North-South reconciliation ran deeper than ever before.

A key source of this optimistic nationalism was President Woodrow Wilson. He enjoyed popularity across the nation, especially in the South, which had not been favorably inclined toward the White House since the 1850s. Even though Wilson drew his public philosophy chiefly from the Progressive nationalism of the urban Northeast, he was considered "southern" by southerners because of his roots in Georgia, North Carolina, and Virginia. Southerners desperately wanted one of their own in the White House, and Wilson encouraged them to think that they had such a leader.[2] To them, Wilsonian progressivism had brought improvements in commerce, education, and health. When they considered the international scene, especially in the light of their own reformative optimism, southerners felt encouraged to believe that in great part because of Wilson their Dixie was well on its way to regaining a secure, respected role in the nation and the world. Not since the early nineteenth century, when "another Virginian" occupied

1. Quoted in Dewey W. Grantham, *Southern Progressivism: The Reconciliation of Progress and Tradition* (Knoxville, 1983), 338.
2. On Wilson's southernism, see Arthur S. Link, "Woodrow Wilson: The American as Southerner," *Journal of Southern History*, XXXVI (February, 1970), 3–17.

the White House, had southern leaders felt so confident about their section. Equally important, with Wilson's presidency and the re-emergence of the Democratic party, they gained what they were lacking as late as 1911—access to national political power. In this sense, the final merging of New South expansionism with that of the Northeast was an important element of the return of the South to national affairs often associated with the Wilson presidency.[3]

Reverence for the Anglo-Saxon influence in history played a curious role in the way New South leaders found sectional redemption through Wilsonian progressivism. Positive interest in the trans-Atlantic racial bond had not always been strong. In the antebellum years white southerners had indeed exhibited nothing short of adoration for "the English-speaking people"—a regard based on common families, the cotton trade, and a romantic, cavalier view of the planter as English country gentleman. They believed in the white man's manifest destiny.[4] Yet in the postbellum era that attitude gave way to an intense Anglophobia. Senator Morgan and many other former Confederates would not forgive Britain for wavering on aid during the Civil War. Still other southerners viewed Britain's approach to world affairs as unprincipled imperialism, not so different from the Northeast's continuing policies toward the South. Populists revolting in the early 1890s reinforced this Anglophobia. British investments in southern lumber and railroads, not to mention the general British support of the gold standard, represented critical elements in the "foreign capitalist" oppression of southern working classes. Even Senator Morgan, no Populist, shared this nativist response to Englishmen.[5]

Although this Anglophobia continued after the turn of the century, as expressed by such leaders as Mississippi's James K. Vardaman and North Carolina's Claude Kitchin, it soon was displaced as the domi-

3. Grantham, *Southern Progressivism*; George Brown Tindall, *The Emergence of the New South, 1913–1945* (Baton Rouge, 1967), 33–69; C. Vann Woodward, *Origins of the New South, 1877–1913* (Baton Rouge, 1951), 481.

4. See, for example, Reginald Horsman, *Race and Manifest Destiny: The Origins of American Racial Anglo-Saxonism* (Cambridge, Mass., 1981), 122–25, 140–42, 164–75, 280–83.

5. Edward P. Crapol, *America for Americans: Economic Nationalism and Anglophobia in the Late Nineteenth Century* (Westport, 1973); Charles S. Campbell, Jr., *Anglo-American Understanding, 1898–1903* (Baltimore, 1957), 130–32, 186–89; Woodward, *Origins of the New South*, 118–20; Joseph A. Fry, "John Tyler Morgan's Southern Expansionism," *Diplomatic History*, IX (1985), 340.

nant sentiment by a resurging Anglophilism. Confederate veterans died. The silver issue lost out, and cotton prices improved. British investment in Dixie textiles suddenly was perceived as helping New South businessmen compete with northeastern textilists. Although New South textilists saw British exporters as competitors, the Dixie businessmen also understood that Britain's power in the world economy helped keep trade outlets open. Most important, Britain's expansionist approach to world affairs increasingly stood as a model, not as an object of criticism, as New South advocates embraced expansionism.[6]

Perhaps, too, America's general acceptance of Jim Crow in the South encouraged southerners to believe that, after all, their section's traditional advocacy of white superiority had a legitimate place in the national and international mainstream. Certainly, as many southerners advanced the Progressive reforms of segregation and disfranchisement, so did they seek to extend the idea of racial progress to the international scene by advancing Anglo-American preeminence.[7] As Walter Hines Page, newly appointed ambassador to Britain, wrote his fellow Progressive Edwin A. Alderman, "I can't get over the feeling . . . that the English-speaking folk must rule the world."[8] Thus, when war opened in Europe in 1914, New South Anglophiles such as Page, Alderman, and the Mississippi senator John Sharp Williams were primed for the task at hand. Granted, the New South's developing prowar, pro-League stance derived from some essentially nonracial currents, some old and some new in the section's history: a sectional

6. Patrick J. Hearden, *Independence and Empire: The New South's Cotton Mill Campaign, 1865–1901* (De Kalb, 1982), 132, 138, and *passim*. Even when the cotton crisis of 1914 and 1915 arose, it represented only a temporary intrusion on the new sense of bond. See Link, "The Cotton Crisis, the South, and Anglo-American Diplomacy, 1914–15," in J. Carlyle Sitterson (ed.), *Studies in Southern History in Memory of Albert Ray Newsom, 1894–1951* (Chapel Hill, 1957), 122–38. On the persistent dislike for the British, consult William F. Holmes, *The White Chief: James Kimble Vardaman* (Baton Rouge, 1970), Chaps. 11–13, and Alex Mathews Arnett, *Claude Kitchin and the Wilson War Policies* (Boston, 1957).

7. For focus on American racism as a national phenomenon and the reemergence of the Anglo-American bond, see Bradford Perkins, *The Great Rapprochement, England and the United States, 1895–1914* (New York, 1968), 311–12, and Stuart Anderson, *Race and Rapprochement: Anglo-Saxonism and Anglo-American Relations, 1895–1904* (Rutherford, 1981).

8. Cited in John M. Cooper, Jr., *Walter Hines Page: The Southerner as American 1855–1918* (Chapel Hill, 1979), 267.

eye focused tightly on free trade, certain to follow the establishment of the League; loyalty to the Democratic party; and the powerful image of Woodrow Wilson in the mind of the New South.[9] Still, the racial current—one that could subsume and unite all the others—found expression in the section's strong ethnic and cultural affinity for an Anglo-American mission to regenerate the warring world of the early twentieth century.

This devotion to the spreading of white paternalism had a questionable hold on President Wilson's own mind, but it did indeed find strong representation among Wilson's advisors and other appointees. And not all were southerners. There was no greater Anglophile in this era than Secretary of State Robert Lansing of New York. A disproportionate number of the noted Anglophiles, however, were from the South. In the Cabinet there was the Tarheel-turned-Texan David F. Houston; another North Carolinian, Josephus Daniels, and two other Texans, Albert Sidney Burleson and the president's most influential advisor, Edward M. House.[10] The diplomatic corps, still a victim of patronage, also bore the southern Anglophile mark. No fewer than twenty of Wilson's forty-two diplomatic appointments went to southerners considered enlightened by the standards of progressivism. Most notable were South Carolina's William E. Gonzales (minister to Cuba, then Peru), Virginia's Thomas Nelson Page (ambassador to Italy), and of

9. Tindall, *The Emergence of the New South*, 63–64; Robert Hoyt Block, "Southern Opinion of Woodrow Wilson's Foreign Policies, 1913–1917" (Ph.D. dissertation, Duke University, 1968); Timothy Gregory McDonald, "Southern Democratic Congressmen and the First World War, August 1914–April 1917: The Public Record of Their Support for and Opposition to Wilson's Policies (Ph.D. dissertation, University of Washington, 1962); Dewey W. Grantham, "Southern Senators and the League of Nations, 1918–1920," *North Carolina Historical Review*, XXVI (1949), 187–205; Richard L. Watson, "A Testing Time for Southern Congressional Leadership: The War Crisis of 1917–18," *Journal of Southern History*, XLIV (1978), 3–40; Carl N. Degler, "Thesis, Antithesis, Synthesis: The South, the North, and the Nation," *Journal of Southern History*, LIII (1987), 16.

10. On Wilson's racial and social views, see Joel Williamson, *The Crucible of Race: Black and White Relations in the American South Since Emancipation* (Chapel Hill, 1984), 364–65; Arthur S. Link, *Wilson the Diplomatist: A Look at His Major Foreign Policies* (Baltimore, 1957), 14–15; Link, "Wilson: The American as Southerner," 2–11; John M. Cooper, Jr., *The Warrior and the Priest: Woodrow Wilson and Theodore Roosevelt* (Cambridge, Mass., 1983), 210–11; and Lloyd C. Gardner, *Safe for Democracy: The Anglo-American Response to Revolution, 1913–1923* (New York, 1984), and on the Cabinet also, Tindall, *The Emergence of the New South*, 2, 143–44.

course the former North Carolinian who had made a career as a New York editor, Ambassador Walter Hines Page.[11] Still, there remains no more fascinating example of the New South Progressive advocating Anglo-Saxon leadership in the context of Wilsonianism than the man who, in 1918, succeeded Page at the Court of St. James's—John W. Davis.

Historians have generally regarded Davis as the "straight-thinking" West Virginia lawyer who served three years in Congress before becoming President Wilson's solicitor-general. When Page resigned as ambassador to the Court of St. James's, just as Wilson was preparing to leave for Versailles, Davis assumed the London post. By 1921, however, he had returned to the practice of law. From his firm on Wall Street, he ran as the Democratic nominee for president in 1924, served as president of the American Bar Association, helped establish the Council on Foreign Relations, opposed governmental centralization in the New Deal, and completed his career by arguing against Thurgood Marshall in the desegregation cases of the mid-1950s. When Davis died in 1955, he was unquestionably "the lawyer's lawyer." Yet his contemporaries also considered him very much an Anglophile of the New South.[12]

In view of his reputation and self-image as "categorically a Southerner," Davis' roots are intriguing. His origins were in mid-nineteenth-century West Virginia. In the 1860s that state held a complex array of people, from Union veterans to those who had consciously sought to be neutral in the Civil War, and on to those who lived deep in the state's isolated mountain ranges, disconnected from much of the flow of history. However, because of the state's proximity to Virginia, one of the two principal seedbeds of the South, stereotypical southerners also lived in West Virginia and well beyond the Old Virginia towns of the eastern section. At one such place, Clarksburg, in the north central

11. *United States Chiefs of Mission, 1778–1973* (Washington, D.C., 1973); Cooper, *Walter Hines Page,* 255–404; Tindall, *The Emergence of the New South,* 5, 285. Thomas Nelson Page is included as a Progressive, despite his extolling of certain social values of the old order, because he advocated expanded industrialism and improved education. See Wayne Mixon, *Southern Writers and the New South Movement, 1865–1913* (Chapel Hill, 1980), 36–41.

12. Charles Warren, "Our Ambassador to St. James'," broadside [February 1918?], in Charles Warren Papers, Library of Congress. See William H. Harbaugh, *Lawyer's Lawyer: The Life of John W. Davis* (New York, 1973).

part of the state, there lived not only the family of Confederate hero Stonewall Jackson but that of John W. Davis.[13]

The trauma of the Civil War dominated Davis' Clarksburg youth. In 1860 his Scots-Presbyterian father, a lawyer, joined other prominent Clarksburg residents in opposing West Virginia's separation from Virginia. Ironically, the father also opposed the secession of West Virginia from the Union. A full secession movement, he argued, surely would result in open civil violence; and as the northern "fanatics" invaded, they would eliminate slavery and thus the southern way of life. An aggressive Jeffersonian Democrat of renowned strict constructionist rhetoric, the elder Davis went on to Congress after the war, where he fought against the Fourteenth and Fifteenth amendments as encroachments upon states' rights and efforts to destroy "white man's government." Considering that Davis' father "yielded to no one in [his] devotion to the South," it is not surprising that John, born in 1873, grew up hating Thaddeus Stevens' Republican party and the Reconstruction that had reduced the white South "to rags."[14] Equally unsurprising, the son matured to revere Stonewall Jackson, Claude G. Bowers' *Tragic Era*, and that novel in which southerners "come alive," Margaret Mitchell's *Gone With the Wind*.[15]

Other early influences only solidified this emerging sectional viewpoint. Educated and genteel, his parents urged the disciplined study of literary classics, especially those of England. Young Davis' education at Washington and Lee University provided a similar influence. When he enrolled at this "Athens of the South," located in Lexington, Virginia, Robert E. Lee had been its president only a few years before.

13. James M. Callahan, *History of West Virginia, Old and New* (3 vols.; Chicago, 1923), I, 399ff.; Richard O. Curry, *A House Divided: A Study of Statehood Politics and the Copperhead Movement in West Virginia* (Pittsburgh, 1964), 135. Although in his biography Harbaugh does not emphasize Davis' southernism, he does concur with the emphasis reflected here. William H. Harbaugh, telephone interview with author, January 11, 1984.

14. Harbaugh, *Lawyer's Lawyer*, 3–10, 497. Davis' daughter, Julia, would recall that her father was raised in an area where the war had wrought great destruction, where people felt "invaded . . . occupied . . . defeated . . . ruined," and "depressed." Davis, *Legacy of Love* (New York, 1961), 6, 102–109.

15. John W. Davis' Ambassadorial Diary, July 22, 1919, in John W. Davis Papers, Sterling Library, Yale University. Hereinafter this work will be cited as Diary; the collection will be cited as Davis Papers. In 1954, Davis appeared before the United States Supreme Court on behalf of the State of South Carolina, stating that South Carolina had not come to Washington, D.C., "as Thad Stevens would have wished, in sackcloth and ashes." Quoted in Harbaugh, *Lawyer's Lawyer*, 515.

There Davis encountered the magnetic professor John Randolph Tucker, grandson of Thomas Jefferson's teacher, George Wythe. Tucker extolled the superiority of governmental institutions Americans had inherited from England.[16] In Davis' later life—as a Washington and Lee law professor, an attorney, and a public servant—he would bear the enduring mark of Tucker's teachings. He would exhibit a continual scholarly interest in the "advanced" legal institutions of England and focus intently on the Angles, Saxons, and Jutes as well as the Magna Charta and Parliament. With an admitted "life-long admiration for the British people," moreover, he would view nonwhites, including American Negroes, as inferior (though he always avoided the term *nigger* and despised the Ku Klux Klan), and he would urge that the world needed the stabilizing, progressive influence of British and American whites.[17] Nevertheless, he would part with Tucker on matters of economic productivity. Although he always revered Thomas Jefferson, Davis would oppose maintenance of the small-farm economy and instead advocate "the creative force of industry" in "the cause of his [own] region." In fact, Davis would use his own finely honed talents as a corporate attorney to foster Yankee-style industrial growth in West Virginia.[18]

Other elements of the postbellum South also affected Davis' developing persona. Even by his late thirties, when he headed for Washington, he acted, indeed *appeared*, in every respect "the distinguished southern gentleman," and one "good to look at." With premature silver hair and twinkling blue eyes set deeply in a "long Anglo-American face," he stood straight and dignified at just under six feet. Those recalling his personality invariably hit on the stereotype: "a raconteur . . . without rival," with "a gentle manner," "courtliness," "charm," and "a ready, soft smile," "well turned out" in a conservative, vested suit, complete with watch chain.[19] Much like Joseph T. Robinson,

16. Harbaugh, *Lawyer's Lawyer*, 10–14, 15–28, 31–34, 108, 173; Davis, *Legacy of Love*, 15, 18.

17. On his admiration for the British, see, for example, Washington *Post*, September 19, 1918. On this prejudice applied to American Negroes, see New York *Times*, March 31, 1955; Harbaugh, *Lawyer's Lawyer*, 36, 47, 52, 234, 273, 495; Davis, *Legacy of Love*, 225–26.

18. Beckles Willson, *America's Ambassadors to England* (London, 1928), 463; Harbaugh interview, January 11, 1984.

19. Harbaugh, *Lawyer's Lawyer*, 28 and *passim*; *Washington Wife: Journal of Ellen Maury Slayden from 1897–1919* (New York, 1962), 340–41 and *passim*; Washington *Post*, March 29, 1955.

Cordell Hull, Edwin Alderman, and his other southern friends, Davis possessed, beneath his genuine gentleman's exterior, an equally real interior, as if grafted from the Yankee ways he sought to emulate. Noted for his photographic memory, he was "master of his emotions," cool, calculating. Perhaps the *Times* of London came closest to Davis' complexity when it stated that he had "the ease and quiet finish of the South and its mellow humor, mingling with the sterner qualities, the competence, the decisiveness of the North."[20] If so, Ellen Graham Bassell ("Nell"), whom he married in 1910, provided the perfect complement. This prominent lady from Charlottesville, Virginia, had "classic Anglo-American beauty . . . [with] golden hair, blue eyes [and] perfect, if chiselled, features." At ease in any social setting, she seemed to combine the drive of a Scarlett O'Hara with the concern of a Melanie Wilkes as she urged her husband onward in his rapidly developing professional life.[21]

Finally, the roots and influences of Davis' role as a diplomat from the New South can be traced specifically through his ideas about Americans and the world in the years before Wilson. Along with many others of the New South, he opposed Republicans from Benjamin Harrison to Theodore Roosevelt for their party's reluctance to lower the tariff. He also refused to jump headlong into the "Splendid Little War" mentality of 1898. He connected the war fever of that year to the "Republican demagogues" who elected a president as weak "as a human fishing worm." He decried the "power of brute force" as still the "recognized . . . final arbiter of quarrels." As late as April 14, 1898—a week before the Spanish-American War broke—Davis thought like a pacifist and anti-imperialist: "I am filled with genuine sadness at the thought of the war which seems on us at last, and I regret it because all war is horrible at best, because I believe it to be wholly unnecessary if not wholly unjustifiable, and because I think no matter what the outcome may be this country will be the loser—not in money and blood alone but even perhaps in liberty, which cannot long survive when a nation goes upon

20. Willson, *America's Ambassadors*, 463; London *Times*, as quoted in Harbaugh, *Lawyer's Lawyer*, 130–31; David Vann, interview with author, Birmingham, Ala., January 20, 1984. Vann, who clerked for Justice Hugo Black at the time Davis was making his last appearances before the United States Supreme Court, recalled that all Supreme Court clerks would come to the Court to witness Davis' "awesome mind and memory in action."

21. Harbaugh, *Lawyer's Lawyer*, 80–81; Washington *Post*, September 19, 1918.

a 'war-footing.'" Even in the midst of the conflict, he believed that history would "place [the war] among the greatest of mistakes" and professed opposition to "all land-grabbing and imperialism." By the time Spain sued for peace in July, the attorney was exasperated: "I hope . . . the war is nearly over."[22]

Still, like so many people of the New South looking outward at the turn of the century, Davis seemed torn in different directions by the events of 1898. As early as February, though he opposed the war, he had begun to adjust to the unpleasant reality before him: "I cannot give up the conviction that there will be no war—[but] perhaps the wish fathers the thought." By early April, despite his continued criticism of warmongers, he believed that "after war comes there must be but one sentiment, and we must all be *pro patria*." And in late April, with war under way, he took the same approach: "If we have to fight, let's give them thunder. We must all be *pro patria*." Finally, by May he joined the growing wave of New South patriotism. Before a West Virginia group celebrating George Washington's birthday, he integrated Confederate experiences of 1865 with national feelings of 1898: "For the first time since the war drums ceased to thunder over thirty years ago, decoration day finds us listening to the roar of cannon and the tramp of armed men. But today it is no longer brother against brother, American against American, but humanity against cruelty and liberty against despotism." Then, still caught in limbo between the dynamics of expansionism and isolationism, he concluded the address with stern warnings about "those who think the time is ripe for us to enter upon a colonial policy, forgetting that liberty is best preserved in small places, and that men—not acres—make a country great."[23]

Some twenty years later, his career having expanded from West Virginia attorney to solicitor general of the United States, Davis had much the same reference point in regarding world affairs: his section's history and culture. As Congress resolved to enter World War I, Davis wrote his daughter that "we shall set out on what may be the hardest task of our national life—certainly since the [eighteen] sixties." Yet

22. Harbaugh, *Lawyer's Lawyer*, 65, 70–73; Davis to Julia Davis, February 24, July 26, 1898, and to Julia McDonald, April 14, 21, June 26, July 15, 26, 1898—all in Davis Papers; Davis, *Legacy of Love*, 14, 151.

23. Davis to Julia McDonald, February 24, April 3, 1898—both in Davis Papers; Harbaugh, *Lawyer's Lawyer*, 43; *Decoration Day Speech*, May 30, 1898, in Davis Papers.

during the previous two decades his beacon—the South—had begun to emit a dramatically different signal. The patriotism in the signal had grown to a spurious intensity, drowning out the earlier antiexpansionist sentiments. Domestic trends were the key cause. The South's involvement in the Progressive Era and Davis' own dynamic role in the New Freedom of Woodrow Wilson provided him with a southern-based patriotism emphasizing Anglo-Saxonism, free trade, the enforcement of the Monroe Doctrine, and the general American mission to help the world find progress. If Davis would not always see eye to eye with Wilson, he was like John Sharp Williams, Oscar W. Underwood, and many others of his region in no longer being ambivalent about American power abroad. He looked out upon the world as a missionary expansionist, and in a general sense Wilson the "southerner" was his leader.[24]

Specifically, Solicitor General Davis viewed World War I with "an unwavering faith in the civilizing force" of Britain and its liberal expansionist role in world affairs. As the progenitor of Anglo-Saxon legal institutions, Britain appeared in Davis' eyes as the symbol of "reason" and "the reign of law," the defender of international economic activity and order. Against a world setting of economic instability and conflict, he viewed the Commonwealth as an agent of cultural superiority and uplift. Because the attacking Germans were "a people without either manners or morals," this Victorian gentleman deemed a British victory essential.[25]

Moreover, in Davis' view (if not Wilson's) Britain's mission was America's. The two nations had the same predestined role as progressive, white societies. As early as 1914, he had confessed to his father, "I have never had less neutrality in my soul in any war than I have in this one." By 1917 he was even more emphatic. When the stakes were so

---

24. Davis to Anna K. Davis, February 2, April 6, 1917—both in Davis Papers. *Cf.* Grantham, *Southern Progressivism*; Tindall, *The Emergence of the New South*; Woodward, *Origins of the New South*. See also Diary, August 20, 1919, Davis to Anna K. Davis, February 6, 1917—both in Davis Papers; George Colman Osborn, *John Sharp Williams: Planter-Statesman of the Deep South* (Baton Rouge, 1943), 254–310; Evans C. Johnson, *Oscar W. Underwood: A Political Biography* (Baton Rouge, 1980), 215–74.

25. Davis to Anna K. Davis, February 11, 1917, in Davis Papers; Harbaugh, *Lawyer's Lawyer*, 421–22, 431. See also E. David Cronin (ed.), *The Cabinet Diaries of Josephus Daniels, 1913–1921* (Lincoln, Nebr., 1963), 227.

high, he wrote, there were "things far worse than war," for America was helping to "defend the rights of the world" to progress under Anglo-American guidance and helping to "set the day of democracy and peace far ahead." Davis had always had reservations about President Wilson's "insensitive" and "petty" ways of dealing with people. But he nevertheless considered Wilson's war message the "most thrilling scene" he would ever witness, and throughout World War I he reveled in the president's "devotion" to civilization, democracy, and a postwar world receptive to the "superior" influence.[26]

Although the president was never personally close to Davis, he knew the West Virginian's patriotism from his role as solicitor general— particularly from his nationalistic defense of the Selective Service Act. Wilson also had a clear impression of Davis from Colonel House and from Davis' close friend, Secretary of State Lansing. So, with the war virtually over and Ambassador Page resigning at London, Wilson turned to Davis—the sophisticated Anglo-Saxonist, the easy-talking yet hard driving southern gentleman, the scholarly attorney—to help extend progressivism into the postwar world.[27]

Actually, the administration was already moving Davis into the international arena when the London job opened. Having decided in August, 1918, that he was ready to leave the solicitor general's position, Davis had agreed to serve as one of four high commissioners representing America at an international conference on German prisoners of war. To be held in Berne, Switzerland, the conference excited Davis. On September 1 he headed to Europe filled with notions of bringing order and civilization to a chaotic situation. Therefore, Davis

26. Davis to John J. Davis, October 14, 1914, and to Anna K. Davis, February 5, 1917—both in Davis Papers; Harbaugh, *Lawyer's Laywer*, 161; Davis to Anna K. Davis, February 3, April 4 (?), 1917—both in Davis Papers; Davis to Charles Warren, March 1, 1919, in Warren Papers; Robert Lansing, *War Memoirs of Robert Lansing* (Indianapolis, 1935), 244; Harbaugh, *Lawyer's Lawyer*, 123–27, 138, 157–60.
27. Thomas W. Gregory to Davis, July 23, 1917, and Davis to Gregory, July 25, 1917—both in Department of Justice Straight Numerical File—Gregory Papers, National Archives; See also Davis, "Address . . . at the Eclipse," October 27, 1917, general collection, LC; Davis to Woodrow Wilson, July 5, 1912, Edward M. House to Wilson, August 24, 25, 1918—all in Woodrow Wilson Papers, LC; Daniel M. Smith, *Robert Lansing and American Neutrality, 1914–17* (Berkeley, 1958), 196 n.65; Arthur Clarence Walworth, *America's Moment* (New York, 1977), 39 n.26; EMH [House] to Wilson, July 7, 1915, in E. M. House, *Intimate Papers of Colonel House* (2 vols.; Boston, 1926), II, 9–10; Washington *Post*, September 19, 1918.

was less than pleased when Secretary Lansing's cable reached him, on September 6 at Claridge's Hotel in London, urging him to take the ambassadorship. Even the accompanying cable from Nell—"You must not decline"—failed to ease his reservations. He saw the ambassadorship, unlike the Berne conference, as peripheral to the American war and peace effort. He also viewed it as a "tinseled honor," of little help in his ultimate plan of returning to private law practice and making some money. When he declined, however, Nell and Lansing shot back cables resisting the decision. The secretary urged duty. The savvy wife depicted the Court of St. James's as increasing his reputation and his money-making abilities as an attorney.[28]

On September 11 Davis accepted Wilson's invitation to serve as ambassador to the Court of St. James's and on December 4 embarked for London with Nell.[29] As it turned out, he sailed on the ship carrying President Wilson and other members of the American delegation to the Paris Peace Conference. This permitted Davis his only conversation with Wilson that was even vaguely related to his duties at London. The president stated his own well-known views on the League and other pending international matters but never addressed the specific assignment that Davis would soon discover was his—pursuing the vision of Anglo-American influence in the postwar world with an American policy that often worked against such harmony.[30]

Granted, as Davis took charge of the embassy on December 14, 1918, Anglo-American relations appeared bright in the immediate afterglow of Allied victory. Armistice was thirty-three days old. However, if November had brought cessation of hostilities, it had also seen Wilson's urging for strong American leadership go unsupported by the

28. See Harbaugh, *Lawyer's Lawyer*, 121–36, 562; and Klaus Schwabe, *Woodrow Wilson, Revolutionary Germany, and Peacemaking, 1918–1919: Missionary Diplomacy and the Realities of Power* (Chapel Hill, 1985), 102, which asserts, incorrectly, that Davis and Wilson were close friends.

29. American press reactions to Davis' appointment were quite favorable. For example, see Washington *Post*, September 19, 1918. Southern papers were especially pleased. See Atlanta *Constitution*, September 19, 1918; Memphis *Commercial Appeal*, September 19, 20, 1918; Richmond *Times-Dispatch*, September 19, 1918; Louisville *Courier-Journal*, September 19, 1918; Nashville *Banner-Herald*, September 19, 1918; New Orleans *Times-Picayune*, September 20, 1918.

30. Charles Seymour, *Letters from the Paris Peace Conference* (New Haven, 1965), xxxi-xxxii. Seymour quotes Davis as having said he received "no instructions from first to last."

American congressional elections. Republicans now controlled both houses. At first Davis did not seem to comprehend this omen. As he wrote his friend Charles Warren in Washington, postwar problems were basically European: "It requires no stretch of the imagination to see the whole of continental Europe [as] one of seething bedlam."[31] By early September, 1919, however, Davis had a full appreciation for the complexity of the situation he faced. Against the background of the opening sessions of the Paris Peace Conference, he appraised the scene.

> What a witches stew it is when one comes to contemplate it—a crushed but revengeful Germany, a disappointed but nonetheless ambitious France, . . . a Russia in chaos, . . . and . . . an American Senate which seems to have no realization of the volcanic forces with which it is seeking to deal or how urgently time is the essence of the situation. I still have faith in the ultimate [condition] of a world ordered by law and reason, based on the common consent of the nations; but you call upon me to vindicate the grounds of my belief, [and] I must fall back on the monastic dogma—"*Credo, quia impossibile est.*"[32]

Davis actually held to an additional "right to hope": "the resisting power of the human animal" coupled with "the basic common sense of the British breed."[33] Thus one of the first and always principal strategies of this polished Anglophile was to use essentially informal ways of fostering friendly relations between his people and those of Great Britain.

To this end, Davis artfully employed club memberships, speaking engagements, and other facets of his fast-paced London social life. Quickly he appeared on the membership lists of no fewer than sixteen English clubs. This included five major sporting groups—the Croom Hill Golf Club, the Royal Thames Yacht Club, the Turf Club, the Phyllis Court Club, and the Sir Izaak Walton League—through which

31. For a survey of these events see Robert D. Schulzinger, *American Diplomacy in the Twentieth Century* (New York, 1984), 104–24. Also consult Seth P. Tillman, *Anglo-American Relations at the Paris Peace Conference of 1919* (Princeton, 1961), 35–37; Diary, December 18, 1918; Davis to Warren, March 1, 1919, in Warren Papers.

32. Davis to Charles Warren, September 8, 1919, in Warren Papers. See also Diary, February 11, 1920, and Davis, *Legacy of Love*, 171. These problems, plus others related to Irish independence, prohibition, Mediterranean oil, and the islands of Yap, are discussed in H. Maureen DeJure, "The Diary of a Diplomat: A Study of Anglo-American Relations, 1918–1921" (Honors thesis, Bucknell University [1966]).

33. Davis to Thomas W. Gregory, February 3, 1919, copy in Davis Papers.

he putted, sailed, galloped, volleyed, and cast himself into the company of British royalty and diplomats from around the world. Above all, he adored his "golf sticks." With his regular partner, Lord Reading, he could easily go thirty-six holes on a Saturday—even in the rain.[34]

Davis also used other clubs and gentlemanly professional groups for contacts. More important, before them he delivered formal remarks, often covered in the press, designed "to keynote the community of sentiment between Great Britain and America." After all, he confided to his diary, "I am the guardian of that sentiment." He made his first public appearance before the Pilgrim's Club at the Savoy Hotel on January 10, 1919. That night he wrote, "Am glad the first dip is over." Davis also addressed ranking levels of British academia and law—the faculties and students of Oxford University and of the universities of Birmingham, London, Glasgow, and Edinburgh. So effective was his appearance at Glasgow that students captured him after the speech and "carried [him] on their shoulders around the triangle, chanting, "We want Davis, We want Davis." His greatest such success involved the prestigious jurists of the Middle Temple, Inns of Court. Admitted to this group as an "honorary bencher," Davis addressed the lawyers "on the unity of the British and American Bar, and the lasting friendship of the people whom they serve." The American seemed genuinely excited about the remarkable honor of being only the second foreigner ever admitted to this bar. Although he remained privately struck by the "cold black negroes" among their membership, he still perceived the Middle Temple as "more entitled than any other spot on the two continents to be regarded as the shrine of Anglo-Saxon Liberty." As master par excellence of the after-dinner toast and as dedicated "revolver of ideas" and researcher and writer of the Anglo-American message, Davis often took the podium five nights out of seven and averaged one major address a week for two and a half years.[35]

34. Diary, January 31, August 28, 1919, October 3–4, 1920. Davis to Warren, September 8, 1919, in Warren Papers; Washington *Post*, September 19, 1918. His daughter recalls that golf was not a diversion for him—indeed, his only "diversion" was work. Davis, *Legacy of Love*, 213. The diary confirms this. For example, regarding several days of golf with Lord Reading, he recorded: "Golf with Reading at Coombs Hall. Much talk of British-American politics." Diary, November 27, 1920.
35. Diary, February 22, January 2, 11, March 21, April 7, November 24, 1919, February 25, 28, 1921; Harbaugh, *Lawyer's Lawyer*, 139, 161, 165; Davis to Warren, September 8, 1919, in Warren Papers; Diary, January 10, 30, September 18, Novem-

Such activities resulted in the constant expansion of Davis' social life. This was a mixed blessing. Raised on strong talk about the need for frugality to recover from the ravages of the Civil War, Davis approached diplomatic entertaining with ambivalence. The smallest home ever occupied by an ambassador to the Court of St. James's and a used Pierce Arrow purchased from an army officer and repainted black were the types of economies he felt compelled to pursue in order to fund the often lavish parties expected of a man of his post. Yet what made this social life palatable was more than the coolly calculated perception that "acquaintanceship" was essential to his mission. He and Nell clearly believed they were in their own social element, and they had a genuine, conscious appreciation of the basic humanity and sense of history of the British elite. With minimal compunction, they sprinkled their conversation with "requisite numbers" of *sirs* and *royal highnesses*. Invited to Buckingham Palace on many occasions, Davis found the queen "not at all difficult" in talk and "charming in manner."[36] Prime Minister David Lloyd George, a constant social companion, Davis found to be "one of the most vital of living politicians." More to the point, English society perceived Davis, the southern gentleman, as one of its own. For the trusted American ambassador, weekend and holiday invitations were endless. The king regarded Davis as "the most perfect gentleman I have ever met."[37]

That was good. For during 1919 and 1920, as Davis well knew, American relations with Britain as well as with Europe in general needed every touch of personal diplomacy available. Few issues of these relations taxed his talents more than the future of Germany, and few issues demonstrated more clearly his attitudes as a southerner.

---

ber 18, December 20, 1919, January 3, February 7, 1921; Davis to Gregory, February 3, 1919, copy in Davis Papers; Davis to Warren, March 1, 1919, and Charles Warren to Robert Lansing, February 5, 1919—both in Warren Papers; "Resume of the Speech Made at the Innes Temple" by JWD, included in Davis to Major Henry Beresford, February 12, 1919, copy in Davis Papers.

36. Davis, *Legacy of Love*, 102–109, 162; December 16, 18, 26, 1918, August 6, 1919, April 7, 1920, January 16, 1921; Harbaugh, *Lawyer's Lawyer*, 145–49, 163–64; Cronin (ed.), *Cabinet Diaries of Josephus Daniels*, 399.

37. Davis to Charles Warren, December 13, 1919, in Warren Papers; Diary, November 13–15, 1920; Harbaugh, *Lawyer's Lawyer*, 146. Davis was so well accepted that one day he spent teatime helping Rudyard Kipling develop the "ideal name" for the "American soldier"; they settled on two, *Ed Baker* and *Tommy Adkins*. Diary, January 3, 1919.

Specifically, Davis opposed any force increasing either the intensity or geographical scope of nationalism not aligned with the Anglo-American bond. He was thus strongly critical of French efforts to levy undue penalties on defeated Germany, believing such reparations could easily result in the spread of France's "barbaric" approach to colonialism.[38] More important, he held that a Germany beaten and occupied must be treated with sensitivity or the reconstruction process would produce a German nationalism equally as dangerous as that just defeated. Although he never forgot that wartime Germans had employed considerable brutality, he looked to "the education of a new generation" rather than retribution as the way to improve German "national character." He considered France's hot pursuit of "800 war criminals"—a regenerated Gallic mission rooted in Prussia's defeat of France in 1871—as "a mess" that, fortunately, America had avoided. He was "horrified at the suggestion to hold the trial of the kaiser in London, which [was] simply carrying the insane folly of the whole proposition to further extreme." Facetiously, he inquired of his diary: "Why do they not hold a Roman tribunal and drag him through the city in chains? . . . The growth of democratic sentiment in Germany is to be *stifled* to make a British holiday." In essence, he considered punishment of Germans in the name of progress to be "The Great Myth—allied victors crying to the moon."[39]

Not surprisingly, when Wilson approached Davis in the spring of 1919 about heading an American delegation to a convention on the future of the Rhineland, an area over which the French wanted tight control, Davis jumped at the opportunity. During early June he joined Pierrepont B. Noyes and other American counselors to soften the Rhineland formula espoused by the French. Under Davis' strong leadership, the convention established a civilian commission to administer the territory. However, after an excruciating impasse with French general Ferdinand Foch, Davis and other "soft reconstruction" delegates had to acquiesce to strong French influence in the occupying military

<hr />

38. Diary, July 19, 1920. To Lloyd George, Davis confided that he considered the French to have been "crazy" ever since the demise of Charlemagne. Diary, November 13–15, 1920. See also George W. Egerton, *Great Britain and the Creation of the League of Nations* (Chapel Hill, 1978), 85–87, 156.

39. *Ibid.*, July 3, 1919; Davis to Charles Warren, July 8, 1922, in Warren Papers.

forces and a French presidency of the civilian commission.[40] Nothing suggests that Davis consciously made the connection between the rise of a spurious nationalism in the post-Reconstruction South and his fear of a similar attitude developing in postwar Germany. Yet he did appear acutely sensitive to what could happen to a people who were defeated and placed under tightly controlled military reconstruction. He seemed well attuned to the loser's defensiveness and sense of be-siegement. He sought to minimize these forces for fear that they might ultimately crystallize into a German nationalism opposing Anglo-American leadership.

For primarily the same reason, the future of the Anglo-American connection, Davis wished for a nonviolent though steadfast solution to the problem of Bolshevik Russia. He privately dissented from the intervention of American and other Western troops in Russia; he con-sidered the action "a miserable failure" and wished that "we might soon be well of it." The intervention not only failed to bolster White, anti-Bolshevik forces but also served as a defensive rallying point for the further development of Communist nationalism. Thus Davis judged the withdrawal of foreign forces following the spring of 1919 to be "a propriety" and "a necessity."[41] On the other hand, the ambassador strongly concurred with Wilson's efforts to deny international recog-nition to the emerging Soviet state and denigrated any action by the Paris Peace Conference that indicated respect for Bolsheviks "even by implication." In November, 1919, during a weekend visit to The Firs, Prime Minister David Lloyd George's country estate, British diplomats urged Davis to reconsider Soviet recognition. When Sir Aukland Ged-des, British ambassador to the United States, protested that the argu-ment against "shaking hands with murderers did not impress him, especially as [America] has concluded peace with the Germans whose submarine atrocities were as bad or worse than the Bolshevik horrors," the dedicated Wilsonian countered that "it was impossible to enter

40. Diary, May 31, June 5, December 4, 1919; Harbaugh, *Lawyer's Lawyer*, 141ff.; Schwabe, *Wilson, Revolutionary Germany, and Peacemaking*, 278–79, 422 n. 32. See also A. Lentin, *Lloyd George, Woodrow Wilson and the Guilt of Germany* (Baton Rouge, 1984).

41. Diary, February 4, September 2, 1919. See also Betty M. Unterberger, *America's Siberian Expedition, 1918–1920* (New York, 1969).

into a covenant with a government which declared that it would respect no treaty and would use any breathing space simply to send its emissaries to disturb the internal peace of other nations."[42]

What should be done to block the spread of bolshevism? Again, Davis seemed at one with the president. He praised Wilson's June, 1920, decision to allow individual Americans to trade everything but war materials with Soviets. Like the withdrawal of the Western troops, this would minimize the Soviet leadership's ability to rally internal forces against foreign opposition and "leave on the [Soviets'] shoulders the burden of their inevitable failure." Davis also doubted that Aleksandr Vasilyevich Kolchak, the White Russian leader, could succeed, even with American recognition.[43]

When Wilson assumed the same stance regarding Soviet expansion into Poland, Davis still concurred: "Neither France, England, nor the United States should send a single soldier to the Polish front." In fact, while Davis continually worried about the Soviets' bad faith, double-dealing, and refusal to be checked, and saw the Polish position as increasingly desperate, he never showed any personal wavering from the official American policy of nonintervention. Ultimately, in August, 1920, Polish soldiers with the aid of the French stopped the Soviet advance outside Warsaw. Even in the midst of that stand, as Lloyd George and Sir Winston Churchill inquired about an American battleship appearing in the Baltic, Davis responded: "If [the ship] were sent the question would be raised as to whether it was sent for peace or war."[44]

Here is dramatic testimony to the degree to which Davis and other Wilsonians thought communism to be doomed. Davis clearly believed

42. Diary, January 21, November 30, 1919. On the no-win nature of the dilemma Wilson faced, see Betty Miller Unterberger, "Woodrow Wilson and the Russian Revolution," in Arthur S. Link (ed.), *Woodrow Wilson and a Revolutionary World, 1913–1921* (Chapel Hill, 1982), 49–104. On British policy, consult Egerton, *Great Britain and the Creation of the League of Nations,* 156–58.

43. Diary, June 26, December 15, 1919. See also *ibid.,* December 31, 1919, June 18, 1920; and see N. Gordon Levin, Jr., *Woodrow Wilson and World Politics: America's Response to War and Revolution* (New York, 1968), Chap. 7; Gardner, *Safe for Democracy,* 264–65.

44. Diary, January 19, August 3, 5, 8, 11, 14, 1920. For a concise summary of the complicated postwar situation in Poland, see Kay Lundgreen-Nielson, "Woodrow Wilson and the Rebirth of Poland," in Link (ed.), *Wilson and a Revolutionary World,* 109.

in the inherent weaknesses of the undemocratic, anticapitalist Bolshevik approach. Although he agonized over the fact that the "military power of the Soviet grows," he assumed that the internal ideological weaknesses of the Bolsheviks would ultimately undermine and destroy them—if the Bolsheviks were left alone and not given reasons to be defensive.[45] Another critic of communism, diplomat George Kennan, would posit similar thoughts some three decades later.

Davis also confronted British defensiveness in the postwar period. More so than the Soviet situation, this was a problem of immediate intrusion on the Anglo-American bond. The war had helped America emerge from a predominantly debtor status to become a society of powerful international creditors. This had direct bearing on England. Because the wartime government of Britain had not only borrowed from America but required British citizens to turn over to public control all foreign holdings, by the end of the war British businessmen had lost virtually all of their historic advantages over American counterparts involved in trade in Latin America, Asia, and the Middle East.[46] This reversal of the Anglo-American economic relationship, while memories of "Rule, Britannia" remained so vivid, produced two problems Davis had to confront daily: British paranoia about America's growing economic power and British fear that the Royal Navy, still considered essential to Britain's economic influence abroad, would be outstripped by American vessels.

Davis comprehended this complicated problem as it was developing. In September, 1919, he had a long discussion on the matter with Henry Morgenthau. The two Americans agreed. With Wilson's Fourteen Points emphasizing free trade, Davis wrote, "Competition between [America and Britain] is inevitable and might be expected to create some sentiment which would require careful watching." The next day he cabled the State Department that "dread of American competition was widespread. . . . It would lead to unfriendliness when economic depression settled down on England, which many would seek to explain as due to American pressure," or high prices. It was, he counseled, "the most serious menace to continued sentiments

45. Diary, August 11, 1920; *cf*. Levin, *Wilson and World Politics*, Chap. 7.
46. For these developments explored in a context of revisionism, see Carl Parrini, *Heir to Empire: United States Economic Diplomacy, 1916–1923* (Pittsburgh, 1969).

of good will between the two nations." He understood how the declining value of the British pound placed "a severe burden on the British consumer of American foodstuffs and raw materials." His central point was that "This [situation] is being exploited as one of American absorption of Europe's wealth during the War."[47]

To help ease these developing tensions, Davis took to the podium. Before a broad spectrum of groups—from the Pilgrim's Club to an amalgamation of Manchester merchants—he spread the (questionable) verity that Americans and Britishers had enjoyed a long mutual heritage of living by free trade, and that free trade remained the "best hope for peace" in the twentieth century. He even evoked the memory of Britain's great laissez-faire liberal, John Bright, to support this message.[48]

Davis also worked privately to modify American behavior. He urged members of the American Shipping Board to avoid indiscriminate statements and actions advertising America's burgeoning economic influence. He sent word through Morgenthau that American manufacturers should systematize their overseas lending procedures so that British citizens who were bad credit risks would never be allowed to buy on credit. Only in this way, he reasoned, could inordinate numbers of assumptions and foreclosures—acts intensifying British dislike for Americans—be avoided.[49]

Not surprisingly, in this environment of trans-Atlantic economic tension, America and Britain also vied over "control of the seas," an issue inseparable from trade in an era of world transportation still dependent on the high seas. Through the press and social contacts, Davis immediately perceived the source of Britain's sensitivity. Although the war had taken a heavy toll on British military and commercial bottoms, it had helped America expand its maritime influence. In the context of prevailing economic tensions Britain feared this trend; national ego, as well as ledger sheets, was at stake. Early on, therefore,

47. Diary, September 27, 1919, February 11, 1920.

48. See, for example, *ibid.*, December 11, 14, 1919; Harbaugh, *Lawyer's Lawyer*, 142–43, 166.

49. Jeffrey J. Safford, *Wilsonian Maritime Diplomacy* (New Brunswick, N.J., 1978), 214; Diary, June 23, 1919, February 11, 1920. Davis also struggled to minimize Anglo-American tensions developing out of the *Imperator* affair, a case involving retention of vessels. See Diary, October 20, 25, November 25, December 2, 19, 1919.

Davis cautioned his Washington superiors about "England's chronic sensitiveness." To Frank L. Polk, chief State Department legal counsel, he wrote that British business and naval experts wonder "what it is that we are about." Davis prescribed caution, for "every [nationalistic] speech made at home re-echoes on this side of the Atlantic."[50]

Navy Secretary Josephus Daniels, one of Davis' old friends, failed to heed the warning. Time and again during late 1918 and early 1919 Daniels publicly extolled the virtues of America's expanding navy. Davis managed British responses as effectively as possible. He noted in his diary: "Lunch with Lord Beresford, who suddenly turned on me with the question, 'How long are you going to support your man Daniels?' I coloured and fenced the question." When Daniels visited London in the spring of 1919, Davis invited him to dinner and then for two hours afterward coached the secretary on the proper way to address naval matters before such groups as the Anglo-American Society. Relieved, Davis noted that in speaking to the society on Thursday, May 1, Daniels had taken the "rather obvious suggestion" and devoted his message to "deprecating competition in naval building."[51]

Even as the ambassador helped mute Daniels' braggadocio, other incidents kept the issue alive. Before the Senate Foreign Relations Committee, Admiral William S. Sims testified that in 1917 as he had prepared to leave for the war zone, a high-ranking officer in the Navy Department had warned him "not to let the English pull the wool over your eyes as we would as soon fight England as Germany." The British press immediately criticized the American navy's lack of entente spirit and its inflated self-image. Although Davis believed that the British articles generally reflected a "sane and rational view," he worried about the *Post Express* and other John Bull papers that would "ring the charges" on in public. At a dinner at the Savoy given by the Pilgrim's Club in honor of the Prince of Wales, Davis worked to ease these tensions. "I took occasion," he wrote of his speech, "to make indirect reference to Admiral Sims's indiscretion, saying that with so many millions of English-speaking people and all speaking, it was not sur-

50. Egerton, *Great Britain and the Creation of the League of Nations*, 98, 159–63; Safford, *Wilsonian Maritime Diplomacy*; Davis to Frank L. Polk, January 4, 1919, copy in Diary.

51. Diary, January 4, April 24, May 1, 1919; Cronin (ed.), *Cabinet Diaries of Josephus Daniels*, 399, 405.

prising that an occasional indiscretion occurred. . . . Sometimes even a distinguished Brother Pilgrim said things which had better been left unsaid." He invoked the Anglo-American bond to heal the wound.[52]

Just as Davis rechanneled the Daniels and Sims affairs, a similar episode surfaced. General John J. Pershing noted in public that "America won the war," a statement prompting a rash of John Bull editorials and newspaper cartoons depicting a haughty, insensitive America "insulting our dead." Exasperated, in the spring of 1920 Davis confided to his diary, "It is such things as this which make American popularity in England impossible."[53]

Despite that feeling, Davis never stopped trying to make the impossible become possible. At a farewell luncheon for Davis at Buckingham Palace in 1921, the king expressed concern about American maritime expansion, and Davis concurred: "A race in building *would* ruin both of us." He proceeded to use British logic to explain American aggressiveness: "With [our] outlying possessions and the Canal [we] must be supreme in our own waters . . . and [also] there is Japan, which is arming." Still, he "pressed the hope that the proposed naval conference between Great Britain, the United States, and Japan might be brought about."[54]

His commitment to world peace and international economic activity well attuned to joint Anglo-American leadership also provided the framework in which Davis advanced what he perceived to be his greatest cause during his London assignment and for many years afterward—the cause of the League of Nations. As with other diplomatic issues he confronted, Davis the devoted southern Anglophile found that he often had to exceed the limits of Wilson's foreign policy to advance what he perceived to be the ultimate Wilsonian vision.

From January, 1919, when Davis set to work on League affairs, to

52. Diary, January 19, 21, February 11, 1920.
53. *Ibid.*, February 11, May 13, 1920.
54. *Ibid.*, March 5, 1921. See also Davis, "Anglo-American Relations and Seapower," *Foreign Affairs*, VII (1929), 345–55. Davis' wife, Nell, also felt the intensity of Britain's concern and responded with cool aplomb. At a dinner party, a British general seated on her right bore down on "freedom of the seas" and the matter of Americans' seeking "naval supremacy." Fully aware that any substantive response could mean trouble, Nell said she knew little about "freedom of the seas" but always assumed "it had something to do with mixed bathing." Quoted in H. C. F. Bell, *Woodrow Wilson and the People* (Garden City, N.Y., 1945), 238.

the following November, when the League began to meet defeat in Congress, Davis conveyed to the British public a cautiously conceived optimism about America's willingness to help shoulder the burden of world leadership. He perceived Wilson's personality and general approach to diplomacy as problematic. The president, he believed, suffered from a severe lack of human warmth and sensitivity, making it difficult for him to deal intuitively with Europeans, Britains, or even Americans on the matter of the League.[55]

However, Davis was convinced that the rightness of the president's vision would enable it to prevail. During late January and early February, 1919, as Wilson joined Georges Clemenceau, Lloyd George, and Vittorio Orlando at the Paris Peace Conference and hammered out a draft covenant for the League, Davis looked upon his president "as the great outstanding figure and mastermind of the gathering . . . , [a leader] slowly but surely bringing all the divergent elements to his point of view." Davis confided to Thomas Gregory, attorney general and his former boss, that he shared Gregory's "sense of humiliation that it is in America alone that he [Wilson] is belittled and decried." Davis' main fear, however, was not that Americans would reject the League but rather that, "as usual, [Wilson] is trying to do it all himself and I feel some apprehension on that score."[56]

Events of late February and March increased his optimism about the League's future. With the League covenant developed and submitted to the plenary session of the peace conference, Wilson sailed for home to confront developing Republican opposition to the League. Various meetings and speeches convinced Davis even more of the virtue of Wilson's vision: "He is playing for great stakes and I hope and believe—for the sake of mankind—that he will win." But his caution about Wilson's personality and his overwork was joined by a third fear, that of resistance by Henry Cabot Lodge. After reading reports of Lodge's hostile reception of Wilson's plan to connect the covenant to

55. For examples of Davis' concern over Wilson's lack of warmth, see Diary, December 27, 31, 1919, November 13–15, 25, 1920, and Davis, *Legacy of Love*, 181. To help compensate, Davis went out of his way to praise various speeches made by British dignitaries and pushed diplomatic protocol to the limit by applauding from the diplomatic gallery whenever Lloyd George addressed the House of Commons on the virtues of the Anglo-American bond. Diary, July 3, 1919.
56. Davis to Gregory, February 3, 1919, copy in Davis Papers.

the peace treaty, Davis concluded that the Massachusetts senator was determined to defeat the League forever. The ambassador wrote to Henry White urging immediate effort at ratification in America before the Republican opposition could gain force.[57]

That was a prescient message. During the spring of 1919, Davis devoted long hours helping to edit the League covenant.[58] But what increasingly concerned him during this time was the rapid movement of events resulting ultimately in America's rejection of that document. His earlier concern over Wilson's liabilities appeared justified. Wilson returned to America in midsummer. This crossing led to the twenty-two day marathon of speeches in September and, at the end of that month, Wilson's collapse and the October 2 stroke. For Davis, the future of "the cause" became bleaker, and he wrote that Wilson's "collapse feeds my anxiety" over ratification.[59]

Then came the fateful Senate vote of November 19, 1919. Senator Lodge offered a resolution of ratification with fourteen reservations. Although these provisos limited American obligations under the covenant, in Davis' view they did not dramatically impair the League. Still, upon Wilson's instruction Democrats joined with irreconcilable Republicans, and the Lodge version of American membership in the League—the only version with a chance of passage—went down to defeat. Virtually all southern senators supported Wilson's ironic tactic; and some of the most influential ones were such New South leaders as Mississippi's John Sharp Williams, Alabama's Oscar W. Underwood, and Davis' good friend from Arkansas, Joseph T. Robinson.[60]

Hurt and distraught, the ambassador now witnessed what in cautious moods he always had feared: his president and the Progressives' world order were failing. He wrote in his diary that Wilson's

57. Davis to Warren, March 1, 1919, in Warren Papers; Denna Frank Fleming, *The United States and the League of Nations, 1918–20* (New York, 1932), 139n; Diary, March 20, 1919.

58. For Davis' work on the covenant, see, for example, Diary, March 20, 23, 1919; Harbaugh, *Lawyer's Lawyer*, 563 n.2.

59. Thomas A. Bailey, *Woodrow Wilson and the Great Betrayal* (New York, 1945); Diary, August 25, 30, October 4, 9, 1919; Davis to Warren, September 8, 1919, in Warren Papers.

60. Link, *Wilson the Diplomatist*, 127–55; Grantham, "Southern Senators and the League of Nations"; Osborn, *John Sharp Williams*, 335–60, 384–93; Johnson, *Oscar W. Underwood*, 27–73.

strategy "seems . . . to postpone indefinitely any new order of things." He kept these thoughts to himself, and in public he continued to serve as the optimistic ambassador of the Anglo-American bond. At the University of Edinburgh he spoke on the night of November 19, "dwelling on the moral unity between Great Britain and America" and emphasizing their common ideals. On a weekend visit to The Firs, he found himself cornered by the prime minister, who, Davis wrote, told him that "America was offered the leadership of the world and [threw] the sceptre into the sea" and that "the trouble with the League is that it was drawn up by men who are used to written constitutions, especially Woodrow Wilson." Davis politely deflected the first shot by "describing as frankly as [he] could the different [political] elements which entered into the difficulties and of course the tremendous disadvantage of the President's illness." As to the second point, Davis would recall, "I held my tongue, but the truth is I entirely agree with him. Lansing had the right idea in his skeleton form of general principles which the President so curtly brushed aside."[61]

That continued to be Davis' private assessment. Other than a flurry of excitement over the visit to the United States by Edward, prince of Wales, Anglo-American relations were not encouraging for him.[62] Throughout the winter and spring of 1919 and 1920, until May when Wilson even vetoed a joint resolution ending the war, Davis' mind played on the causes for the League's defeat: Wilson's sickness and rigid approach; the complex, seemingly insoluble problems of the postwar world; the inability of the Senate to deal successfully with matters of foreign relations; and the fickleness of America, which had "dragged Europe into the League covenant" and then disengaged itself. Davis' sense of depression finally hit rock bottom in early spring when news of Secretary Lansing's resignation reached London. "In the present state of affairs, it is difficult to maintain robust faith in the final survival of the League." Looking upon Lansing's action as an unex-

61. Diary, November 19, 22, 29, 30, 1919. See also Egerton, *Great Britain and the Creation of the League of Nations,* 189, 204, on British reactions.

62. New York *Times,* October 3, November 9, 11, 27, 1919, gives a running account of the visit. See also Diary, December 1, 5, 1919. On December 1 Davis notes: "Had I not urged the matter I believe his invitation, if it came at all, would have been so delayed that it would have been refused; and if I had not pressed it after the President's illness, I think that the authorities here would have cancelled it."

plained "sensation of the first magnitude," Davis sat down on the night of March 24 and poured out to Charles Warren his inner feelings about American foreign relations: "My chief feeling is one of deep humiliation at the demonstrated ineptitude of the U.S. in foreign affairs. The position apparently is that we refuse to cooperate with the rest of the world for fear of involving ourselves in their affairs or permitting their intrusion into our own; reserving to ourselves, however, the sovereign privilege of meddling in other people's business as offensively as we choose. . . . With its growth in wealth, in population, and in commerce, the U.S. must have foreign relations whether it wishes them or not. Hermit Kingdoms are out of date."[63]

Davis' intense depression was relatively short-lived. His longtime hatred for Republicans—those who had freed the slaves, defeated the South, and operated according to the dictates of Thaddeus Stevens and the carpetbaggers—provided the key vehicle for his resurging faith in the Wilsonian mission to the world. With the developing presidential election back home, partisan attacks on Wilson activated a siege aggressiveness within Davis which renewed his advocacy of Mr. Wilson and "the cause."

The rally was gradual. From June, 1920, until his final departure from London in March, 1921, the ambassador continued to exhibit lingering signs of defeat. He firmly believed that "the state of the world becomes daily more, rather than less, alarming." On the other hand, Davis increasingly blamed this state of affairs not on Wilson but on the Republicans. Although Davis had wished for the success of Lodge's reservationist version of the covenant, he had never stopped perceiving the Massachusetts senator and his colleagues as Wilson's personal opposition. Now, throughout the summer and fall of 1920, Davis began to believe that the world around him was chaotic for the same reason that the American South of 1865 had been: the Republicans.

---

63. Diary, December 8, 9, 18, 19, 1919, February 11, 13, 14, December 9, 16, 1920; Davis to Charles Warren, December 30, 1919, March 24, 1920—both in Warren Papers. There is little indication that Davis understood the specific reasons for Lansing's resignation—that is, that Davis knew of any dissatisfaction the president might have had with Lansing's loyalty or "intellectual submission and agreement." Link, *Wilson the Diplomatist*, 27. Had Davis known of this, however, he would not have been surprised, for he clearly understood Wilson's "heady" view of the presidency. See, for example, Diary, April 3, 1919, and Harbaugh, *Lawyer's Lawyer*, 149–50.

When Republican campaigners attacked the Democratic contender, James M. Cox, by criticizing Wilson's Democratic appointments to the peace commission, Davis descended on the British Museum to plow through dusty issues of the *Congressional Record*. There he found that Republican president William McKinley had shown almost equal partisanship in establishing the 1898 peace committee.[64] How Davis used this information is unclear; what does appear clear is that it intensified his negativism toward the hypocritical party of Lincoln. After Republicans won the presidential election in November, Davis seemed unsurprised about America's withdrawal from the Supreme Council in Paris: "Nothing remains for our complete divorcement from Europe except to withdraw the Army at Colbenz. I should imagine that this should soon follow under the [Warren G. Harding] administration." Indeed, Harding's Republicans would now complete their pernicious victory over Woodrow Wilson. "The American election was *not* a verdict on the League"; it was only further indication of the manipulative powers of the Republicans—"contemptible" obstructionists and people of "egotism and partisanship," consisting of more than one "sneak."[65]

The emerging corollary, of course, was that Wilson, after all, would have prevailed in his enlightened mission had only the "tragic illness" not hampered his ability to repulse the Republican attack. With no further references to Wilson's basic personality flaws, Davis more and more blamed the vicious circumstances for Wilson's vacillation between rigidity and "lack of decision" in advancing the League. He reflected upon how different things might have been—American membership in the League, world progress—had there been no stroke. Thus, when the Nobel committee awarded the peace prize to Wilson in December, Davis easily acknowledged it as "a deserved tribute."[66]

Davis' renewed excitement about Wilson's cause grew so rapidly

---

64. Diary, June 20, 1920. Davis spoke at Oxford University and the University of London defending Wilson's right to appoint members of the peace commission. He cited McKinley's 1898–1899 actions as precedent, although there is no indication that he included McKinley's appointment of George Gray, a Democrat, as he explained the "precedent." Davis to Charles Warren, March 24, June 21, 1920—both in Warren Papers.

65. Diary, July 28, 1920, January 12, 24, 1921.

66. *Ibid.*, June 22, September 2, December 7, 1920.

during the summer and fall of 1920 that he began thinking again in terms of American membership in the League and how this was the key to world progress in the context of Anglo-American friendship. In July he was invited to serve on a League-sponsored international tribunal to settle the Åland Islands controversy. He wanted badly to accept so that there would be an "American of some repute as a member of the Commission . . . to show the American people that the League is a going concern," and he certainly would have accepted if his State Department appointment had not prohibited such service. That same month he dined at the Garrick Club with Edward M. House, Sir William Wiseman, and Sir Eric Drumond to discuss how best to "present the League of Nations to the American people." In mid-August, anticipating a Republican victory in November and ready to relinquish his post, he and Nell crossed the Atlantic for a month's leave of absence in New York, Washington, D.C., and West Virginia to make plans for their life after London. While home, he made a point of visiting with Lansing and persuaded him to postpone publication of a strong indictment of Wilson's leadership. If this appeared, Davis argued, "it would furnish ammunition to enemies" of a revived effort at American membership in the League.[67]

He also spent several days at the State Department researching for a speech advocating American membership in the League. Delivered at the opera house in his hometown of Clarksburg, West Virginia, before the largest audience ever gathered in Harrison County, the speech reflected the heart and the mind of a resurrected New South Progressive. Whether to join the League, he pronounced, was "the greatest question confront[ing] the people since the Civil War." If Americans failed to join, they would have to arm themselves "with every means which mankind can devise," for there would be perpetual war so long as the League lacked America's influence. He argued there had been too much debate about small matters: "If the principles which underlie the League are sound . . . the League will survive any shortcomings in outward form and will correct any mistakes in its structure." Finally, he sounded the Wilsonian trumpet: "To stay out . . . is not only false to

67. *Ibid.*, July 13, 22, 23, September 5, 1920.

America's ideals [and] untrue to her professions of humanity and service, but fraught with utmost dangers to [our] vital interests."[68]

In November the Davises returned to London. There the ambassador sorrowfully followed press accounts of the presidential election and promptly rededicated himself to "the cause" despite the Republican victory. On more than one occasion during his last winter abroad he connived with Huntingdon Gilchrist, secretary to the League, to move Senator Medill McCormick and other influential Americans into "League circles" when they visited in Britain or Europe.[69]

The same tone marked his final departure from London, not to mention most of his subsequent career. On March 9, 1921, he and Nell boarded the *Olympia* at Southampton and headed for home. As his diary shows, Davis may have been relieved to be returning to the practice of law, but he did not fail to apply his noted personal touch to the departure scene.

> The admiralty sent out a convoy of nine destroyers flying the stars and stripes at the peak. . . . When they left they sailed alongside cheering, with the rails manned. I sent them this message: "Mr. Davis . . . is glad to have as his last sight of England the representatives of the valiant British navy which has done so much to make the seas secure for the commerce of the world. Good by and good luck forever." They sent [back]: . . . "Everyone greatly regrets your departure. . . . We are greatly honored [for] the pleasure of escorting you our ally's representative from the British shores for those of your own country." A stop at Cherbourg—out to the open sea and home! It is the end of a great adventure.[70]

In a broader sense the adventure continued for some thirty years more. With his expanded reputation Davis quickly established a prosperous law practice in New York City. From that prestigious base, he declined nominations for the presidencies of the University of Georgia and the University of Virginia and then, grudgingly, futilely ran for president of the United States on the 1924 Democratic ticket.[71] The

---

68. *Ibid.*, September 9, 11, 23, October 6, 18, 1920; Wheeling (W. Va.) *Register*, October 19, 20, 1920.

69. Davis to Huntingdon Gilchrist, December 9, 1920, in Huntingdon Gilchrist Papers, LC; Diary, November–December, 1920.

70. Diary, March 9, 1921; Harbaugh, *Lawyer's Lawyer*, 166–67.

71. Harbaugh, *Lawyer's Lawyer*, 166–250. Davis had also been considered a dark

1924 loss to Republicans, like the 1920 defeat, only intensified his Wilsonianism. From the offices of the Carnegie Endowment for International Peace and the Council on Foreign Relations, which he had helped establish, Davis wrote and spoke throughout the twenties, thirties, and forties on the need for a League of Nations and ultimately a United Nations. During these years the ingredients of the message never really changed. Against a domestic backdrop of growing federalism and the nascent civil rights movement, both of which he opposed, Davis supported Franklin Roosevelt's war policies and still urged internationalism built upon the principles of the Anglo-American bond and world organization. Only in this way could the world move beyond war and disorder and into the age of conservatively enlightened ("liberal") politics and balanced industrialism.[72]

Finally, the larger adventure did indeed come to a close. Toward the end of his life this New South Progressive, like others, encountered a defeat that could not even be blamed on the Republicans. The consummate creature of Wilsonianism, the United Nations, proved unable to block the return to another period of conflict. And in 1955, the year Davis died, a world of cold war and an America of lingering McCarthyism left him confused about the cause he had so long espoused.[73]

It is doubtful that Davis ever consciously connected the history and culture of his section to his developing role in Wilsonianism. Still, there are relationships between the two separate if intertwined parts of his life which would seem to defy coincidence. Raised on vivid memories

---

horse in the 1920 campaign, the result of a "push Davis" movement that had begun while he was still in London. See also Robert S. O'Keefe, "Davis: The Country Lawyer," *Washington and Lee Alumni Magazine*, XLVIII (April, 1973), 4.

72. Harbaugh, *Lawyer's Lawyer*, Chaps. 12–22; Davis, "Permanent Bases of American Foreign Policy," *Foreign Affairs*, X (1931), 1–12; Davis to Tasker H. Bliss, November 10, 1923, in Tasker H. Bliss Papers, LC; Robert A. Divine, *Second Chance: The Triumph of Internationalism in America During World War II* (New York, 1971), 15, 192, 197–98; Robert D. Schulzinger, *The Wise Men of Foreign Affairs: The History of the Council on Foreign Relations* (New York, 1984), 6, 9, 31–32, 46.

73. Davis was one among many leaders of the American bar who bowed to the inwardness of McCarthyism. More important, he became an advocate of collective security through regional alliances, something that Wilson always denounced. Harbaugh, *Lawyer's Lawyer*, Chaps. 25–26; Link, *Wilson the Diplomatist*, 154–55.

of southern suffering in the violence and chaos of the Civil War and Reconstruction, Davis became an advocate of peace and order and economic progress not just at home but throughout the world. Nurtured on the evil ways of mid-nineteenth-century Republicans, his wariness of Republicans in national office was matched by an intense faith in the virtues of Democrats, living and dead, and especially Thomas Jefferson. Educated at a time when the South was increasingly perceived from both inside and outside as defeated, economically backward, and socially inferior, he presented his section's virtues by exuding a Progressive's "enlightened conservatism," a safe Victorian persona, and a driving professionalism all wrapped up in a resurrected yet genuine version of a southern gentleman—a key element in his style as a diplomat in early twentieth-century London. Raised on "the lesson" of southern race relations, the dictum that the white must control the nonwhite, he advocated the internationalization of white paternalism as a key to an advancing world community. No doubt these are among the principal reasons that John W. Davis embraced Woodrow Wilson, another Victorian gentleman and a man understood to be "a southerner" promising a progressive world order under the auspices of white, Democratic leadership.

This is not to say that Davis, the New South Progressive, was Wilson's clone. Far from it. On the central matters of race, nationalism, and internationalism, the two differed. Upon more than one occasion Davis' preoccupation with the Anglo-American bond moved him further into the worlds of diplomatic compromise and cultural expansionism than Wilson was willing to go. A man whose primary influences can be traced to the nationalistic urban Northeast, Wilson was an *American* of moderate white paternalist race views; while Davis, a Southerner raised never really to trust the government in Washington, was an *Anglo-American* whose strong white paternalism derived in great part from the experience of the American South. Wilson advocated the expansion of the progressive Anglo-American society with a close eye to his nation's self-interest. Davis urged a more transnational and cultural force, one that lacked the national power to turn on him but one that was sufficiently international to advance the white man's mission to bring orderly reform to the traditional political and economic world. In this sense, while neither man should be considered an imperialist, Davis surpassed Wilson as an internationalist-expansion-ist.[74]

If Wilson's nationalistic realism and reluctance to move beyond a broadly defined American self-interest caused Davis problem after problem, the overriding point is that Davis never stopped employing his exceptional diplomatic talents to ease Anglo-American tensions. The ambassador to the Court of St. James's wanted his president's basic foreign policy to succeed. Although, as an insider, he knew Wilson to be petty, Davis joined other New South Progressives in looking upon Wilson as the enlightened, virtuous man from the South, the international leader. Hence, as a New South Wilsonian, Davis needed Wilson to succeed—for the progressive world, for America, for the South, for Clarksburg, West Virginia, and for John W. Davis. In the end Wilson failed. Wilsonianism may have, too. But another generation of New South advocates would sound the trumpet with renewed force before that reality finally hit home.

74. These comparisons are essentially mine. However, on Wilson's nationalism see Link, *Wilson the Diplomatist*, 15–16ff.; and Levin, *Wilson and World Politics*, 182ff., a persuasive statement regarding Wilson's belief in American exceptionalism that complements Link's treatment, though the tones of the two writers are quite different. Wilson's anti-imperialism, coupled with his belief in America's "special role" in the world, is emphasized in Whittle Johnston, "Reflections on Wilson and the Problems of World Peace," in Link (ed.), *Wilson and a Revolutionary World*, esp. 201–202.

5

The Southern Council on
International Relations

In the decade following World War I, the New South movement lost focus. Some programs continued, especially business growth and educational improvement, and there was also the relatively new idea of urban boosterism. But the sudden demise of the leader, Woodrow Wilson, combined with swirling moralistic backlashes against Roaring Twenties "progress," diminished the vitality that the New South cause had known in the Gilded Age and the Progressive Era. Although southerners of this time, such as John W. Davis, were less inclined than were other Americans to turn their backs on Wilsonian internationalism, the splintering of the New South movement makes it difficult to identify this or any other outlook as the New South foreign-affairs sentiment of the 1920s.[1]

Yet the setback was only temporary. In the early 1930s another distinct wave of the movement began to spread over the section, and with it came another call for expansion. This "consciousness of kind," as historian Fletcher Green described it, should not be confused with the ideas of the few young southern reformers who, in the 1930s, began to reject traditional white paternalism. Most New South leaders of the 1930s and 1940s showed persistent acceptance of the old racial absolute. Still, the new wave was in other respects genuinely iconoclastic, compared to its predecessors, and by many standards had a right to call itself "liberal." Including women among their membership and

---

1. Dewey W. Grantham, *Southern Progressivism: The Reconciliation of Progress and Tradition* (Knoxville, 1983), 410–17; George Brown Tindall, *The Emergence of the New South, 1913–1945* (Baton Rouge, 1967), 219ff.; George C. Herring and Gary R. Hess, "Regionalism and Foreign Policy: The Dying Myth of Southern Internationalism," *Southern Studies*, XX (1981), 254–56. For examples of the New South outlook persisting in the form of urban boosterism, see Blaine A. Brownell, "Birmingham, Alabama: New South City in the 1920s," *Journal of Southern History*, XXXVIII (1972), 21–48; and Charles Paul Garofalo, "The Sons of Henry Grady: Atlanta Boosters in the 1920s," *Journal of Southern History*, XLII (1976), 187–204.

openly condemning the lynch mob, these scholars, business people, journalists, ministers, and civic leaders reflected the strong institutional-management (bureaucratic-planning) approach to social change that had begun to emerge in northeastern reform circles during the Progressive Era. Hence in the 1930s, in the context of the depression and the New Deal and in response to still another Yankee idea, the New South movement surged forward again, reflecting a new, bureaucratic approach to expansion.[2]

Sociologist Howard W. Odum is often considered the enigmatic symbol of this generation of New South thought. Although he was both a symbolic and substantive leader, there nevertheless were many other leaders and academic influences. As New South social engineering blended with increasing anxiety over another world war, there emerged at the University of North Carolina—in the very shadow of Odum's office—a regional planning group ostensibly committed to enlightening southerners about the responsibilities and tangible sectional benefits of world power. The leader of this cause was a young political scientist named Keener C. Frazer; the organization he established ultimately took the name of the Southern Council on International Relations.

Frazer's background helps elucidate key sources of the Southern Council's effort. Born in 1900 in the south Alabama town of Eufaula, Frazer was the son of a prominent minister in the Methodist Episcopal Church, South. He completed an undergraduate education at Wofford College (Spartanburg, South Carolina), a master's degree in political

2. Fletcher Green, "Resurgent Southern Sectionalism, 1933–1955," in J. Isaac Copeland (ed.), *Democracy in the Old South and Other Essays by Fletcher Melvin Green* (Nashville, 1969), 290. Recent exploration of 1930s regionalism is reflected in Joel Williamson, *The Crucible of Race: Black and White Relations in the American South Since Emancipation* (Chapel Hill, 1984), 482ff. (where his *New Liberals* should not be confused with my *new wave*); Tindall, *The Emergence of the New South*, Chap. 17; Michael O'Brien, *The Idea of the American South, 1920–1941* (Baltimore, 1979); Daniel Joseph Singal, *The War Within: From Victorian to Modernist Thought in the South, 1919–1945* (Chapel Hill, 1982); and John K. Kneebone, *Southern Liberal Journalists and the Issue of Race, 1920–1944* (Chapel Hill, 1985). On its "Progressive" elements, see Otis L. Graham, Jr., *An Encore for Reform: The Old Progressives and the New Deal* (New York, 1967), 208–13; and Dewey Grantham, Jr., "The South and the Reconstruction of American Politics," *Journal of American History*, LIII (1966), 227, 233. Morton Sosna and Sharon N. Shouse provided important background information on race and southern liberalism of the 1930s and 1940s.

science at the University of North Carolina, Ph.D. course work in international relations at Johns Hopkins University, and further study on international affairs at Geneva. In the early 1930s he returned to Chapel Hill to commence a teaching career in political science that would span four decades. A dapper dresser and one who often used a cane to stroll about the quadrangle, he became known as an incessant talker about the South's future in world affairs. Fascinated with John Tyler Morgan, Frazer tried for some two decades to complete a biography of the noted southern expansionist. More important, Frazer represented a significant body of upper-middle-class southern gentlemen and ladies who revered Woodrow Wilson, urged the "internationalization" of southern education, and argued for American membership in the League of Nations. Some of these individuals, such as educator Francis Pendleton Gaines, had actually worked for Wilsonianism in the era of World War I. Still active but with little group support in the 1920s, they now were poised to respond to the new bureaucratic forces of the 1930s. Others were, like journalist John Temple Graves II, relatively young but, owing to family and educational influences, equally primed for the resurging effort. Frazer fell into this latter category.[3]

The state of the world spurred Frazer and other southern internationalists to action. In the spring of 1937—with Japan moving on Peking, fascism growing steadily in Europe, and President Franklin D.

3. Leon Sensabaugh to the author, September 30, 1980; J. Carlyle Sitterson to the author, October 7, 1980; George I. R. MacMahon to the author, October 20, 1981; Jay Higginbotham to the author, July 31, 1981; George Mowry, telephone interview with author, July 28, 1981; Frances Davies, telephone interview with author, August 13, 1981; Willis A. Sutton to Frazer, March 22, 1937, Frazer to Frank P. Graham, September 21, 1937, Frazer to Henry S. Haskell, July 22, 1937, and Frazer to Malcolm Davis, December 13, 1937—all in Southern Council on International Relations papers, Southern Historical Collection, University of North Carolina, Chapel Hill. I researched these papers just as they arrived at the Southern Historical Collection; they are now integrated into two separate collections in the SHC: the Frank Porter Graham Papers and the University Archives Collection. Hereinafter, all correspondence relative to the SCIR can be found in these two collections, unless otherwise noted. I did not interview Keener Frazer because of his severe ill health; he died in 1983. Frazer's notes and outline for the Morgan biography are included in the SCIR Papers. Many of these Wilsonians' activities in the 1920s can be traced through documents in the James T. Shotwell Papers, Butler Library, Columbia University. See also Robert D. Accinelli, "Militant Internationalists: The League of Nations Association, the Peace Movement and U.S. Foreign Policy, 1934–1938," *Diplomatic History*, IV (1980), 19–38; and Randall Bennett Woods, *The Roosevelt Foreign Policy Establishments and the Good Neighbor Policy* (Lawrence, Kans., 1976).

Roosevelt still committed to neutrality—James T. Shotwell and Nicholas Murray Butler of the Carnegie Endowment for International Peace invited Frazer to tour Europe as a Carnegie lecturer extolling the cause of international organization. They knew that Frazer had espoused the Carnegie Endowment message of "community internationalism" with the goal of a "global oneness" receptive to United States leadership through international organization, free trade, and Christianity.[4] Frazer declined the offer. At a meeting in New York City, he advised Carnegie Endowment officials that his greatest interest lay in organizing articulate southern internationalists into a planning group devoted to the South's "education in international relations." It is unclear whether Shotwell perceived the central domestic goal Frazer represented. What is clear is that leaders of the Carnegie Endowment saw Frazer's proposal as an opportunity. Two years earlier they had established the Midwest Council on International Relations under the guidance of Jesse Unruh—a group designed to pressure President Roosevelt into more aggressive efforts at world peace. In Frazer they saw the ideal individual to organize a similar effort in the South. Out of that meeting, accordingly, came a Carnegie Endowment commitment for around $3,000 per year and the resultant organization of the Southern Council on International Relations.[5]

The Southern Council took shape in Chapel Hill. In addition to Carnegie funds, small grants were obtained from the Rockefeller Foundation and from private individual sources, such as the Alabama textile company of Donald B. Comer. Individual membership dues ran

4. See Harold T. Josephson, *James T. Shotwell and the Rise of Internationalism in America* (Rutherford, 1975); and Joseph Frank Greco, "A Foundation for Internationalism: The Carnegie Endowment for International Peace, 1931–1941" (Ph.D. dissertation, Syracuse University, 1971).

5. Frazer to Virginius Dabney, January 28, 1947, and Eugene Pfaff to Dabney, August 12, 1944—both in Virginius Dabney Papers, Alderman Library, University of Virginia; Henry S. Haskell to Frazer, May 7, 10, July 19, 1937, Frazer to Haskell, May 19, 1937; Mowry, telephone interview; New York *Times*, January 30, 1938; Frank P. Graham to Frank Purser, May 3, 1938, Frazer to Leon Sensabaugh, February 11, 1938, in Leon F. Sensabaugh Papers, in possession of Tennant S. McWilliams, Birmingham, Ala.; Greco, "A Foundation for Internationalism," 147–55; Robert H. Ferrell, "The Peace Movement," in Alexander DeConde (ed.), *Isolation and Security* (Durham, N.C., 1957), 99–100. The council would also receive small grants from the Rockefeller Foundation to work on specific educational projects related to inter-American affairs. Pfaff to Dabney, January 24, 1944, Dabney Papers.

$3.00 annually. Frank P. Graham, president of the University of North Carolina, provided office space, clerical assistance, and occasional leaves of absence for an executive secretary, who was usually Frazer.[6] More significant, Graham offered use of his name and that of his university. Offices, or "The Bureau," were located in the old YMCA building on the campus.[7] On University of North Carolina stationery and with the signature of the leading educator in the South—Graham was always listed as president of the group—Frazer sent out invitations for executive committee service, city directorships, and regular memberships. The three hundred acceptances came from every urban center of the South, and they usually included white, well-educated Protestants, loyal Democrats, and products of families that had been in the South for at least one generation. A disproportionate number of the members had received college educations in the East, especially at Princeton and Johns Hopkins universities. The original executive committee consisted of the following people: Frank R. Ahlgren, editor of the Memphis *Commercial Appeal*; Amry Vandenbosch, University of Kentucky political scientist; Will R. Manier, Nashville attorney; Henry Plant Osborne, Sr., Jacksonville, Florida, attorney; Francis P. Gaines, president of Washington and Lee University; Theodore H. Jack, president of Randolph-Macon College in Ashland, Virginia; Charles Pipkin, dean of the Graduate School, Louisiana State University; Mrs. Rowland H. Latham, president, North Carolina Federation of Women's Clubs; Donald B. Comer, Orville Park, Macon, Georgia, judge; E. R. Malone, Pensacola banker; Frank P. Graham; John Temple Graves II, Birmingham journalist; and Alfred H. Stone, Jackson, Mississippi, attorney.[8]

6. Haskell to Frazer, July 19, 1937; Eugene E. Pfaff, telephone interview with author, August 15, 1981; Fletcher Green, "The South Looks Abroad," *South and World Affairs*, V (September, 1943), 7. There are numerous financial statements in the SCIR papers. Frazer's leaves of absence were made possible through the Kenan Fund. Memorandum to Frank P. Graham, "The Southern Council on International Relations," October 14, 1937, Frazer to Henry S. Haskell, May 14, 1938, November 11, 1940, Frazer to Graham, August 8, 1940; Federico G. Gil, telephone interview with author, August 24, 1981.

7. Although Graham's pressing schedule at this time prohibited his significant involvement in the organization, his activism as an internationalist would become dramatically apparent when he went to the United States Senate in 1949. See Warren Ashby, *Frank Porter Graham: A Southern Liberal* (Greensboro, 1980), 171–223.

8. Two notable exceptions to the southern Protestant tone of the group were New

Frazer and the wartime executive secretary, Eugene Pfaff (once a student under Carl Becker at Columbia University), guided this membership in fieldwork modeled on activities earlier introduced in the South by the League of Nations Association and in other sections by the Carnegie Endowment. Workers in the Chapel Hill office mailed to center directors an assortment of internationalist materials received from Carnegie officials in New York City. There were reading lists and recommendations for curriculum changes in public education; topics and often scripts for radio call-in shows; designs for displays at county fairs and public libraries; news releases to permit local newspaper coverage of international events; and lists of speakers available for commencement exercises and religious and professional meetings.[9] Pfaff, on leave from North Carolina Women's College (Greensboro), traveled extensively throughout the South during the war years to advise center directors on the use of these materials and the organization of local membership. Within his own state, he also introduced radio symposia or panel discussions. Bannered as "Carolina Roundtable," the broadcasts usually consisted of three or four University of North Carolina professors analyzing a recent turn in the war.[10]

Yet the few periods of intense, efficient effort by the Southern Council fail to offset the impression that such fieldwork had little measurable impact. Southern Council members recall that their meetings were often small and their influence "limited," "vague," and "inconsequential." Frazer had little ability as a daily administrator. Even when the Southern Council received good management, as it did when Eugene Pfaff took charge during 1944 and 1945, the problems of molding grass-roots public opinion, combined with travel and communication difficulties during wartime, prohibited any measurable success. As Pfaff would recall, "I suppose we touched a few people." Concurring is a substantial body of scholarship evaluating the effect of public opinion groups on foreign policy.[11] In short, there does not seem to

---

Yorker James T. Shotwell, serving on the committee as a representative of the Carnegie Endowment; and Rabbi Joseph Rauch, of Louisville.

9. The SCIR papers are filled with drafts and typed carbon copies of these materials.

10. Pfaff, telephone interview. There is considerable correspondence on this activity in the SCIR papers.

11. Pfaff, telephone interview; Mowry, telephone interview; Amry Vandenbosch to the author, August 20, 1981. For pertinent parallel studies, see, for example, Lester M.

have been a cause-and-effect relationship between the Southern Council's internationalist fieldwork and the strong, so-called internationalist votes cast by southerners in Congress between 1938 and 1948.[12]

Nonetheless, the Southern Council had significance. In addition to its fieldwork, the Council published a journal that provides important insights into how some New South advocates reacted to the chaotic world beyond them. Initiated as a mimeographed fortnightly called *Memoranda on International Problems*, the publication, by February, 1941, had developed into a full journal—slick paper, photographs, diagrams— and bore the title *The South and World Affairs*. Principal editors included American historian George Mowry (1941), American historian J. Carlyle Sitterson (1941 and 1943), Keener Frazer (1942), European historian Eugene Pfaff (1944 through 1945), Latin American historian Federico G. Gil (1946 through 1947), and political scientist George I. R. MacMahon (1948).[13] Although they occasionally ran material by authors not associated with the Southern Council, the editors normally published pieces written for them by the Carnegie Endowment staff—pieces with a southern appeal—together with articles by a broad range of Southern Council members and sympathetic scholars located in southern universities. Many articles originated as speeches and resolutions presented before the organization's annual meetings. Considering the image of scholarship and objectivity the Southern Council sought to project, it is not surprising that articles rarely focused on specific politicians and congressional votes on specific foreign policy issues. What is curious is the journal's reflection of community internationalism adjusted to the evolving interests of the New South.

Milbrath, "Interest Groups and Foreign Policy," in James N. Rosenau (ed.), *Domestic Sources of Foreign Policy* (New York, 1967), 231–51; and Greco, "A Foundation for Internationalism," 266–68.

12. On "internationalist" votes during this period, see Tindall, *The Emergence of the New South*, Chap. 20, which cites research by Alexander DeConde, Charles O. Lerche, Jr., Paul Seabury, Wayne S. Cole, and Alfred O. Hero, Jr. See also Herring and Hess, "Regionalism and Foreign Policy," 256–61.

13. Mowry and Sitterson were of course associated with the History Department of the University of North Carolina. Gil, who arrived from Havana in 1945, held an appointment in the Political Science Department of the University of North Carolina. Pfaff taught European history at what would become the University of North Carolina at Greensboro. MacMahon, who obtained an M.A. under Frazer's direction, later taught history and political science at Homerton College, Cambridge, England.

From its inception, the Southern Council journal echoed the Carnegie Endowment litany: a firm American commitment to some international peace-keeping organization, combined with the international
cooperation fostered by free trade, could stem the tide of fascist advances and avert another world war. Prospects for American military
action represented only a further breakdown of world order.[14] In October, 1937, for example, Shotwell and Butler praised Roosevelt's recent "quarantine" speech and speculated on how much more effective
such moral and economic suasion could be if the United States were in
the League of Nations. In turn, Frazer wrote Henry S. Haskell, executive secretary for the Carnegie Endowment, that the Southern Council
aimed to encourage this same sentiment among all southerners and
would start with church organizations. This design immediately appeared in the journal. In early 1938 the journal published an article by
Frank P. Graham entitled "Keep the Flag Flying," which argued that
the League of Nations, if strengthened by American membership,
could have stopped Japan's movement from the beginning.[15]

The journal reflected an equally intense interest in international
trade. Frazer advised Haskell: "Our immediate objective is to make
articulate that element in our southern population which is able to
view the trade agreement program in the light of its benefit to the
whole section" (the South). That "program" was Secretary of State
Cordell Hull's reciprocal trade plan. Hull's 1939 trade treaty with
England found glowing approval in the journal, for it restored cotton,
tobacco, and rice markets lost after a 1932 tariff revision. But the
Good Neighbor or Latin American phase of Hull's program generated
the greatest enthusiasm. It was interpreted as final realization of a long-
espoused southern position on foreign policy. From Thomas Jefferson
and James Monroe, to Henry Clay, to Woodrow Wilson, and on to
Tom Connally and Claude Pepper, traditional Southern leadership
stood for closer economic ties with Latin America. Appreciative that

14. The general foreign policy positions of the Carnegie Endowment during the years
1937 and 1939 are treated in Greco, "A Foundation for Internationalism," 194–95,
209, 214, 233.

15. *Ibid.*, 212–13; Frazer to Henry S. Haskell, October 28, 1937, in SCIR Papers;
Frank P. Graham, "Keep the Flag Flying," *Memoranda on International Problems,* I
(February 21, 1938), 1–2.

still another southerner, Cordell Hull, now carried the mantle, the journal urged the case of continued reciprocity.[16]

Yet the journal connected economic Good Neighborism to more than profits. Writers argued that a strong inter-American bond, as represented in the Lima Conference, would discourage Old World fascism from seeking to cross the Atlantic. The "spiritual unity of the Americas," as enunciated so clearly by James Monroe, would stay intact and the Western Hemisphere would remain peaceful.[17] In case there were doubters about the diplomatic and ideological advantages of inter-American trade, the journal printed elaborate statistical reports tracing the dramatic loss of scrap iron, cotton, and tobacco markets as a result of German expansion in Eastern Europe and Japanese advances in Manchuria; both represented an "alarming prospect" for the closing of "the open door" and thus for freedom.[18] In short, southerners had both an ideological and a fiscal stake in a strong, if nonmilitary, American effort on behalf of peace through trade. John Temple Graves II capsuled this sentiment by advocating a "Three Paths to Peace" plan—"free economics," "collective action," and "passion" for "democracy's institution" in the face of "the dictator countries."[19]

16. Frazer to Henry S. Haskell, March 1, 1938; "John Bull and the South," *Memoranda on International Problems,* I (January 15, 1939), 1–5; "The United States and Latin America," *Memoranda on International Problems,* I (December 1, 1938), 1–5; Frank R. Ahlgren to the author, September 22, 1981. On Hull's trade plan, see Bryce Wood, *The Making of the Good Neighbor Policy* (New York, 1961).

17. Henry S. Haskell to Frazer, January 9, 1939, as cited in Greco, "A Foundation for Internationalism," 253–54; "The Lima Conference," *Memoranda on International Problems,* I (February 1, 1939), 1–5; "Decline in World Trade," *Memoranda on International Problems,* I (March 7, 1938), 1–5; "The United States and Latin America," 1–5.

18. For examples from *Memoranda on International Problems,* see "Czechoslovakia and the South," I (September 28, 1938), 1–4, "The Trade Agreements Program," I (October 15, 1938), 1–6, "The United States and the Far East," I (December 15, 1938), 1–5, "The South Loses a Customer," I (March 15, 1939), 1–5; from *South in World Affairs,* see "The South and the Far East," I (May 1, 1939), 1–5, "War and the South," I (September 1, 1939), 1–5. The journal criticized German fascism chiefly from the standpoints of economics and political ideology, but occasionally it carried an article on persecution of Jews. See "Immigration and the South," *Memoranda on International Problems,* I (November 15, 1938), 1–8; and "The South and the Refugees," *South in World Affairs,* I (June 1, 1939), 1–5.

19. John Temple Graves II, "Three Paths to Peace," *Memoranda on International*

European developments, however, soon caused a change in the formula of peace through trade and international organization. By September, 1939, Germany had attacked Poland; France and England had responded with force; and World War II had begun. In view of these events, Shotwell and others at the Carnegie Endowment had to alter their position on free trade and international organization. As Butler put it, "We must hope for a non-military solution, although I do not see how we can avoid letting some of these matters be settled by force." They thought that American military action might be necessary. This does not mean that a hawkish sentiment had suddenly replaced the broad idealism of community internationalism. Rather, there was a new context for the idealism. Free trade and international organization would be achieved after the appropriate action, perhaps a military one, had created the appropriate environment. Realistically, community internationalism had been forced to embrace what might be called "militant internationalism."[20]

Southern Council members made this adjustment to moderate militarism as easily as did any internationalists in the nation. Like most, they openly admitted that America might need to enter the war, but they also focused on what the world should be like after the fighting had stopped. Reflecting this perspective were articles and printed speeches by Phillip Weltner, former chancellor of the University of Georgia; Charles M. Destler, then at Georgia Teachers' College, and Keener Frazer himself.[21] More instructive are the journal's printed proceedings of the Southern Council's first annual meeting, convened in Nashville in late March, 1940. The one hundred members present gave unanimous approval to three key documents. "A Report on the Organization of Peace," drafted by Judge Blanton Fortson of Athens, Georgia, and Denna F. Fleming of Vanderbilt University, called on

Problems, III (March 21, 1938), 1–4; Frazer to Henry S. Haskell, February 15, March 8, 1938, Haskell to Frazer, March 1, 1938.

20. Greco, "A Foundation for Internationalism," 255–57, 263; Mark Lincoln Chadwin, *The Warhawks: American Interventionists Before Pearl Harbor* (New York, 1968), Chap. 3; Accinelli, "Militant Internationalists," 1938. On the movement after 1938, consult Josephson, *James T. Shotwell*.

21. "Report on the Organization for Peace," *South in World Affairs*, II, No. 8 (n.d.), 1–8; see also "After the War," *ibid.*, II (October 15, 1939), 1–5, and "The United States in a World War," *ibid.*, II, No. 6 (n.d.), 3.

southerners to support an organization like the a League of Nations in the postwar period. A second resolution, framed by Vanderbilt chancellor O. C. Carmichael and Frank R. Ahlgren, implored southerners to endorse a postwar "extension . . . of the Reciprocal Trade Agreements program." Although the drafters admitted that certain southern interests—sugar, for example— could experience "temporary hardship" with a continued flexible tariff, they argued that "the ultimate benefit to the whole nation" was involved; and as the nation prospered, it was "the sense of the Conference" that the South ultimately would, too.[22] Finally, the conference approved a document on education. Written by William Whatley Pierson, dean of the Graduate School at the University of North Carolina, and Guy E. Snavely, president of Birmingham-Southern College, the document urged planning for a greater study of world cultures and particularly for Latin American languages and institutions. This could represent an essential step toward Good Neighbor internationalism so important to postwar order. Their rationale, it seems, extended beyond cultural pluralism: a region could not benefit from the world if its people did not know what was in the world; thus the southerners' "traditional position" on exporting could be greatly reinforced by "a more informed understanding" of the people of Latin America. Like most of Snavely's work with the council, the report was the product of Birmingham-Southern's Latin Americanist Leon Sensabaugh. He was a former student under John H. Latané at Johns Hopkins, and Sensabaugh's association with the noted Wilsonian scholar in Baltimore clearly showed in this case.[23]

Such focus on the future did not prohibit an equally intense interest in the contemporary ramifications of mobilization. The years 1940 and 1941 brought dramatic developments for the Allies: the fall of France, the Battle of Britain, and the Battle of the Atlantic. The Allied effort desperately needed more American assistance. Hence, as Roos-

22. "Report on the Reciprocal Trade Agreements," *ibid.*, II, No. 9 n.d.), 1–3; "Conference on the International Interests of the South," *ibid.*, II, No. 7 (n.d.), 1–5; "The Trade Agreements Program," *ibid.*, II, No. 5 (n.d.), 1–5; Frazer to Henry S. Haskell, February 7, May 2, 1940, Haskell to Frazer, April 11, 1940.
23. "The United States in a World at War," *South in World Affairs*, II, No. 6 (n.d.), 1–2; "Report on the South and Latin America," *ibid.*, II, No. 10 (n.d.), 1–5; Frazer to Leon Sensabaugh, February 20, 1940, and Frank P. Graham to Sensabaugh, April 6, 1940—both in Sensabaugh Papers.

evelt's "undeclared war" took shape with the destroyer deal, lend-lease, and selective-service extension, Southern Council members rallied around the president as never before. Repeating a Carnegie Endowment message, Frank P. Graham advised readers of the journal that "our responsibility is to aid Britain with our natural resources."[24] For some Southern Council members, the best "natural resource" that could be offered by a region considered "economic problem no. 1" was manpower—enlistment. Others heralded the potential aid of Birmingham's iron and steel, Kentucky's coal, and Tennessee's aluminum. The two perspectives found connection in New South boosterism. The higher the southern enlistment rate, the more patriotic the region's image. And the greater that tone of nationalism, the greater the economic benefits southerners could anticipate from the location of war industries and military camps in their section. Because these political rewards could provide immeasurable assistance in the southern drive for a balanced, modern economy, the journal printed statistics showing southern enlistments as the highest in the nation and urged an even greater turnout. At this juncture in world affairs, these southern internationalists had ideals and self-interest in perfect synchronization.[25]

As the United States moved closer to formal involvement in the war, this outlook intensified. In the spring of 1941, for example, John Temple Graves II—two years before publishing his noted book, *The Fighting South*—announced that "preparedness" and inter-American trade were contributing so much that the South appeared no longer "the shank end of the continent" but, instead, the "heart of the hemisphere." He referred chiefly to the phenomenal growth of Mobile and New Orleans as ports. Although Donald Comer also praised these developments, he remained unsatisfied—the New South hinged on textile markets, and the Japanese still stymied this expansion.[26] At the 1941 annual conference in Atlanta an excited group of more than one

24. Robert A. Dallek, *Franklin D. Roosevelt and American Foreign Policy, 1932–1945* (New York, 1979); Greco, "A Foundation for Internationalism," 260; Frank P. Graham, "Gaps in Our Defense," *South in World Affairs,* III (February, 1941), 13. The Graham article contains a theory about "fifth column" infiltration and poverty among lower class blacks and whites in the South, a theory that reflects the more traditional side of Graham's New South social values.

25. "The South's Part in National Defense," *South in World Affairs,* II, No. 14 (n.d.), 1–3; "The South Aids Defense," *ibid.,* II, No. 19 (n.d.), 1–5; "Western Hemisphere Incorporated," *ibid.,* II, No. 16 (n.d.), 1–5; *ibid.,* II, No. 18 (n.d.), 1–5.

26. John Temple Graves II, "The South: Heart of the Hemisphere," *South and World*

hundred persons bounded back and forth among "three different parlors" of the Biltmore Hotel to hear talks on intercultural understanding and international organization. Under Pierson's guidance, in the summer of 1941 the University of North Carolina implemented a popular international exchange program. Aimed at liberal arts students as well as businessmen and others involved in continuing education, the program had a strong Latin American emphasis and received considerable praise at the 1942 annual meeting held at the Carolina Inn in Chapel Hill.[27]

The bombing of Pearl Harbor in December, 1941, and American entry into the war further reinforced these views. With the help of the Carnegie Endowment and southern chambers of commerce, writers for the journal published a barrage of statistics on port expansion at New Orleans, Mobile, Jacksonville, and Norfolk. Similar reports documented the heavy-industry boom at Birmingham and soaring timber profits all along the coastal plain and in the Piedmont. Sheer joy echoed from the black belt and textile towns. Under the title "King Cotton Joins Up," the journal declared: "Overnight the South's great cotton surplus was lifted from the depths of 'economic problem number 1' into the realm of national blessing. . . . For clothing purposes alone, the average soldier consumes 124 yards of cotton a year."[28]

Affairs, III (April, 1941), 4–6; Mark Taylor Orr, "The South and Inter-American Agriculture," *ibid.*, III (October, 1941), 10–11, 14; M. Clifford Townsend, "The South and Defense Contracts," *ibid.*, III (June 1941), 3–4, 18; "The South in the News," *ibid.*, III (October, 1941), 12; "Our Foreign Trade," *ibid.*, III (November, 1941), 5; Graves, *The Fighting South* (New York, 1943); Donald Comer, "Textiles and Southern Life," *South and World Affairs*, III (May, 1941), 8–9. See also Michael A. Breedlove, "Comer, Cotton and the World of the 1930s" (Seminar paper, University of Alabama at Birmingham, 1980), and the voluminous collection of Comer papers in the archives of the Birmingham Public Library, Birmingham, Ala. Mr. Breedlove currently is writing a dissertation on Comer's life.

27. Atlanta *Constitution*, April 5, 1941; "Southerners and the World Today," *South and World Affairs*, III (April, 1941), 3; "Conference on the International Interests of the South," *ibid.*, III (February, 1941), 7; J. Coriden Lyons, "Summer School for South America," *ibid.*, III (March, 1941), 3–19; Howard A. Dawson, "Public Education and National Defense in the South," *ibid.*, III (June, 1941), 12–16; Leon Sensabaugh to W. W. Pierson, March 12, 1941, Chess Abernathy to Sensabaugh, March 25, 1941, Sturgiss Leavitt to Sensabaugh, March 26, 1941, Tom Wallace to Sensabaugh, March 25, 1941—all in Sensabaugh Papers; assorted clippings and drafts of resolutions pertaining to the 1942 meeting, in Dabney Papers.

28. Scott Wilson, "Port of New Orleans," *South and World Affairs*, IV (January, 1942), 10–14; Maurice Ries, "New Orleans and the Caribbean," *ibid.*, 408; Chester

With the renewal of southern economic prosperity came power and responsibility. At least this was the context in which the journal crusaded for southern support for a postwar order. The "Four Freedoms," the Atlantic Charter, the Dumbarton Oaks Conference, and finally the San Francisco Conference in 1945 were steps to the realization of Woodrow Wilson's organizational plan for a peaceful spreading of American influence. In November, 1944, with the inception of the United Nations at hand, the journal bore a full-cover portrait of Woodrow Wilson. Through international organization first espoused by the "southerner" Wilson, the opportunities of democracy and Christianity would be offered to the postwar world. To encourage southerners to shoulder that burden of world progress, the journal also reminded its readers of the tangible benefits of international organization: working through the UN, Americans could crack Japanese hegemony over the Pacific and regain access to the important markets of that area.[29]

Still, many members of the Southern Council believed that American responsibility in the postwar period might have to go beyond participation in the UN. The Chapel Hill international studies program offered a model of cultural understanding that all people could follow regardless of UN politics. Indeed, if Western Europeans were unable to accept cultural differences between themselves and the Russians, asserted Robert L. McLemore of Mississippi Southern College, then Americans were all the more obliged to honor these differences—that is, so long as Russians delivered on promises to dismantle the expansionistic Communist International Agency.[30] As an extension of

---

Lyons Chandler, "The South's Inter-American Commerce," *ibid.*, IV (August, 1942), 7–8, 15; J. K. Taussig, "Hampton Roads," *ibid.*, IV (February, 1952), 7–8; M. A. Touart, "The Port of Pensacola," *ibid.*, IV (April, 1941), 11–14; John Temple Graves II, "Birmingham—The Magic City," *ibid.*, IV (May, 1942), 406; Gene Holcomb, "King Cotton Joins Up," *ibid.*, IV (September, 1942), 2–5, 19; and Holcomb, "King Cotton and the War," *ibid.*, IV (October, 1942), 11–15.

29. Eugene Pfaff, "Our Stake in the Peace," *ibid.*, VI (November, 1944), 1–4; "For What Do We Fight," *ibid.*, III (December, 1941), 13–14; "Why We Fight," *ibid.*, IV (December, 1942), 1, 13; "The United Nations," *ibid.*, V (January, 1943), 3, 14; "Pacific Paradise—Lost," *ibid.*, IV (March, 1942), 14–15; "United Nations Plan for a Post-War World," *ibid.*, VI (January, 1944), 10–11; Malcolm Davis to Frazer, March 31, 1943, and Frazer to Davis, April 9, 1943, telegram.

30. Eugene Pfaff, "The South and Tomorrow," *South and World Affairs*, VI (March, 1944), 9–12; R. L. McLemore, "Preserving a United Front," *ibid.*, V (November, 1943), 2–3, 14. See also "The Consolidation of Soviet American Friendship," *ibid.*, V (December, 1943), 2–3, 17; "British Peace Aims," *ibid.*, IV (January, 1942), 8–10, 14.

World War I views, the notion of going it alone or of at least acting outside the UN was also applied to Britain. That country's war aims clearly included free trade, and southerners and other Americans must stand by Britain in this cause at all costs. Graves felt so strongly about the need for a unilateral American commitment to Britain that he even reinterpreted origins of the Monroe Doctrine to show an exaggerated tradition of Anglo-American friendship. "It is with Britain . . . that the United States ventured upon its greatest foreign policy of the Nineteenth Century—Pan Americanism. . . . It will be with Britain . . . that the United States goes into the post-war world."[31] With the ending of the war in 1945, the vibrancy of the Southern Council's internationalism showed all signs of continuing. Good Neighborism and foreign trade commanded the usual monolithic support, and so did the education theme, particularly in view of the Fulbright Act, which systematized foreign experiences for scholars.[32] Atomic energy, however, proved to be a critical problem.

One month after the bombing of Japan, John Bothwell McConaughy, of the University of South Carolina, wrote on behalf of UN regulation of atomic weapons. In line with Shotwell and Butler, he suggested that America's atomic power, if left to America's control, would spawn intense insecurity in an already paranoid Russia. This insecurity, in turn, could trigger a surge of Soviet expansionism that would be met by Western opposition and therefore become the cause for another period of world conflict. At about the same time, William G. Carleton, of the University of Florida, argued in the journal that power politics, instead of the UN, offered the only effective means of regulating atomic weaponry. "It is exceedingly childish," he wrote, "to believe that treaties to outlaw the new weapon can be effective." Although they took opposite views, these scholars shared concern for the

31. John Temple Graves II, "The Fighting South is a World-Minded South," *ibid.*, V (June, 1943), 3–23. See also "Latin American Notes," *ibid.*, IV (August, 1942), 14; "Good Neighbor Deeds in War Time," *ibid.*, V (January, 1943), 9–11; "They Fight with Us," *ibid.*, V (February, 1943), 11, 20; Frazer to Lewis Hanke, April 11, 1942, Tom Wallace to Frazer, March 31, 1942.
32. F. G. Gil, "What Does Latin America Hope from the Post-War World," *South and World Affairs*, VII (October, 1945), 10–13; "Sectionalism and Internationalism," *ibid.*, IX (February, 1947), 2–3; John A. Thompson, "Inter-American Progress at LSU," *ibid.*, VIII (April, 1946), 1–4; Lucien P. Gidden, "Education for Peace," *ibid.*, VIII (May, 1946), 11–14, 16; "A Genuine Approach to the Problems of Peace: Educational Exchange," *ibid.*, X (April, 1948), 4–6.

UN's future in the volatile postwar world, a concern becoming even more apparent in the summer of 1946. American-Russian tensions over the future of Europe and the Mediterranean area, combined with fears about atomic power, defeated the movement for an effective UN atomic energy commission.[33] Yet most who wrote for the journal failed to articulate the impact of these developments. No one focused on the development of an American atomic energy commission as a setback for the cause of international organization. Instead, most continued to argue for UN regulation of atomic energy and to denounce world federalism as an alternative to the UN. The 1946 annual conference, held in Birmingham, passed a resolution affirming these established opinions. Those drafting the resolution included Edward R. Malone and Alabama Methodist minister John Frazer, Keener Frazer's brother. Conference attendance came close to one hundred, about average, and Guy E. Snavely was elected president of the council.[34]

Despite this resolve, the Southern Council effort soon dissipated. From late 1946 through the spring of 1948, heightening Russian-American tensions moved the world toward a frightening polarity. United States diplomacy embraced "containment" and regional alliances—the Truman Doctrine, the Marshall Plan, the Vandenburg Resolution, the Organization of American States. Although the journal indicated that pro-UN resolutions captured the support of the small group attending the 1947 conference in Atlanta, the proceedings of this meeting received only scant coverage. Instead, the journal focused on inter-American relations and the virtue of American aid to Britain and France.[35] In the spring of 1948, when an apparently small-

33. McConaughy's article deserves attention as a fascinating precursor of psychological interpretations of the cold war. See John Bothwell McConaughy, "Atomic Energy and International Relations," *ibid.*, VII (October, 1945), 1–9, 13; and McConaughy, "Russia—Psychological Problem Number 1," *ibid.*, VIII (August, 1946), 1–10. See also William G. Carleton, "Progress Toward Peace," *ibid.*, VII (November, 1945), 1–7, and Walter LaFeber, *America, Russia, and the Cold War 1945–1984* (New York, 1985), 42ff.

34. "Toward an Economic Basis for Peace," *South and World Affairs*, VIII (October, 1946), 1–2, 16; "World Federalists," *ibid.*, 1–2; "Fallacies of the World Federalists," *ibid.*, IX (January, 1947), 3–7; "Plans for the Southern Council on International Relations," *ibid.*, X (March, 1948), 1; "New Program of the Southern Council on International Relations," *ibid.*, VIII (April, 1946), 8–19, 16. See also Frazer to Virginius Dabney, April 1, 1946, in Dabney Papers.

35. LaFeber, *America, Russia, and the Cold War*; Gil, telephone interview; "Excerpts from Winston Churchill's Speech," *South and World Affairs*, IX (April, 1947), 6–7;

er group convened for the last time, in Louisville, Kentucky, the journal carried only a notice that the meeting would be held. The May issue
marked the end. Federico Gil assessed the impact of the cold war on
inter-American relations: people in the United States no longer looked
to the Southern climes with Pan-American excitement, they looked to
the East with fear. And Frank Graham, in one final, futile surge, called
for active UN influence in the recurring nationalistic movements in
Indonesia before some other influence prevailed.[36]

Some members explain the demise in terms of money. With Carnegie
funds drying up, the journal shrank from about twenty pages in 1946
to around five pages in 1948. Others believe that "the Cold War probably defeated us." The two explanations are no doubt the same. Once
the core of community internationalism, the Carnegie Endowment
had become a weak anachronism in the developing context of the cold
war. Splintering and loss of focus paralyzed the New York operation
by the late 1940s; this in turn reduced the funds that the foundation
could send to such groups as the Southern Council. The same loss of
enthusiasm showed among the ranks of the Southern Council. In
short, by 1948 they had no viable cause, and they would not have one
again until they did as Shotwell did in the 1950s: move to the right and
embrace a moderate cold warriorship.[37]

Although it is clear that the Southern Council rose and fell as part of
the broad story of the Carnegie Endowment for International Peace,
there are other, deeper implications of its history. One wonders if many
New South internationalists did not fall farther in 1948 than did their
counterparts in New York City. In addition to a national and international cause, southerners had regional esteem and identity at stake in

---

R. S. Hecht, "Letter from Argentina," *South and World Affairs,* IX (May, 1947), 6–8;
Gaspar C. Bacon, "Our National Interest in Aiding Europe," *South and World Affairs,*
X (March, 1948), 2–5.

36. Federico G. Gil, "Repercussions of Bogota," *South and World Affairs,* X (May,
1948), 1–6; Frank P. Graham, "Truce in Indonesia," *ibid.,* 6–8.

37. Frazer to Dabney, April 1, 1946, in Dabney Papers; Pfaff, telephone interview;
Gil, telephone interview; Leon Sensabaugh, telephone interview with author, August
24, 1981; Greco, "A Foundation for Internationalism," 149–243, 271, 284; Charles
DeBenedetti, "Peace Was His Profession: James T. Shotwell and American Internation-
alism," in Frank J. Merli and Theodore A. Wilson (eds.), *Makers of American Diplomacy:
From Theodore Roosevelt to Henry Kissinger* (2 vols.; New York, 1974), II, 95–100;
Robert Griffith, "Old Progressives and the Cold War," *Journal of American History,*
LXVI (1979), 334–47; Joseph Herzenberg to the author, October 1, 28, 1980.

the movement for international organization. Not so long ago H. L. Mencken had assailed their region as a cultural Sahara, a section of "barbarism." Such "South-baiting" persisted into the 1930s and "spread through the academy," where "jeers and taunts" focused on the basic inferiority of the South. Further, no more than a decade had passed since President Roosevelt had announced to the world that the South was America's "number one economic problem." Although many devotees of the New South cause admitted the accuracy of these images, they still flinched when confronted with such realities.[38] Then relief came. It was not relief in the form of the New Deal, for that effort barely touched the surface of many southern problems. Instead, it was relief in the form of a revived Wilsonianism. As the journalist Graves put it, Wilson is the man "that leads all others of this century in Southern esteem." More to the point, considering the Wilsonian image in the continuing movement for a New South, it is not surprising that Graves and others of the Southern Council actually thought of Wilsonian internationalism as earlier New South Progressives had—as a "Southern idea."[39] They seemed to rejoice in the possibility that their benighted region had, after all, produced an idea that would rescue the world from itself and establish a new order under a progressive American leadership. They had long awaited this resurging sense of sectional virtue, and they would make the most of it with new techniques of social planning. When events of 1939 resulted in war and the conflict broadened to include America in 1941, there was even more optimism, indeed, anticipation. The ideology simply expanded, as it had in 1917, and embraced the necessity of war as a means to the greater peaceful expansion of American influence in the postwar world. But the effort failed. The UN proved unable to manage the first test of postwar peace, atomic weaponry, and this was only a forecast of future frustrations for the "Southern idea."

38. The quoted passages are from C. Vann Woodward, *Thinking Back: The Perils of Writing History* (Baton Rouge, 1986), 16. See also Tindall, *The Emergence of the New South*, Chap. 6 and 599ff.; George B. Tindall, "The Benighted South: Origins of a Modern Image," *South Atlantic Quarterly*, XL (1964), 281–94; and Fred C. Hobson, *Serpent in Eden: H. L. Mencken and the South* (Chapel Hill, 1974).
39. Graves, "The Fighting South is a World-Minded South," 23; Tindall, *The Emergence of the New South*, 668; Gil, telephone interview; Mowry, telephone interview. See also Herring and Hess, "Regionalism and Foreign Policy," 249–50, 253, 258–61; and Arthur Link, "Woodrow Wilson: The American as Southerner," *Journal of Southern History*, XXXVI (February, 1970), 3–17.

Hence the dramatic reappearance and then demise of Wilsonianism marks an important juncture in the evolving story of New South views about the world. The ideal that during a half century had become one of the central rallying points for the New South identity had been virtually eliminated. For these preachers of progress, recalled George Mowry, "the Southern failure now loomed in the shadow of rising fears about Russia." Moreover, following this "defeat," there soon would commence the second Reconstruction—the civil-rights movement. Attacked by Russia from the outside, the civil-rights movement from the inside, and without Wilson, they felt compelled to seek sectional redemption by turning to the sole remnant of their foreign policy outlook, an explicitly ethnocentric nationalism. The New South embraced cold warriorship.[40]

40. By 1945 George Mowry had become an observer of the Southern Council rather than a participant (Mowry, telephone interview). Leon Sensabaugh, who expressed the same sentiment about the demise of the organization, was still active in the Southern Council (Sensabaugh, telephone interview). On the swing "to the right," the cold warriorship of old Southern Wilsonians, see Paul Seabury, *The Waning of Southern "Internationalism"* (Princeton, 1957); Alfred O. Hero, Jr., *The Southerner and World Affairs* (Baton Rouge, 1965); Norman Graebner, *The New Isolationism* (New York, 1956), 1–31; and Griffith, "Old Progressives and the Cold War," 334–47. On the most extreme side of southern cold warriorship, but a side that nevertheless included some individuals of the New South persuasion, consult, for example, Jack A. Salmon, "The Great Southern Commie Hunt," *South Atlantic Quarterly*, LXXVII (1978), 433–52. John Kneebone addresses cold warriorship and desegregation in *The Southern Liberal Journalists*, 217–18.

6

The Expanding South

In retrospect, when advocates of the New South joined in the super-patriotism of the cold war period, they were capitulating to a sense of self they had long sought to reject. They were giving up on the idea that something positive from their own sectional experience could be injected into American life. This suggests that New South leaders down through the generations indeed had reflected various cultural elements that might actually be associated with what C. Vann Woodward called the "burden of southern history." These influences did not exist just in the worlds of metaphor and folkmind. They existed in the form of concrete ideas—ideas about national mission and expansion certainly articulated and on occasion even translated into governmental record. Thus, though Woodward's hypothesis was inherently murky, there are certain New South thoughts about American foreign relations that emerge as a distinct and traceable current in the developing idea of the burden. More important, the story of the New South and American expansion helps explain why the countervailing current in Woodward's tragic story—"spurious nationalism"—survived as a dominant strain of late-twentieth-century southern thought.

Over the course of some seventy-five years, different generations of New South advocates sought to offer the nation and the world something from their section that would be considered good and worthy of respect. At a time when America was rising to world power, their sectional cause became intertwined with that power. At first, most of them dissented from American expansion in an effort to put the nation back on the proper moralistic footing, a foundation they believed they understood in view of their own experiences with an invading force in the era of the Civil War and Reconstruction. That relatively iconoclastic influence, however, collided with the more forceful notion that America, as one of the comparatively new and dynamic elements in Western civilization, *was to be* an expanding society.

The resultant demise of the anti-imperialism of a James H. Blount and the ambivalence of an Erwin Craighead was accompanied by a surging expansionist sentiment among New South leaders such as John Tyler Morgan and Daniel A. Tompkins. Morgan, the old expansionist, often legitimated this nationalism with lessons from the antebellum southern experience, and most New South advocates of the early Progressive Era did, too. In Tompkins' view, Jefferson and the other national leaders from Virginia had steered America onto a course of power and expansion via the first and second wars with Britain, the westward movement, the acquisition of Florida, and the enunciation of the Monroe Doctrine. Uniting tradition with progress, these Progressives invoked the Sage of Monticello to enhance their creed; they hoped that southern involvement in national expansion would help provide the key to a respectable, prosperous future. Nevertheless, throughout the 1890s and well into the early Progressive Era, Yankees controlled national power circles, took full advantage of retarded economic development in the South, and on occasion employed classic colonial tactics in manipulating labor and business in the section.

Then came Woodrow Wilson. Here was a man with a dramatic though convoluted influence on the New South's relationship with American expansion. Not long after Wilson's election in 1912, New South leaders and others of the section began to perceive this man's crusade for a world order based on multilateral American expansion as a clear indication of the South's long-sought return to national and international prominence. This sectional resurrection did not involve gray uniforms and flashing sabers or white robes and lynch ropes; it sprang from the prestige and power of Wilsonianism. A "southerner" was in the White House. They gloried in the perception that their man and their idea, Wilsonianism, would permit America its most expansive, uplifting experience ever, an enlightened, multilateral role in the world.

During World War I this sentiment reached a feverish pitch. North Carolina's Josephus Daniels, Mississippi's John Sharp Williams, and a host of other New South Progressives easily eclipsed the few remaining preachers of caution, such as James K. Vardaman. Enthralled with their new image and political clout, New South Progressives worked hard for Wilson as he targeted his diplomacy from neutrality, to belligerency, to open diplomacy, and finally to the League of Nations. Although party politics and free trade help explain this enthusiasm, so does an intense southern interest in the Anglo-American bond. Indeed, New South Progressives such as John W. Davis and Walter Hines Page appeared far more devoted to Anglo-American cultural expansion than did Wilson himself. Hence the Senate's rejection of the League fired New South Wilsonians to even greater fervor. Republicans had defeated the South in 1865, helped to restrain their economic growth throughout the late nineteenth and early twentieth centuries, and now stymied the southerners' plan for a League of Nations that in their minds would internationalize white paternalism. In some ways the League became another Lost Cause.

Beneath this experience ran currents still deeper than the mid-nineteenth century fall from power and prosperity. Beyond race, beyond the defeat of 1865, Wilsonianism lived as a "Southern idea," a positive southern contribution to American life that had returned southerners to heights of dignity and power they had not known since Jeffersonian days. Previous waves of New South leadership had turned to Jeffersonianism as an expansionist connection between past and present. The generation of the late Progressive Era went even further. Focused on the Wilsonian as well as Jeffersonian notion that America was to be a beacon for the world, they viewed the League as something resurrected from the man who led the South when the South led the nation—Mr. Jefferson. This connection elucidates the drive for sectional redemption through expansionism as a factor in the New South creed and diminishes the significance of international organization in the historiographical debate over the legitimacy of southern "internationalism." It also offers a provocative illustration of how historical myths develop and function in a people under severe stress. The Jefferson-Wilson connection obviously had little basis in fact. Although born and raised a southerner, Wilson derived his sense of multilateralism and other aspects of his public philosophy from the urban Northeast—the source of so much that had frustrated the New South movement. Moreover, Jefferson never advocated international organization or anything else resembling the League of Nations. Still, the New South's longing for a positive sectional self-image and determination to find it through expansionism subsumed these matters of historical reality. Its leaders mythologized Jefferson's approach to foreign affairs as well as Wilson's sectional identity and returned themselves to the center of American life.

Although frustrated by the rejection of the League, New South leaders refused to admit defeat. They struggled to advance the League throughout the years following World War I. Granted, Progressive foreign policy projects often identified with Republican Charles Evans Hughes did indeed encounter the opposition of certain southern politicians, among them Wilsonians; this resistance derived from party hostilities as well as a developing protectionist sentiment in the South. Then, too, amid the hectic materialism and backlashes of moralism in the 1920s, it is difficult to trace a cohesive New South sentiment. Yet, the League of Nations Association and the Carnegie Endowment for International Peace, two organizational bridges between the Wilsonianism of the first and second world wars, recruited far more effectively in the South than in any area other than certain urban pockets in the Northeast. Against a backdrop of Mencken's assailing southerners for their cultural backwardness, Senator Claude Swanson of Virginia was joined by a substantial southern company, not the least of whom was John W. Davis, as he urged American membership in the World Court as well as the League itself.

Moreover, when war came again to Europe in 1939, the Southern Council on International Relations, applying the new bureaucratic techniques of northeastern progressivism, worked through southern churches, businesses, and schools to convert this Wilsonian sentiment into political support for President Franklin D. Roosevelt's developing war policies. The impact of the council appears similar to that of other bureaucratic efforts at molding public opinion—minimal. Even so, the activities of the council, particularly the general policy positions urged in *The South and World Affairs*, attest to the strength and renewed focus of New South expansionist sentiment in the era of World War II. That sentiment found ready complement in Washington, D.C. Senator Tom Connally of Texas and other national leaders from the South, such as Tennessee's Cordell Hull and South Carolina's James F. Byrnes, often provided the cutting edge for Roosevelt's war programs. As Connally put it, Wilson's "body [may sleep] out there in the great cathedral but his spirit stands today among the great figures of history."[1] True to

1. Connally quoted in John E. Wiltz, *In Search of Peace: The Senate Munitions Inquiry, 1934–36* (Baton Rouge, 1963), 205.

this spirit, when the war ended in 1945, southern senators such as Connally joined New South advocates of the council in urging another chance at realizing the Wilsonian dream, the United Nations. Perhaps at last the "Southern idea" would prevail.

This was not to be. New South leaders now had the wrenching experience of seeing their influence finally implemented in the form of the UN, only to be proven hollow within three years. The new enemy of Wilsonianism, communism, began to spread beyond the boundaries of Soviet Russia. Unable to stop this menace to American progress in the world, indeed, unable even to regulate atomic weaponry, the United Nations lost supporter after supporter. A polarity descended on the world, not a multilateral Wilsonian order. What New South leaders since the late Progressive Era had perceived as a sectional idea that could uplift America and the world, and therefore themselves, became increasingly labeled in the irrational days of McCarthyism as a Communist plot to weaken America's unilateral action against Russia. A few New South advocates of the New Deal generation, such as Alabama's John Sparkman and Arkansas' J. William Fulbright, continued to espouse the cause of Wilsonian internationalism by supporting various UN projects. But these senators often had to lower their profiles and actually disguise their views when campaigning back home. Their constituency had given up on Wilsonianism. Historically, these "forward thinking" southerners had been stigmatized as former slave owners, as leaders of a defeated, poor, ignorant section, and as racists. On top of this, they were on the verge of being called un-American in the frantic atmosphere of the cold war and Soviet aggressiveness. So New South leaders shifted to the right. Forsaking a multilateral approach to expansionism, they joined other frustrated Wilsonians in expressing a unilateral cold warriorship—a stance more often than not attributed simply (and erroneously) to the martial and racial traditions of southern society.

At the deepest level, the New South's movement to cold warriorship in the 1950s may well have been another psychic crisis in which many southern leaders did indeed give up on offering a significant southern influence to the polity of national society. Yet on another level this transformation probably was quite easy. After all, the New South had reembraced expansionism by the turn of the century and since that time had only been seeking different ways to make the idea work for sectional progress and esteem. In the 1950s, 1960s, and 1970s, all the

New South advocates did differently was to cease looking for something truly positive in southern history that could be joined to the national experience. They focused on country music and a few other nonideological residues of the past that other Americans would accept as curious and worthwhile. Otherwise, they offered themselves more and more as conforming Americans.

This story both clarifies and extends the analysis of the South's spurious nationalism as presented in Woodward's burden thesis. Woodward emphasized the pressure felt by southern leaders such as Lyndon Johnson to advocate a mainline American patriotism in order to escape the stigmas of defeat and backwardness. Clearly this process, so apparent among New South advocates in the 1960s and 1970s, had been evolving for a long time. Evidenced by southerners of 1898, 1917, and 1941, it perhaps found greatest intensity in those of the early 1950s, when the sectional influence increasingly seemed hollow. Lyndon Johnson's spurious nationalism in the Vietnam era had the force of history behind it.

Woodward also emphasized the role of the "bulldozer revolution," the surge of industrialization and other types of domestic economic expansion during the era of World War II. It seems, however, that even by the turn of the century the New South had connected this form of sectional uplift with nationalism and expansionism. Thus from the perspective of sheer southern business growth, the missionary nationalism engendered in the South by this economic modernization represented a culmination, rather than an initiation, of domestic development attuned to world affairs.

Woodward focused on the civil-rights sentiment of white southerners in the late 1960s, their "treasury of virtue" outlook, as a further source of their support for the mythological American mission to expand and uplift others. From one perspective, this attitude represents a significant break with the earlier postbellum southern experience. From the early post–Civil War years, indeed from the start of southern history, white control over nonwhite had prevailed as a central ingredient of the southern viewpoint. Whether this traditional race view had surfaced in the Gilded Age as a function of imperialism or anti-imperialism among New South leaders, the belief in racial inequality played a powerful role in the continuing New South effort to inject something positive into the American outlook. Then, abruptly, increasing numbers of white (and, ironically, black) southerners emerged from the tumultuous 1960s calling for an expanded American influence in the world, because their nation had demonstrated still another sign of its virtue: its ability to bring a degree of *equality* to domestic race relations. Here, as Woodward implied, was a radically new role for race in the New South world view.[2]

To extend this analysis, one might argue that these "radical" New South advocates moved beyond the traditional racial absolute of the Victorian value system and accepted the nontraditionalist, modernist reality of racial equality. This contention, however, is misleading. It misses the point that racial responses of earlier New South leaders had always shown as much change as continuity. The racial factor evolved from an Anglo-Saxonist argument against expansion apparent in the first New South wave; to an Anglo-Saxonist argument for expansion among New South advocates at the turn of the century and on through the Progressive Era and World War II; at last to an anti-Anglo-Saxonist argument for expansion in the post-1960s period. In essence, race as a central theme in the history of southern attitudes toward foreign policy has reacted to other forces as much or more than it has generated actions of its own. And the larger forces it has responded to are the dynamics of mission and expansion, ideas of fifteenth-, sixteenth-, and seventeenth-century Western culture that developed into a powerful ethnocentricity in the American experience. Claude Pepper and J. William Fulbright, in his later career, possibly may stand as exceptions. But Jimmy Carter and others of the most recent New South wave, those supportive of the civil-rights movement and sophisticated urban development, have a great deal in common with people such as Frank Graham, Keener Frazer, John W. Davis, Daniel A. Tompkins, and Erwin Craighead, if not the anti-imperialist Blount. Over the decades little has indicated that the New South, like the rest of America, could look clearly through history and see reality, or that its spokesmen could see through the ideas of American exceptionalism and expansion.

The power of culture and nationalism, and the fact that many alternative ways of life in the world are not especially appealing, makes all this understandable. Nevertheless, it is interesting that the story of the

2. Alfred Hero, "Changing Southern Attitudes Toward US Foreign Policy," *Southern Humanities Review*, VIII (1974), 281–89; C. Vann Woodward, *The Burden of Southern History* (Rev. ed.; Baton Rouge, 1970), 223–31.

cold-war South is in some ways the chronicle of New South leaders not only modernizing their region but giving it "enhanced illusions of *national* virtue." Well-educated in the conventional sense, charming in public, powerful in private conversations, now increasingly involved in both Democratic and Republican politics—these middle class leaders offer with greater and greater intensity the expanding South.[3] The diminishing of southern distinctiveness has resulted, as have the extraordinary benefits of increased racial harmony, economic mobility, and improved social services.[4] Still, the impact of this process on American foreign affairs in an age virtually begging for catastrophe—its reinforcement of American exceptionalism—is not as comforting.

3. Woodward, *The Burden of Southern History*; Tennant S. McWilliams, "Expansionism in Southern History: A Speculative Essay" (Paper presented before the Society for Historians of American Foreign Relations, Washington, D.C., August 3, 1984); C. Vann Woodward, "The Aging of America," *American Historical Review*, LXXXII (1977), 588–90.
4. *Cf.* Charles P. Roland, "The Ever-Vanishing South," *Journal of Southern History*, XLVIII (1982), 3–20.

Essay on Sources

General Studies

There is no full and detailed study of the recent South and world affairs. Wayne S. Cole, *An Interpretive History of American Foreign Relations* (Homewood, Ill., 1974) is a survey focusing on the interaction between foreign affairs and domestic forces, with considerable attention to southern sectionalism. Useful for general data is Edward W. Chester, *Sectionalism, Politics, and American Diplomacy* (Metuchen, N.J., 1975). George C. Herring and Gary R. Hess, "Regionalism and Foreign Policy: The Dying Myth of Southern Internationalism," *Southern Studies*, XX (1981), 247–77, focuses on the post-1920 period but is still quite helpful in sorting out the broader postbellum foreign policy experience of the South. The same is true for Paul Seabury, *The Waning of Southern "Internationalism"* (Princeton, 1957); Alexander DeConde, "The South and Isolationism," *Journal of Southern History*, XXIV (1958), 5–18; Charles O. Lerche, *The Uncertain South: Its Changing Pattern of Politics in Foreign Policy* (Chicago, 1964); Alfred O. Hero, Jr., *The Southerner and World Affairs* (Baton Rouge, 1965); and Carl N. Degler, "Thesis, Antithesis, Synthesis: The South, the North, and the Nation," *Journal of Southern History*, LIII (1987), 3–18.

American concepts of exceptionalism, mission, and expansion, with few references to the South, have been explored by many scholars for a relatively long time. Most helpful to me have been Laurence Veysey, "The Anatomy of American History Reconsidered," *American Quarterly*, XXXI (1979), 455–77; Ernest L. Tuveson, *Millenialism and Utopia: A Study in the Background of Progress* (New York, 1964); Robert Nisbet, *History of the Idea of Progress* (New York, 1980); Edward McNall Burns, *The American Idea of Mission: Concepts of National Purpose and Destiny* (New Brunswick, N.J., 1957); Loren Baritz, *City on a Hill* (Westport, 1964); Robert E. Osgood, *Ideals and Self-Interest in American Foreign Relations* (Chicago, 1953); Frederick Merk, *Manifest Destiny and Mission in American History: A Reinterpretation* (New York, 1963); Lloyd C. Gardner *et al.*, *Creation of the American Empire: U.S. Diplomatic History* (2 vols.; Chicago, 1976); Bernard Fensterwald, "The Anatomy of American 'Isolation' and Expansionism,"

Journal of Conflict Resolution, II (1958), 111–39, 280–309; William Appleman Williams, *Contours of American History* (Cleveland, 1961); and Morrell Heald and Lawrence S. Kaplan, *Culture and Diplomacy: The American Experience* (Westport, 1977).

The experience of the American South since the era of the Civil War and Reconstruction is treated in a wide variety of literature. Studies include Michael Perman, *The Road to Redemption: Southern Politics, 1869–1879* (Chapel Hill, 1984); C. Vann Woodward, *Origins of the New South, 1877–1913* (Baton Rouge, 1951); George Brown Tindall, *The Emergence of the New South, 1913–1945* (Baton Rouge, 1967), strong on the two world wars; I. A. Newby, *The South: A History* (New York, 1978); Charles P. Roland, *The Improbable Era: The South Since World War II* (Lexington, Ky., 1976); Dewey W. Grantham: *Southern Progressivism: The Reconciliation of Progress and Tradition* (Knoxville, 1983); James C. Cobb, *Industrialization and Southern Society, 1877–1984* (Lexington, Ky., 1984); and Gavin Wright, *Old South/New South: Revolutions in the Southern Economy Since the Civil War* (New York, 1986), which refutes the "colonized South" thesis found in writings by Woodward and others. The New South movement can be pieced together in these works as well as in Paul M. Gaston, *The New South Creed: A Study in Southern Mythmaking* (New York, 1970), in George Brown Tindall, *The Persistent Tradition in New South Politics* (Baton Rouge, 1975), and in Carl N. Degler, *Place over Time: The Continuity of Southern Distinctiveness* (Baton Rouge, 1977).

C. Vann Woodward's hypothesis of the burden of southern history can be seen evolving in four essays. In original form they appeared as "The Irony of Southern History," *Journal of Southern History*, XIX (1953), 3–19; "The Search for the Southern Identity," *Virginia Quarterly Review*, XXXIV (1958), 321–38; "A Second Look at the Theme of Irony," Chap. 10 in Woodward's *The Burden of Southern History* (Rev. ed.; Baton Rouge, 1970); and "The Aging of America," *American Historical Review*, LXXXII (1977), 583–94. *The Burden of Southern History* (Rev. ed.) includes reprints of "The Search for the Southern Identity" and "The Irony of Southern History." Some of his other key thoughts about cold war Americans and "free security" appear in "The Age of Reinterpretation," *American Historical Review*, LXVI (1960), 1–19, and are extended in "The Fall of the American Adam," *New Republic*, CXXXV (December 2, 1981), 14–16.

For critiques of the burden thesis per se, consult Michael O'Brien, "C. Vann Woodward and the Burden of Southern Liberalism," *American Historical Review*, LXXVIII (1973), 589–604; Robert B. Westbrook, "C. Vann Woodward: The Southerner as Liberal Realist," *South Atlantic Quarterly*, LXXVII (1978), 54–71; Jan DeBlieu, "A Past Apart," *Emory Magazine*, LI (October, 1984), 6–12, James R. Green, "Rewriting Southern History: An Interview with C. Vann Woodward," *Southern Exposure*, XXII (November–December, 1984), 87–92; Daniel Joseph Singal, *The War Within: From Victorian to Modernist Thought in the South, 1919–1945* (Chapel Hill, 1982); and John Herbert Roper, *C. Vann Woodward, Southerner* (Athens, Ga., 1987). In June, 1982, Professor Woodward gave me his own critique of the burden thesis in a wonderful two-hour conversation in New Haven. Also see Woodward's *Thinking Back: The Perils of Writing History* (Baton Rouge, 1986).

James H. Blount, the New South and America's Outward Thrust

No scholar has yet tackled the writing of a full biography of James H. Blount, probably because of a lack of his personal papers. Such a collection apparently existed in Macon, Georgia, in the early 1930s but had vanished by the time J. G. de Roulhac Hamilton of the University of North Carolina entered the area searching for manuscripts to build the Southern Historical Collection. Blount's congressional career can be traced in the *Congressional Record*; in biographical sketches in *The South in the Building of the Nation* (12 vols.; Richmond, Va., 1909); and in numerous state and local studies chronicling the history of Macon. For a fascinating memoir written by Blount's long-living and influential daughter, Dolly Blount Lamar, consult *When All Is Said and Done* (Athens, Ga., 1952). On Blount's career, particularly useful newspapers are the Macon *Daily News*, the Atlanta *Constitution*, the New York *Times*, and the New York *Daily Tribune*. Osmos Lanier, Jr., gives a brief overview of Blount's Hawaiian assignment in "'Paramount' Blount: Special Commissioner to Investigate the Hawaiian Coup, 1893," *West Georgia College Studies in the Social Sciences*, XI (1972), 45–55.

The New South movement of the Blount era—the 1870s, 1880s, and early 1890s—is treated in Woodward, *Origins of the New South*, and Gaston, *The New South Creed*. On American expansion and antiexpansion during these years, three important works are Walter LaFeber, *The New Empire: An Interpretation of American Expansion, 1860–1898* (Ithaca, N.Y., 1963); Julius W. Pratt, *The Expansionists of 1898: The Acquisition of Hawaii and the Spanish Islands* (Baltimore, 1936); and E. Berkeley Tompkins, *Anti-Imperialism in the United States: The Great Debate, 1890–1920* (Philadelphia, 1970). Works focusing chiefly on the issue of Hawaiian annexation include Thomas J. Osborne, *"Empire Can Wait": American Opposition to Hawaiian Annexation, 1893–1898* (Kent, Ohio, 1981); William Adam Russ, *The Hawaiian Revolution (1893–94)* (Selingsgrove, Pa., 1959); and Charles W. Calhoun, "Morality and Spite: Walter Q. Gresham and U.S. Relations with Hawaii," *Pacific Historical Review*, LII (1983), 292–311.

On southern opposition to the annexation of Hawaii and other expansionist causes of this era, see Gregory Lawrence Garland, "Southern Congressional

Opposition to Hawaiian Reciprocity and Annexation, 1876–1898" (M.A. thesis, University of North Carolina at Chapel Hill, 1983); Edwina C. Smith, "Southerners on Empire: Southern Senators and Imperialism, 1898–99," *Mississippi Quarterly*, XXXI (1977–78), 89–107; Osmos Lanier, Jr., "Anti-Annexationists of the 1890s" (Ph.D. dissertation, University of Georgia, 1965); Lala Carr Steelman, "The Public Career of Augustus Octavius Bacon" (Ph.D. dissertation, University of North Carolina, 1950); and Christopher Lasch, "The Anti-Imperialists, the Philippines, and the Inequality of Man," *Journal of Southern History*, XXIV (1958), 319–31. Lasch emphasizes racist sources of southern anti-imperialism; Steelman, not denying the factor of race, documents a broader view. Key primary documents on Blount's opposition to Hawaiian annexation are *Senate Reports*, 53rd Cong., 2nd Sess., No. 227, and Blount's "Report of the Commissioner to the Hawaiian Islands." This "report" rests in original form in the National Archives. Blount apparently finished writing the document on July 17, 1893; he mailed it on the first appropriate vessel heading for the mainland, on July 25. It was first published in *House Executive Documents*, 53rd Cong., 2nd Sess., No. 47, and later in U.S. Department of State, *Foreign Relations, 1894*, Appendix II. For the most recent study of southern expansionist sentiment, an attitude often associated with Senator John Tyler Morgan, see Joseph A. Fry, "John Tyler Morgan's Southern Expansionism," *Diplomatic History*, IX (1985), 329–46. Professor Fry is writing a biography of Morgan and has shared his fascinating research with me. See also O. Lawrence Burnette, Jr., "John Tyler Morgan and Expansionist Sentiment in the New South," *Alabama Review*, XVIII (1965), 163–82, a seminal application of Walter LaFeber's arguments to the postbellum South; Tennant S. McWilliams, "The Lure of Empire: Southern Interest in the Caribbean, 1877–1900," *Mississippi Quarterly*, XXIX (1975–1976), 43–63; and Patrick J. Hearden, *Independence and Empire: The New South's Cotton Mill Campaign, 1865–1901* (De Kalb, 1982).

The Mobile Register, *the New South, and 1898*

Erwin Craighead and John L. Rapier receive short biographical treatment in *The South in the Building of the Nation* and in Marie Bankhead Owen (ed.), *The Story of Alabama* (5 vols.; New York, 1949). More on Rapier as an influential Mobilian can be found in Tennant S. McWilliams, *Hannis Taylor: The New Southerner as an American* (University, Ala., 1978). There are no major manuscript collections for either man, though relatives and others in Mobile have some pertinent documents (as cited in the notes). For other New South newspapermen of the era—Henry Watterson, Henry W. Grady, Richard H. Edmonds, Francis W. Dawson—there are biographical studies in both published and dissertation forms and also treatments in Woodward's *Origins of the New South* and Gaston's *New South Creed*.

The newspaper in late nineteenth-century America reflected far more than just one journalist's opinion at a given moment. For the broader cultural significance of newspapers consult Gerald F. Linderman, *The Mirror of War: American Society and the Spanish-American War* (Ann Arbor, 1974), which represents Robert Wiebe's "search for order" thesis applied to American culture at the turn of the century. Studies of newspapers and the Spanish-American War include Marcus W. Wilkerson, *Public Opinion and the Spanish-American War* (Baton Rouge, 1932); Joseph E. Wisan, *The Cuban Crisis as Reflected in the New York Press* (New York, 1934); and Charles H. Brown, *The Correspondents' War* (New York, 1967). Diplomatic issues of this time are treated in Ernest R. May, *Imperial Democracy: The Emergence of America as a Great Power* (New York, 1961); Charles S. Campbell, *The Transformation of American Foreign Relations, 1865–1900* (New York, 1976); and David F. Trask, *The War with Spain in 1898* (New York, 1981).

In addition to a wide range of M.A. theses and articles in state and local journals, some of which are cited in the notes, consult the following works on 1898 prowar sentiment among southerners: McWilliams, "The Lure of Empire"; Richard E. Wood, "The South and Reunion, 1898," *Historian*, XXXI (1969), 415–30, an important extension of Paul Buck's emphasis on the "road to reunion"; Burnette, "John Tyler Morgan and Expansionist Sentiment in the New South"; and William A. Williams, *The Roots of the Modern American Empire* (New York, 1969). David E. Alsobrook emphasizes antiwar sentiment in "'Remember the Maine!': Congressman Henry D. Clayton Comments on the Impending Conflict with Spain, April, 1898," *Alabama Review*, XXX (1977), 229–31, as do Steelman, "The Public Career of Augustus Octavius Bacon," and Smith, "Southerners on Empire." The post-1898 interest in foreign markets is traced in Hearden, *Independence and Empire*; Thomas J. McCormick, *China Market: America's Quest for Informal Empire, 1893–1901* (Chicago, 1967); and Tennant S. McWilliams (ed.), "New Southerner Abroad: General Joe Wheeler Views the Pacific and Beyond," *Pacific Historical Review*, XLVII (1978), 123–27. Southerners and the psychic crisis of the 1890s is a fascinating subject, one deserving of full exploration in the historiographical context of Richard Hofstadter's "Cuba, the Philippines, and Manifest Destiny," in Hofstadter, *The Paranoid Style in American Politics and Other Essays* (New York, 1966).

Daniel Augustus Tompkins, the New South and the Era of Theodore Roosevelt

Although there is no scholarly, published biography of Daniel Augustus Tompkins, there is a strong dissertation on him: Howard B. Clay, "Daniel Augustus Tompkins: American Bourbon" (Ph.D. dissertation, University of North Carolina, 1948). There also are full collections of Tompkins' papers at

Duke University and in the Southern Historical Collection of the University of North Carolina at Chapel Hill. The latter collection proved most useful in this study because of its broad-ranging biographical materials. It contains hundreds of letters to and from international business contacts; many of them include orders for, or discussions of, Tompkins' writings on industry and foreign markets. The Duke collection is primarily internal business materials.

A number of studies implicitly categorize Tompkins as only a Bourbon, a member of the "conservative regime." Woodward's *Origins of the New South* portrays him in this light, as does Dwight Billings, Jr., *Planters and the Making of the New South: Class Politics and Development in North Carolina, 1865–1900* (Chapel Hill, 1979). Other studies would permit many of his post-1900 activities the label of Progressive. Such is the case in George T. Winston, *A Builder of the New South: Being the Story of the Life and Work of Daniel Augustus Tompkins* (Garden City, N.Y., 1920), and in Grantham's *Southern Progressivism*. The latter is a comment not so much on Tompkins' "liberal" elements as on the complexity and often conservative nature of progressivism in the South as well as nationwide. For Bourbon sources of southern progressivism, see Grantham, *Southern Progressivism,* and also Tindall, *The Persistent Tradition in New South Politics*. One can hardly read Tompkins' various pamphlets (cited in the notes) and not conclude that he does indeed fit the conservative, "ex-Bourbon" strain of New South progressivism. His role as a New South advocate, and that of others of his time, is treated in Woodward, *Origins of the New South*, Gaston, *The New South Creed*, and Grantham, *Southern Progressivism*.

North-South political and economic rivalry in the late nineteenth and early twentieth centuries, a rivalry that absorbed much of Tompkins' energy, is discussed in Woodward, *Origins of the New South*, Grantham, *Southern Progressivism*, and Patrick J. Hearden's superb article, "New England's Reaction to the New South," *South Atlantic Quarterly*, LXXV (1976), 371–88. The New South's involvement in the American Asiatic Association can be reconstructed with close analysis of the journal of that organization and with careful reading of James John Lorrence, "The American Asiatic Association, 1898–1925: Organized Business and the Myth of the China Market" (Ph.D. dissertation, University of Wisconsin, 1970). Also useful is Salvadore Prisco III, *John Barrett, Progressive Era Diplomat, 1877–1920* (University, Ala., 1973). On key New South leaders and foreign policy issues of the Roosevelt era, consult Chester, *Sectionalism, Politics, and American Diplomacy*; Grantham, *Southern Progressivism*; Hearden, *Independence and Empire*; Jerry Israel, *Progressivism and the Open Door: America and China, 1905–1921* (Pittsburgh, 1971); and Robert Neal Seidel, "Progressive Pan Americanism: Economic Development and United States Policy, 1906–31" (Ph.D. dissertation, Cornell University, 1973). The South's experience with Chinese immigration is especially interesting. This subject has been probed from the perspective of the New South by a number of scholars (cited in the notes); but for a new analysis emphasizing Chinese responses to Dixie, see Lucy M. Cohen, *Chinese in the Post-Civil War South: A People Without a History* (Baton Rouge, 1984).

John W. Davis, the New South and the Era of Woodrow Wilson

What surely will stand as the definitive biography of John W. Davis is William H. Harbaugh's, *Lawyer's Lawyer: The Life of John W. Davis* (New York, 1973). There is also a solid study of Davis' diplomatic career in Maureen DeJure, "The Diary of a Diplomat: A Study of Anglo-American Relations, 1918–1921" (Honors thesis, Bucknell University, 1966), though Davis' southernism is not addressed there either. Of course the key source for Davis' diplomatic work is his four-volume Ambassadorial Diary, located in the original at Yale University, in the John W. Davis Papers, Sterling Library. Microfilm copies of the diary are available at Yale and Columbia universities and at the University of Alabama at Birmingham. The diary stands as a key document of Wilsonian diplomacy chiefly because Davis was so analytical, articulate, and consistent. Other key primary materials on Davis are located in the Charles Warren Papers at the Library of Congress.

Grantham's *Southern Progressivism* covers the varied literature on the New South and domestic reform during the Wilson years. There is also a wide range of important secondary material now available on southerners and Wilsonian diplomacy, and this includes strong focus on the orientation of New South Progressives—people such as Josephus Daniels, John Sharp Williams, and Walter Hines Page. Important general analyses include Robert Hoyt Block, "Southern Opinion of Woodrow Wilson's Foreign Policies, 1913–1917" (Ph.D. dissertation, Duke University, 1968); Timothy Gregory McDonald, "Southern Democratic Congressmen and the First World War, August 1914–April 1917: The Public Record of Their Support For and Opposition to Wilson's Policies" (Ph.D. dissertation, University of Washington, 1962); Dewey W. Grantham, "Southern Senators and the League of Nations, 1918–1920," *North Carolina Historical Review*, XXVI (1949), 187–205; and Richard L. Watson, "A Testing Time for Southern Congressional Leadership: The War Crisis of 1917–18," *Journal of Southern History*, XLIV (1978), 3–40. Integrative analyses are also found in Tindall, *Emergence of the New South,* and Grantham, *Southern Progressivism*. Although virtually every noted New South Progressive has been treated with biography, none has been analyzed more carefully than Walter Hines Page. John Milton Cooper's *Walter Hines Page: The Southerner as American, 1855–1918* (Chapel Hill, 1979) is a masterful biography. There is no adequate study of southern Anglophobia and

Anglophilism, an ironic gap considering the emphasis on race as a central theme of southern history.

On Wilson as a southerner the most incisive study is Arthur S. Link, "Woodrow Wilson: The American as Southerner," *Journal of Southern History,* XXXVI (February, 1970), 3–17. Link does not develop the southern "stake" in the Wilsonian image as much as might be done, though he clearly provides the framework for the thesis. For many examples of New South leaders revering Wilson—and connecting him with Jefferson— see Robert Dallek, *Democrat and Diplomat: The Life of William E. Dodd* (New York, 1968), as well as Dodd's various monographs; O'Brien, "Woodward and the Burden of Southern Liberalism"; and Michael O'Brien, *The Idea of the American South, 1920–1941* (Baltimore, 1979). On Wilson and the diplomacy of the Paris Peace Conference and the League, works of considerable importance include E. David Cronin (ed.), *The Cabinet Diaries of Josephus Daniels, 1913–1921* (Lincoln Nebr., 1963); Seth P. Tillman, *Anglo-American Relations at the Paris Peace Conference of 1919* (Princeton, 1961); Klaus Schwabe, *Woodrow Wilson, Revolutionary Germany, and Peacemaking, 1918–1919: Missionary Diplomacy and the Realities of Power* (Chapel Hill, 1985); George W. Egerton, *Great Britain and the Creation of the League of Nations* (Chapel Hill, 1978); N. Gordon Levin, Jr., *Woodrow Wilson and World Politics: America's Response to War and Revolution* (New York, 1968); Arthur S. Link (ed.), *Woodrow Wilson and a Revolutionary World 1913–1921* (Chapel Hill, 1982); Arthur S. Link, *Wilson the Diplomatist: A Look at His Major Foreign Policies* (Baltimore, 1957); John M. Cooper, Jr., *The Warrior and the Priest: Woodrow Wilson and Theodore Roosevelt* (Cambridge, Mass., 1983); and Lloyd C. Gardner, *Safe for Democracy: The Anglo-American Response to Revolution, 1913–1923* (New York, 1984).

The Southern Council on International Relations, the New South, and the Era of World War II

The papers of the Southern Council on International Relations (SCIR) are a relatively recent addition to the Southern Historical Collection of the University of North Carolina at Chapel Hill. The council materials are integrated into the Frank Porter Graham Papers and the University Archives Collection. Copies of the council's publication—from its inception as *Memoranda on International Problems* to its full appearance as *The South and World Affairs*—are located in the Wilson Library of the University of North Carolina. Photocopies are available at the University of Alabama at Birmingham. Issues of the journal appearing after 1941, when the council expanded its subscription list, are available in many university libraries. Also useful were the Virginius Dabney Papers in the Alderman Library of the University of Virginia. Dabney was too involved in other operations to play an active role in the council, but he corresponded with council leaders.

On the New South and domestic reform in the 1930s and 1940s, general information is located in Tindall, *Emergence of the New South*, and Grantham, *Southern Progressivism*. Singal's *The War Within* deepens and broadens such knowledge in a striking way. Also most useful is John K. Kneebone, *Southern Liberal Journalists and the Issue of Race, 1920–1944* (Chapel Hill, 1985). On New South leaders of this era and key foreign policy issues there is a wide body of significant secondary literature. Perhaps most important on years leading up to World War II, when the New South movement temporarily lost focus, is Herring and Hess, "Regionalism and Foreign Policy"; Charles M. Dollar, "The South and the Fordney-McCumber Tariff of 1922: A Study in Regional Politics," *Journal of Southern History*, XXXIX (1973), 45–66; Alexander DeConde, "The South and Isolationism," 332–46; and Seabury, *The Waning of Southern "Internationalism."* On foreign affairs sentiment of the New South movement as it resurged in the World War II years, consult Hero, *The Southerner and World Affairs*; Seabury, *The Waning of Southern "Internationalism"*; Irving Howard, "The Influence of Southern Senators on American Foreign Policy, 1939–50" (Ph.D. dissertation, University of Wisconsin, 1955); Robert A. Divine, *Second Chance: The Triumph of Internationalism in America During World War II* (New York, 1971); and DeConde, "The South and Isolationism." Much of this literature is summarized in Tindall's *Emergence of the New South*. For an alternative southern viewpoint, opposition to much of Roosevelt's approach to World War II, see especially Wayne Cole, "America First and the South," *Journal of Southern History*, XXII (1956), 36–47.

The New South and the Emerging Cold War

For some thirty years the growing historiographical trend with respect to the cold war has been toward analyses of the passing of southern internationalism in the late 1940s and early 1950s and arguments that leaders and others of the New South region really never were honest internationalists. Accounts reflecting this trend in interpretation include Seabury, *The Waning of Southern "Internationalism,"* and more recently, Herring and Hess, "Regionalism and Foreign Policy." It is my contention, however, that New South advocates were probably no more and no less honest internationalists than northeasterners such as James T. Shotwell and Nicholas Murry Butler. All were cultural expansionists; all believed in the American mission—even more so, ironically, than their leader, Woodrow Wilson. Indeed, most aggressive internationalists of the periods of the two world wars considered "the cause" of American internationalism to be one of establishing an international organization receptive to a "progressive" American influence in the world. When that dream was consummated, then proved empty in the critical early years of the United Nations, they all—not just southerners—appeared to move to the right by dropping the international organization (multilateral) part of their message while sticking with the more unilateral, missionary litany. In moving to the right, New South leaders probably were unique by virtue of the sectional (including racial) stake they had had in Wilsonianism.

Studies showing New South leaders and other internationalists dropping their cause and embracing cold warriorship include Norman Graebner, *The New Isolationism* (New York, 1956); Robert Griffith, "Old Progressives and the Cold War," *Journal of American History*, LXVI (1979), 334–47; "Victory and a Shift," *Newsweek*, (June 24, 1957), 31; Lerche, *The Uncertain South*; Hero, *The Southerner and World Affairs*; and works by Seabury and Herring and Hess cited above. Also helpful in understanding this move to the right is Carl Degler's article, "Thesis, Antithesis, Synthesis," which suggests that the South was never outside the mainstream—there was no mainstream to be outside of.

Index